Fictions of Female Adultery, 1684–1890

Fictions of Female Adultery, 1684–1890

Theories and Circumtexts

Bill Overton
Reader in Literature
Loughborough University

First published 2002 by
PALGRAVE MACMILLAN
Houndmills, Basingstoke, Hampshire RG21 6XS and
175 Fifth Avenue, New York, N. Y. 10010
Companies and representatives throughout the world

PALGRAVE MACMILLAN is the global academic imprint of the Palgrave
Macmillan division of St. Martin's Press, LLC and of Palgrave Macmillan Ltd.
Macmillan® is a registered trademark in the United States, United Kingdom
and other countries. Palgrave is a registered trademark in the European
Union and other countries.

ISBN 0–333–77080–3

This book is printed on paper suitable for recycling and made from fully
managed and sustained forest sources.

A catalogue record for this book is available from the British Library.

Library of Congress Cataloging-in-Publication Data
Overton, Bill.
    Fictions of female adultery, 1684–1890 : theories and circumtexts / Bill
    Overton.
        p. cm.
    Includes bibliographical references and index.
    ISBN 0–333–77080–3
    1. English fiction—History and criticism. 2. Adultery in literature.
    3. Literature, Comparative—English and French. 4. Literature,
    Comparative—French and English. 5. French fiction—History and
    criticism. 6. Women in literature. I. Title.
    PR830.A37 O94 2002
    823.009'353—dc21
                                                                2002072306

10   9   8   7   6   5   4   3   2   1
11   10   09   08   07   06   05   04   03   02

Printed and bound in Great Britain by
Antony Rowe Ltd, Chippenham and Eastbourne

Produced as camera-ready copy by the author using Impression Publisher
on an Acorn Kinetic RiscPC.

Contents

Preface

This book is a sequel and companion to one first published in 1996. *The Novel of Female Adultery: Love and Gender in Continental European Fiction, 1830–1900*[1] is a comparative study of leading examples of a kind of fiction that flourished in the later nineteenth century. It attempts to chart how and where this tradition originated, and to suggest why it never took root in Britain or North America; but most of it is concerned with analysing nineteenth-century fiction of adultery, chiefly novels, from France, Russia, Germany, Denmark, Portugal and Spain. The wide scope of this enterprise, and the limits on what could go into a single book, made it impossible for me to deal at the same time with several other important matters: in particular, the questions of how the novel of adultery has been and might further be theorized, the role of adultery in earlier British fiction, and the development of the novel of adultery in France after 1860 to the point when it faded out about thirty years later. To treat these topics is the aim of the present book, which is intended to be read alongside its predecessor and to complement it.

A companion study also affords other benefits – I hope for readers as well as author. One of these is the opportunity to take into account work on the subject published since 1996, especially the collection of essays edited by Nicholas White and Naomi Segal, *Scarlet Letters: Fictions of Adultery From Antiquity to the 1990s*, and White's *The Family in Crisis in Late Nineteenth-Century French Fiction*.[2] Another is the chance to refine the phrase I used in *The Novel of Female Adultery* to identify the type of fiction I am investigating. The reason I employed that phrase, and put it in my title, is that the term used by previous critics, 'the novel of adultery', fails to indicate a fundamental fact about the fiction to which it refers: that it is a gendered form, grounded on the representation of female experience by men. Adultery by men often figures in novels by both male and female writers of the nineteenth and other centuries, but it is very rarely their central subject, and most writers – Tolstoy is an honourable exception – seem to take it virtually for granted. The stock term 'novel of adultery' is therefore at best shorthand and at worst a misnomer. Because that term masks the gender bias inherent in the form, 'novel of female

vi

adultery' is better. However, there is a further complication. As I pointed out in my previous book, 'the great majority of novels of adultery deal with single adultery on the part of the female' – 'single' referring to adultery in which only one of the partners is married.[3] For this reason, as I should have realized at the time, a more precise term is 'novel of wifely adultery'. This first struck me when, researching the present book, I came across the phrase 'wifely adultery' at the start of Lawrence Stone's *Road to Divorce: England 1530–1987*.[4] Because it is more accurate, the term 'novel of wifely adultery' is the one I employ most often here, though where appropriate (as in the title), and to avoid monotony, I sometimes use a phrase referring to 'female adultery', or even the term 'novel of adultery', instead.

This book is divided into two parts, the first of which addresses theory. It begins with a chapter discussing what is at issue in theorizing the novel of adultery and setting out the approach and method adopted in the rest of the study. Two further chapters deal respectively with the most important contribution to the field so far, Tony Tanner's *Adultery in the Novel: Contract and Transgression*,[5] and, through reference to work by Loralee MacPike and Naomi Segal,[6] with ways of theorizing the role in adultery fiction of patterns of childbearing and childlessness. The second part of the book considers 'circumtexts' of the novel of wifely adultery – in other words, narratives of adultery that are more or less 'marginal to the form itself. First, there are three chapters on adultery in British fiction up to the Romantic period. The chief aims of these are to demonstrate the importance of the theme of adultery in British novels up to about the end of the eighteenth century, to show how the theme was increasingly squeezed out, and so to further help account for its subsequent virtual absence from respectable British fiction till near the end of the nineteenth century. Second, there are two chapters on adultery in later nineteenth-century French fiction. Here the main objectives are to show what happened to the treatment of the theme after Flaubert, especially during the Naturalist movement in France of the 1870s and 1880s. Together, the five chapters on 'circumtexts' help define the novel of wifely adultery more closely by considering alternatives in Britain, before it was invented, and in France, once it was all too common. They cast light not only on the history of the form but on the various ideological and other imperatives behind it. I hope they are also of interest as studies of the narratives with which they deal.

Some readers may be puzzled by my decision to combine in the same book a discussion of theoretical issues and, in particular, extended analysis of texts from two very different novelistic traditions – different not only linguistically and culturally but also historically. I hope the theoretical part of the book needs no justification. Although critics have approached adultery fiction from a range of theoretical positions, none has considered what kinds of method and approach are most appropriate, and the complexity of the topic requires that such questions be tackled. At the same time, since the novel of wifely adultery is a cross-cultural form, it demands comparative criticism. Although it developed furthest in France, examples occur in most other European countries in the nineteenth century, and it has important antecedents in Restoration and eighteenth-century Britain. Any attempt to theorize the form or to generalize about it must therefore be based on a wide range of novels from different national traditions. In *The Novel of Female Adultery* I gave part of that basis; here I expand it by considering not only early British and later French adultery narratives, but also, in Chapter 2, Rousseau's *Julie, or the New Heloise* and Goethe's *Elective Affinities*. The importance of the earlier British narratives is in part that, although they did not influence the form, they help illuminate what is at issue in it and why, in Britain and North America, adultery fiction was all but suppressed for most of the nineteenth century.

One way of explaining why there was no Anglophone tradition of adultery fiction in the nineteenth century is to say that it had flourished only too vigorously already – so vigorously that nineteenth-century moralists were determined not only to have no more of it but even to forget, as far as possible, that it had ever existed. The scholarship of the last twenty or so years has done much to restore the loss, and the three chapters in this book on adultery in early British fiction do their best to add to the recovery.

Acknowledgements

I am very grateful for the support and help without which this study could not have been completed within the four years or so it has taken – or even at all. To Loughborough University and to the United Kingdom's Arts and Humanities Research Board I owe not only the year's study leave that enabled progress with the project that would otherwise have been impossible, but also remission from my teaching that, though modest, has eased its latter stages. In particular I thank Maurizio Calbi, Andrew Dix, and Catie Gill, who have carried out various of my teaching responsibilities so well, and Ian Clarke and Elaine Hobby for corresponding care with my administration. I also appreciate greatly the work of staff at the Pilkington Library of Loughborough University, especially in its Inter-Library Loan Department, and of the other libraries I have used, especially the British Library and the libraries of Cambridge, Leicester and Nottingham Universities.

Other kinds of support have helped a lot too. Earlier versions of parts of Chapters 1 and 3 first appeared in the *Modern Language Review*, 94 (1999), and I am grateful for the comments of the anonymous reader, for the advice of Malcolm Cook as editor, and for permission to revise and reprint. It is also a pleasure to acknowledge responses to drafts of parts of Chapters 2 and 3 from colleagues at research seminars in the Department of English and Drama of Loughborough University, and to a draft of part of Chapter 2 from members of the Seminar for Research in Progress at the Arts Faculty of the University of Northumbria, especially Allan Ingram. Others who have given particular help and encouragement are Mary Orr and Jennifer Birkett; Grace, Keith, George, Henry and Julie Overton and Sally Andreasen; and Chris White, who advised on possible cover designs, read and commented on drafts of Chapters 7 and 8, and suggested further reading for the latter. Finally, Elaine Hobby has contributed to the progress of the book in more ways than I can say, not only by reading and commenting on all of it in draft, in the case of some parts several times, but by giving constant companionship and support.

Literary Chronology

1662   Lafayette, *La Princesse de Montpensier*

1669   Guilleragues, *Les Lettres portugaises*; English translation 1678

1678   Lafayette, *La Princesse de Clèves*; English translation 1679

1684   Behn, Part 1 of *Love-Letters Between a Nobleman and his Sister*; Part 2, 1685; Part 3, 1687

1688   Behn, *The Fair Jilt*

1690   Locke, *Two Treatises of Government*

1700   Astell, *Some Reflections upon Marriage*

1705   Manley, *The Secret History of Queen Zarah and the Zarazians*

1709   Manley, *The New Atalantis*

1710   Manley, *Memoirs of Europe*

1714   Manley, *The Adventures of Rivella*

1718   Lafayette, *La Comtesse de Tende* (anonymously)

1719   Haywood, Parts 1 and 2 of *Love in Excess*; Part 3, 1720

1722   Defoe, *Moll Flanders*

1724   Defoe, *Roxana*; Haywood, Volume 1 of *Memoirs of a Certain Island Adjacent to the Kingdom of Utopia*; Volume 2, 1725

1728   Rowe, *Friendship in Death*; Part 1 of *Letters Moral and Entertaining*; Part 2, 1731; Part 3, 1732

1740   Volume 1 of Richardson, *Pamela*; Volume 2, 1741

1741   Henry Fielding, *Shamela*

1743   Anon, *The Fair Adultress: or, the Treacherous Brother*

1744   Anon, *The Fair Adultress. A Novel*

1747   Volumes 1 and 2 of Richardson, *Clarissa*; Volumes 3–7, 1748

1748   Cleland, Volume 1 of *Memoirs of a Woman of Pleasure* [*Fanny Hill*]; Volume 2, 1749

1749   Henry Fielding, *Tom Jones*

1751   Cleland, *Memoirs of a Coxcomb*; Haywood, *The History of Miss Betsy Thoughtless*; Smollett, *The Adventures of Peregrine Pickle*

1752   Henry Fielding, *Amelia*

1759   Sarah Fielding, *The History of the Countess of Dellwyn*

1761   Anon, *Adultery Anatomized*; Rousseau, *Julie, ou la nouvelle Héloïse* and *Eloisa* (English translation); Sheridan, *Memoirs of Miss Sidney Bidulph*

1766   Goldsmith, *The Vicar of Wakefield*

1770	Anon, *A Full and Complete History of His R—l H— the D— of C—d and Lady G—r, the fair Adultress*
1771	Griffith, *The History of Lady Barton*; Mackenzie, *The Man of Feeling*; Anon, *Harriet: or, The Innocent Adultress*
1773	Griffith, 'The Unforced Repentance'
1778	Burney, *Evelina*
1779	Volumes 1–3 of *Trials for Adultery: or, the History of Divorces*; Volumes 4–7, 1780
1780	Griffith, *Novellettes*
1782	Laclos, *Dangerous Liaisons*
1786	Lee, *The Errors of Innocence*
1788	Smith, *Emmeline, the Orphan of the Castle*; Wollstonecraft, *Mary, A Fiction*
1791	Inchbald, *A Simple Story*
1792	Wollstonecraft, *A Vindication of the Rights of Woman*
1796	Hays, *Memoirs of Miss Emma Courtney*
1798	Wollstonecraft, *The Wrongs of Woman*
1801	Chateaubriand, *Atala*
1802	Chateaubriand, *René*
1809	Goethe, *Elective Affinities*; English translation 1854
1811	Austen, *Sense and Sensibility*
1813	Austen, *Pride and Prejudice*
1814	Austen, *Mansfield Park*; Scott, *Waverley*
1816	Austen, *Emma*; Constant, *Adolphe*
1818	Bowdler, *Family Shakespeare*
1829	Balzac, *Physiology of Marriage*
1830	Stendhal, *The Red and the Black*
1832	Balzac, *A Woman of Thirty*; final version 1842; Sand, *Indiana* and *Valentine*
1834	Sand, *Jacques*
1835	Balzac, *Le Père Goriot*
1836	Balzac, *Lily of the Valley*; Musset, *Confession of a Child of the Century*
1839	Stendhal, *The Charterhouse of Parma*
1841	Lucas, 'La Femme adultère'
1842	Balzac, Preface to *The Human Comedy*
1843	Balzac, *The Muse of the Department*
1847	Balzac, *Cousin Bette*; Emily Brontë, *Wuthering Heights*; Charlotte Brontë, *Jane Eyre*
1848	Dickens, *Dombey and Son*; Dumas, *La Dame aux camélias*; Thackeray, *Vanity Fair*

Editions Used and References

References to primary texts discussed are given in parentheses immediately after the quotation or citation; an endnote after the first reference identifies the edition or editions used.

The form of the references is: volume or part number (where applicable), in upper-case Roman; chapter number (again where applicable), also in Roman, lower-case if preceded by volume or part number; and page number in Arabic. Where writing originally in French or German is discussed, the initial reference is to an English translation. This is then followed by a semi-colon, and by the page number of the French or German edition I have used. Where I have modified the translation, this is indicated by the abbreviation 'TM'.

Where more than one English translation exists, I have normally chosen the one most likely to be accessible. Where no translation into English exists, translation of material quoted is my own. As in the cases where I have modified an existing translation, I have aimed for an accurate equivalent, though the result may be more literal than literary.

The date of first publication in book form for each literary work cited is given in parentheses after its title on the first occasion when it is mentioned. The title is normally cited in the form used for the English translation; where there is no translation easily available in English, and translation of the title is needed, this is provided in parentheses. Details of serial publication, if any, are given in discussion or in the notes where this is relevant. Publication dates in the Chronology follow the same convention.

Part I
Theories

1
Theorizing the Novel of Wifely Adultery

In the latter part of the nineteenth century, a type of novel centred on wifely adultery flourished in Continental Europe. Examples include not only Flaubert's *Madame Bovary* (1857), Tolstoy's *Anna Karenina* (1878), and Fontane's *Effi Briest* (1895), but others that are less widely known, such as Jacobsen's *Marie Grubbe* (1876), Eça de Queirós's *Cousin Bazilio* (1878), Leopoldo Alas's *La Regenta* (1884–5), and Pérez Galdós's *Fortunata and Jacinta* (1887). These seven novels came from six different countries: France, Russia, Germany, Denmark, Portugal and Spain. Each is based on a plot in which, with minor variations, a married woman from the middle or upper classes is seduced by an unmarried man of the same class and comes to grief. They are further alike in that each is told in an impersonal narrative voice, and each was written by a man.

There are four main reasons why this type of fiction demands critical investigation. First, there is the question why a significant number of novels with such similar characteristics appeared in several different European countries within so brief an historical period. Second, there is the problem why, at this particular period, so many outstanding novelists should have chosen the theme of wifely adultery, especially because all use it as a vehicle not just for stories of domestic life but for social and political reflection. The third fact to be reckoned with is that of literary value, because nearly all the examples cited above are recognized as classics – if not on a world scale, as with *Madame Bovary* and *Anna Karenina*, then on a national one. The fourth reason springs from two striking anomalies: that no canonical novel of adultery appeared in Britain or North America, and that none was written by a woman.

The importance of adultery as a fictional theme in the nineteenth-century European novel has certainly not escaped critical attention, but few ideas on the subject have won widespread acceptance, and many of the questions it raises still lack adequate definition. There are several reasons why this is so. To begin with, adultery itself is

3

fraught with such moral and ideological consequence that any kind of consensus, even about its literary representation, will never be straightforward. Next, the various theoretical paradigms current and competing in literary studies will always produce different readings – and even different ideas about what is significant. Third, and related to both these problems, there is no agreed definition of what counts as adultery in fiction, or indeed of what a novel of adultery is. Tony Tanner, for example, in the most interesting and far-reaching treatment of the theme, acknowledges that adultery does not even occur in two of the three literary texts that he analyses at length.[1] Similarly, in her book *The Adulteress's Child*, Naomi Segal remarks: 'It is not essential for my purpose for "actual" adultery to have taken place (though it usually has); adulterous desire is enough.' Indeed, Segal asserts that most of the ten examples of the French Romantic confession that she discusses as part of her study are also novels of adultery, although adultery takes place in only two of them and is crucial to none.[2]

As a first step towards theorizing the novel of adultery, it is therefore necessary to distinguish between narratives in which adultery plays different kinds of role. The full-blown novel of adultery is defined in my previous book as 'any novel in which one or more adulterous liaisons are central to its concerns as identified by its action, themes and structure'.[3] Only in this type of novel – which is almost always a novel of wifely adultery – does the theme determine the whole structure and design of the narrative. At the other end of the spectrum are novels in which adultery occurs but in which it is not the principal focus. Elsewhere are novels of adulterous desire, or of adultery avoided. Though both these types of fiction may have features in common with the novel of adultery, they constitute a different kind of text. A further variant is the novel of prostitution. Disputing my point in my previous book that the nineteenth-century novel of adultery 'virtually ignores the adultery of unmarried women', Nicholas White objects that it is in the novel of prostitution that such adultery may be found.[4] However, the prostitute is defined not by her marital status but by the fact that she has sex for money – she may be unmarried, like Nana in the novel Zola named after her (1880), or not, like another eponymous heroine, Rosalía Bringas, in *That Bringas Woman* by Pérez Galdós (1884).[5] The novel of prostitution is therefore a different form. Not only does it raise different questions from those raised in the novel of wifely adultery, but it is much less prominent in the period.

Some examples may clarify the kinds of distinction that are necessary in defining adultery fiction. First, three novels in which adultery occurs but is not the principal focus are Laclos's *Dangerous Liaisons* (1782), Stendhal's *The Charterhouse of Parma* (1839), and Balzac's *Cousin Bette* (1847). So far as I know, *Dangerous Liaisons* has never been classed as a novel of adultery, although both Valmont and Merteuil, the main characters, have affairs with various married partners – in Valmont's case, most significantly with Mme de Tourvel.[6] Instead, Laclos's novel is usually understood as a novel of seduction; an alternative term is Nancy K. Miller's 'libertine text'.[7] The reason it is never considered as a novel of adultery is straightforward: it gives marriage little importance. Tourvel's husband never appears in the action; he does not figure among the correspondents; and she herself refers to him only rarely in her letters and dialogue. His role is, in a word, nominal; so that Tourvel defends her chastity as a value in itself rather than as a duty determined by marriage vows.[8] The limited value given by the novel to matrimony is connected with the widespread practice of arranged marriages among the French aristocracy. This practice the novel obliquely questions, even as it celebrates, with almost equal obliquity, Tourvel's suicidal devotion to her seducer.

The Charterhouse of Parma is also a narrative that is never described as a novel of adultery, even though the liaisons of two pairs of adulterous lovers are central to its action.[9] Again, the reason is that the novel grants little significance to marriage. In keeping with Italian aristocratic tradition, the Duchess Gina Sanseverina's marriage is entirely one of convenience and leaves her free to pursue her affair with the politician Count Mosca. Because of the value Stendhal gives to passion, he conveys no criticism of this – even though, paradoxically, Gina's real passion is for Fabrice, whom Mosca is in a position to protect and foster. For the same reason, what is at issue in Fabrice's affair with Clélia is not adultery but the constraints on passion imposed by politics and religious faith. Despite her love for Fabrice, briefly consummated in a moment of extreme stress while he is in prison, Clélia marries another man after she has helped Fabrice to escape. This she does in deference to the wishes of her father, Governor of the prison, out of filial guilt heightened by the overdose of laudanum he is given inadvertently. Out of the same guilt she vows never to see Fabrice again. Both her vow and her way round it – interpreting it literally, she meets him only at night – are unimaginable in any novel of adultery. This is because the novel celebrates a pre-bourgeois order in which passion and faith can still count for everything, however irrational or even, perhaps, absurd the behaviour they produce. Although both lovers die as a result of Fabrice's wish to have with him the son born of their illicit love, these deaths do not carry the forbidding overtones typical of the novel of wifely adultery: whether in the form of Flaubert's unrelenting irony in *Madame Bovary*, Tolstoy's epigraph 'Vengeance is mine; I will repay' in *Anna Karenina*, or, in *Effi Briest*, the understated deprecation of Fontane.

A different kind of novel in which adultery occurs but is not the central focus is Balzac's *Cousin Bette*. I have argued in *The Novel of Female Adultery* that Balzac contributed more than any other writer to the rise of the novel of wifely adultery, but *Cousin Bette* is no more such a novel than it is a novel of prostitution, even though several of the characters are courtesans. Its action does not centre on the adulteries of Valérie Marneffe, a married woman who becomes the mistress of four of the male characters, but on the ways in which the title character, an embittered spinster, exploits these. Neither is it a novel of husbandly adultery, even though three of Valérie's clients are married, and though the infidelities of one of them, Hector Hulot, give rise to much of the action. Instead, the main focus of *Cousin Bette* is the corruption and downfall of a whole social order, that of the Second Empire, and its supersession on the one hand by the commercial bourgeoisie, on the other by the colourless albeit upright lawyers who, the novel suggests, gained the upper hand after the Revolution of 1830. The adulteries of the various characters, male and female, are symptoms of this corruption, not topics of concern in their own right; and Cousin Bette is a woman driven by the many frustrations she suffers as a slighted relative, not only those of blocked sexual desire.

Second, Lafayette's *The Princesse de Clèves* (1678) is not a novel of adultery at all but one based on adulterous desire in which adultery is avoided. Here marriage is taken seriously, even though it is arranged by the Prince and the Princess's mother, and though the latter knows that the Prince's love for her daughter is not returned. So seriously does the Princess take her commitment to the husband whom she cannot love that, famously, she confesses to him that she is being pursued by another man and, despite herself, is in love with him. Furthermore, despite the frequency of adulterous and other affairs in the court circles she inhabits, she not only resists Nemours but refuses to marry him after her husband dies in despair.

Although the relations between the Princess, the Prince and Nemours constitute a triangle typical of novels of adultery, what is at issue is quite different. Unlike any heroine of a novel of wifely adultery, the Princess not only cares sufficiently for her husband to try to avoid hurting and humiliating him further, but acts in such a way as to preserve the only independent power she possesses. Therefore it is not simply the Princess's refusal to consummate her extra-marital love that distinguishes this novel from classic fiction of adultery; her later refusal to marry Nemours stems not so much from guilt at her husband's death, or from religious conviction, as from a stoic defence of the only real freedom of action left to her.

A third kind of text that differs from the novel of wifely adultery is the French Romantic confession, in which adultery often threatens but rarely occurs. Examples are Chateaubriand's *Atala* and *René* (1801, 1802), Constant's *Adolphe* (1816), Musset's *Confession of a Child of the Century* (1836), Balzac's *Lily in the Valley* (1836) and Fromentin's *Dominique* (1863). Texts in this tradition, which has been discussed extensively by Naomi Segal, are personal narratives told by men, often delivered to an older male.[10] Their characteristic plot is the narrator's escape from an illicit love affair, generally with an older woman, in which the couple relate to each other not only as lovers but to some extent as mother and son. Often the narrator has lost his mother in childbirth; where the father has a role, he is usually distant but worldly-wise and powerful. Although jealousy and infidelity are repeated themes in the Romantic confession, these are clearly not novels of adultery. This is because adultery presupposes matrimony, and in most Romantic confessions neither partner is married – at most, as in Musset's *Confession*, the woman loved by the narrator has been married in the past, or she is married but stays faithful to her husband. Examples in the latter category are Balzac's *Lily in the Valley*, Fromentin's *Dominique*, and Flaubert's *Sentimental Education* (1869), which comprehensively deconstructs the genre. The fact that the central relationship in these texts is quasi-filial distinguishes them from the novel of wifely adultery. They have much to offer to the psychoanalytical approach adopted by Segal, as does a further example, Feydeau's *Fanny* (1858), a manifestly Oedipal text which, cashing in on *Madame Bovary*, grafts on to a Romantic confession a story of adultery.[11]

The reason why it is essential to define clearly the different roles that novelists have given in their fiction to adultery is therefore to do with what those roles signify. Although, as I have shown, they produce different kinds of fiction, at a much deeper level they point to the ideological and other motives behind the literary construction of adultery. An adequate theory of the novel of wifely adultery needs to be capable of defining the genre closely enough both to enable the novels that belong to it to be identified accurately, and, through comparison with other texts, to distinguish it from other genres, especially those that were common in the same period – for example, the *Bildungsroman* as well as the French Romantic confession. It must also be capable of explaining why the form arose and persisted longest in nineteenth-century France, why writers adopted it in other European cultures and in South America, and why, on the other hand, it failed to take root in North America and in Britain.[12] A third requirement is that such a theory must be able to explain the key characteristics of novels within the genre. Examples of these are the type of plot, which is nearly always centred on the seduction of a married woman by an unmarried man; its field of social reference, which is usually bourgeois and sometimes patrician, but very rarely proletarian; its authorship, which is almost always male; its tone, which is sometimes tragic and sometimes ironic or satirical, but almost never comic; and its narrative form, which is usually impersonal.

These three conditions for an adequate theory of the novel of wifely adultery require the generality necessary to any theory – for, it goes without saying, no theory can be valid or useful without a wide sample of data to which it refers and which it attempts to explain. This means studying not only a large number of examples, but, because the form is cross-cultural, examples from more than one literary tradition – the more, the better. At the same time, specificity is also necessary, and for three main reasons. First, the information-base must be deep as well as broad. In other words, the theory needs to be informed not only by a large number of examples, and from different cultural traditions, but also by detailed analyses of each one. It is detailed as well as general information that enables a theory to be developed, tested and modified, and that facilitates the drawing of precise comparisons and distinctions. Second, a novel is a literary artefact of great complexity – partly because of its length, partly because it draws on a wide range of literary techniques and formal conventions, but partly also because novels of wifely adultery were written in the Realist tradition and so constantly refer to the social and historical worlds that the writers and their readers inhabited. It is not possible to do justice to this complexity, or to the novel's own economy and dynamics as an artefact, without detailed textual analysis and reference. Indeed, in any comparative study, it is often the details that count most: the exact nature, for example, of statuses and relationships, of linguistic expressions, or of narrative devices. At the same time, a study that deals with a wide range of examples cannot take for granted that readers will be familiar with them all. For this reason it is necessary, especially in the case of little-known texts, to provide thorough evidence including quotation and even, at times, summary. Such evidence should attempt to represent the text as fully and accurately as possible, and not only supply chapter and verse that the reader can check.

These principles may be illustrated from a brief survey of three studies of the novel of adultery: those by Judith Armstrong, Tony Tanner, and Naomi Segal. Armstrong meets the criterion of range by comparing about fifty nineteenth-century novels from four cultural traditions: French, Russian, British and North American (though she tends to run the last two together). She also offers an historical basis to her study, in that she begins with 'an account of legal, social and religious attitudes to both marriage and adultery' in each of these traditions, concentrating on the second half of the nineteenth century, but prefaced by an outline of how they evolved from the distant past.[13] However, because she approaches her sample texts thematically rather than one by one, she is able to give little detailed analysis and, for example, hardly ever specifies their form or narrative method.[14] The thematic framework Armstrong employs also delivers more costs than benefits. It is based on two assumptions: that marriage represents a generally accepted form of order and that tragedy consists in the breaking of an order, the effects that follow, and the order's ultimate vindication. In accordance with these assumptions, her first chapter, in which she sets out basic attitudes to marriage and adultery, is entitled 'The Establishing of the Order', and the four that ensue 'The Breaking of the Order', 'The Order Broken', 'The Order Vindicated', and 'The Justification of the Order'. One problem with such a structure to her argument is that it fragments the texts she discusses, and so tends to present evidence out of context. For example, in considering adultery in John William De Forest's *Miss Ravenel's Conversion From Secession to Loyalty* (1867), she mentions neither that it is part of a subplot nor that the novel is about the American Civil War; indeed, in citing it she omits the last four words of the title.

Another problem with Armstrong's theoretical framework is that, despite her efforts to provide socio-historical contexts for the novels she discusses, her assumptions about order and tragedy tend to dehistoricize. At the start of her last chapter she poses the question 'whether the reader of the novels, having seen the issue raised and resolved by the various authors, feels the given outcome to be justified or not' (147). This is her way of addressing three issues that are related in complex ways: that of aesthetic achievement; that of tragic form as she conceives it; and that of the relation between the moral assumptions of writer and reader – for she declares, later in the same chapter, 'there is no definitive answer, for a pluralist society, to the question of the nature of the laws transgressed by the adulterer or adulteress' (160). All these questions are important and challenging, and one reason why Armstrong's book is worth studying is that it raises them. In order to resolve them, however, it is necessary to develop a fuller understanding of what is at issue morally, historically, and ideologically in the novels themselves. In particular, this requires much closer attention to a question that Armstrong mentions at times but never investigates, that of the double standard of sexual morality that makes a wife's adultery of much greater concern than a husband's. That question complicates not only the moral questions at stake but the tragic 'universality' she takes for granted.

The approaches taken by Tony Tanner and Naomi Segal differ from each other as well as from Armstrong's, but, because each is discussed in the two chapters that follow, I will only outline them here. Tanner's approach in *Adultery in the Novel* is eclectic, drawing on the history of ideas and on structuralism both in its literary and anthropological manifestations as well as on Freudian-Lacanian theory, but also providing detailed textual commentary on the three novels on which he concentrates. His study therefore meets the criterion of depth of analysis, and its theoretical sophistication not only raises many interesting questions but compensates in part for the limited range of examples. What it lacks, however, is a proper historical perspective on any of the texts discussed at length: Rousseau's *Julie, or the New Heloise* (1761), Goethe's *Elective Affinities* (1809), and Flaubert's *Madame Bovary*. Although Tanner's argument is historical in that it recognizes the novel of adultery as a specifically nineteenth-century phenomenon, it does not take account of the particular historical and ideological conditions of each text. For this reason, although Tanner recognizes the fact that adultery in the nineteenth-century novel is almost always defined as female,[15] he gives no more weight to this than does Armstrong.

There are two main differences between Naomi Segal's study and those by Armstrong and Tanner. First, strictly speaking, Segal's *The Adulteress's Child: Authorship and Desire in the Nineteenth-Century Novel* is a study neither of the novel of adultery nor of adultery as a fictional theme. Instead, as its title and subtitle indicate, its subject is the relationship between authorship, the fictional adulteress and the latter's children. Second, unlike Armstrong or Tanner, Segal bases her study on a single theoretical model, one developed from feminist reinterpretations of Freudian psychoanalysis. She studies a range of novels from France, Russia, Germany and North America, and several late twentieth-century films, but most of her examples are French; and, though her analyses are often detailed, they are also, as her subject requires, quite narrowly focused. This focus produces much of interest, especially when applied to examples of the French Romantic confession, but it is relevant only in part to the study of adultery fiction. For example, as mentioned above, adultery does not even take place in several of the texts Segal analyses; and, by definition, the approach cannot apply to novels in which the adulterous wife is childless, such as Eça de Queirós's *Cousin Bazilio* or Leopoldo Alas's *La Regenta*.[16] There is also a larger difficulty: that, however expertly practised, psychoanalytical criticism cannot in itself account for a type of fiction that manifestly owes its origin to social, historical, political and ideological factors as well as to the operations of the unconscious. Study of the novel of adultery therefore requires a much wider theoretical framework.

The need for such a framework is also evident from Catherine Belsey's study of cultural representations of desire. In her Prologue, Belsey suggests that it is not possible to talk seriously about desire without taking account of psychoanalysis because that, she says, 'is probably the only theory we have that focuses on desire without ignoring the signifier'.[17] Through readings especially of Freud and Lacan, she bears out this claim in detail. She shows that, for Freud, 'Every object of adult desire stands in for an original object which is forever lost, and which it represents' (50); and that Lacan takes this further in that, for him, 'The signifier *replaces* the object it identifies as a separate entity' (55). These arguments lead to the following position: 'Neither natural nor cultural, neither a need at the level of the organism, nor a demand formulated by the *Cogito*, desire is a *difference*. It is an effect of the alienation in the human animal of the requirement for gratification as the demand for love' (60). This in turn, via Derrida's concept of 'differance', leads to the inference that 'Differance gives rise to desire and at the same time prevents its fulfilment', so that 'it is not possible to tell the truth of desire, or about desire' (71). The result, however, is not an impasse, because Belsey also believes that meanings, including 'love, desire, the body' (34), are 'culturally produced and learned' (33), and are thus open to interpretation. Indeed, her book discusses and illuminates a wide range of cultural representations of desire.

As Belsey points out, 'However much sexual practices and preferences are known to differ culturally, the desire that motivates them is tacitly understood to be the same throughout history' (7). The reason she employs an historical as well as a psychoanalytical and a poststructuralist approach is that she rejects this assumption that desire is historically invariable. She grounds in poststructuralist psychoanalysis her theorizing of how desire functions at a general human level, while giving other human sciences the main role in interpreting its specific manifestations. For example, by drawing on textual study and various secondary sources, she is able to contrast the representation of sexual passion in medieval texts such as Chrétien de Troyes's poem *The Knight of the Cart* and Thomas Malory's *Le Morte Darthur* with that in Tennyson's *Idylls of the King* several centuries later. Whereas, in *The Knight of the Cart*, 'It is not so much that love is necessarily adulterous, but rather that love and marriage are not yet indissolubly linked' (107), and, in Malory, 'constancy in love is an absolute value, while a loveless marriage entails only minimal obligations' (113), in Tennyson 'the Queen's sin is also a crime against a husband and a kingdom' (117–18). The only basis on which these contrasts can be explained is not psychoanalytical but historical, involving research into social and cultural institutions and ideology. Thus Belsey employs a fundamentally historical approach when she argues that, 'For respectable people, marriage was the only proper location of desire in the Victorian period. The project, therefore, was to reconcile desire with moral choice, to align it with the *Cogito*, to rational-ize it in the interests of domestic concord' (118). She uses the same approach when she considers the double standard:

One way of sustaining the Victorian ideal of marriage was to differentiate between male and female desire: the sexual impulses of a good man would be held in check by the pure love of a good woman, enabling him to become the Law-giver that civilization required him to be. To this end female desire was brought more firmly than ever before under the control of the law and the Law, legislation and morality. (127)

Belsey's study shows that, while psychoanalysis can illuminate the genesis and the structure of desire, only through historical inquiry is it possible to study the representation of desire in specific times and places in the past. This principle applies all the more strongly to the study of a particular kind of writing such as the novel of wifely adultery. For this literary form sprang not only from the ideal of marriage discussed by Belsey, and the policing of female desire to which it led, but also from the disparate cultural conditions that, among other things, led it to develop differently in various countries and, in Britain and North America, prevented its development altogether.

A study of the novel of wifely adultery must therefore draw on history, sociology, psychology and other human sciences as well as on specifically literary forms of knowledge and analysis, such as those that deal with narrative techniques or with rhetorical figures. And, in the same way that no study based on examples from a single literary tradition would be capable of achieving sufficient generality, approaches based chiefly on one type of theory and method, or, like Segal's in *The Adulteress's Child*, on a single theoretical paradigm, will need to be supplemented by knowledge from other disciplines – in particular, history. Such a study may certainly learn from psychoanalytical theory among the various new forms of knowledge that have arisen over the last hundred or so years. But its richest resource must be literary texts and their social, historical and ideological settings. That is the basic principle on which this book is written.

Those who have sought to explain the currency of adultery fiction in nineteenth-century France, and its virtual absence from contemporary Britain and North America, have often pointed to differences in marital customs.[18] In France, the argument goes, not only were arranged marriages much more common, but, among the aristocracy and upper bourgeoisie, they generally united a husband with a wife younger than himself who might well respond to the advances of a younger lover. In Britain and North America, on the other hand, more account was taken of mutual affection and compatibility, with the result that the wife was less vulnerable to temptation. The practice of contrasting French and British marital customs goes back to the eighteenth century, when, Lawrence Stone has claimed, the arranged marriage gave way in Britain to the 'companionate marriage' based more on affection.[19] Rousseau draws such a contrast in *Julie, or the New Heloise*; and Balzac makes great play of the age difference between French husband and wife in *The Physiology of Marriage* (1829).[20] But it is unwise to assume that fiction directly reflects social fact, or even social perception; or that marital conventions had so great an influence as to produce a type of fiction in one country that they denied in another. Of at least equal, if not greater, importance is what it was possible to offer in fiction intended for a general readership. Chapters 5 and 6 of this book show how it became increasingly difficult to handle the theme of sexual irregularity in British fiction during the eighteenth century, except for a brief interval in the later 1780s and the 1790s; and I have discussed elsewhere the impact of official and unofficial censorship in the century that followed.[21] In France, however, a tradition of libertine writing had long been established, writers such as Merimée and Balzac were able to draw on it more or less discreetly, and literary censorship was less active.[22]

A second way of explaining concern over adultery, and so the novel of adultery itself, is the argument from legitimate inheritance. According to this, the only way of ensuring rights of inheritance and the endurance of the male line was to prevent wives from bearing children by men other than their husbands. Unless a wife's chastity could be guaranteed, no husband could be confident that he had fathered her child(ren); whereas, even if he had issue by another woman, adultery on his part would be less serious, because, although he might make provision for an illegitimate child, such a child could not inherit. However, as Keith Thomas has argued, there are various flaws in this argument, especially the fact that, 'If "confusion of the progeny constitutes the essence of the crime," then the woman should be blameless if there is no confusion or if there is no progeny.'[23] Thomas concludes that the double standard 'is the reflection of the view that men have property in women and that the value of this property is immeasurably diminished if the woman at any time has sexual relations with anyone other than her husband'.[24] Other factors bolstering the double standard included assumptions about normative gender roles and about male and female sexuality. But there is also a socio-political dimension to the question of inheritance and legitimacy.

In her reading of *Julie, or the New Heloise*, Peggy Kamuf argues that Rousseau's heroine is positioned historically and socially between the aristocracy, 'which can no longer sustain its claim to legitimate power', and the bourgeoisie, 'which must succeed to the claim without violence, that is, legitimately'.[25] In other words, wifely adultery is taboo in the new bourgeois order not only to distinguish it from aristocratic sexual licence (actual or assumed), but to ensure bourgeois social legitimacy by providing an incontestable line of descent from father to son. The bourgeoisie's claim to political power was based in no small measure on its pretensions to moral authority. It was therefore a shrewd ideological move on the part of the bourgeoisie to appropriate the care over keeping the blood-line pure that, it was alleged, the aristocracy had neglected. As Rachel Fuchs has emphasized, in forbidding the unmarried mother to pursue for support the father of her child, the Napoleonic Code endorsed Rousseau's position on the problem of paternity and 'accommodated the bourgeoisie's desire to protect marriage, the family, and inherited property'.[26] Nicholas White suggests that 'the analogical power of the notion of legitimacy is undeniable for a developing class obsessed with the assertion of its own political authority', and also goes further: 'threats to the authority of the *paterfamilias* bespeak a fear of more general transgressions – and of the bourgeois insecurity that its own notion of order is the fruit of political transgression'.[27]

White's suggestion further helps explain why wifely adultery is such a common theme in nineteenth-century French fiction, and also accounts in part for its absence from canonical fiction of the period in Britain and North America. However, it was not only in Britain and the United States that the bourgeoisie gained power without political transgression. Literary influence must also have played an important role in spreading the novel of wifely adultery to those European countries such as Germany, Spain and Portugal where it was not taboo and where the bourgeoisie had not taken power through revolution. Nevertheless, the form spread so widely that further explanation is necessary, and this is offered in an essay by Felicia Gordon that supports and goes beyond those of Kamuf and White. 'One function of novels of adultery', Gordon proposes, 'was to legitimise women's exclusion from the public sphere by demonstrating that marriage was their only safe haven and that outside marriage they were doomed.'[28] Drawing on the work of Geneviève Fraisse, Gordon argues that 'democratic cultures faced a new crisis of gender definition', because, if their legitimacy 'rested on the consent of the governed', their exclusion of women from public life could only be justified by 'a renewed theorising of sexual differences'.[29] As Gordon shows, such a justification was supplied in the philosophical realm by Kant and Hegel.

Gordon's thesis works well for *Anna Karenina* and *Effi Briest*, the two texts to which she applies it. This is because, although Tolstoy was influenced by Schopenhauer rather than Kant and Hegel in his thinking on marriage and the family,[30] Schopenhauer's emphases were even more decided than theirs; and because the ideology of the Prussian state was in key respects based on Hegelian thinking.[31] However, two qualifications are necessary. First, while it is true that, as Gordon says, 'The bourgeois novel of adultery may be read simultaneously as a construction of legitimation or an ironic undermining of the ethical double standard on which marriage depended',[32] there is a difference between readings that novels abide, perhaps against the grain, and those they solicit. Rather, Gordon's analysis of *Anna Karenina* and *Effi Briest* suggests that they represent opposing strands within the tradition: in her terms, the one tends to construct legitimation, the other to undermine it ironically. Tolstoy's *The Kreutzer Sonata* (1891) and Fontane's *L'Adultera* (1882), which she also discusses, contrast similarly.[33] Second, the thesis has the additional merit that it applies to French as well as to other Continental European fiction, because women were everywhere excluded from the public sphere; though, for the same reason, it leaves unexplained the absence of novels of wifely adultery from Britain and North America. This absence may be explained only in part by the official and unofficial censorship and the ideology and practice of affective marriage that I have already mentioned.

Another part of the explanation for that absence is that after the Matrimonial Causes Act of 1857, as Barbara Leckie has shown, the topic of adultery flourished in British divorce court journalism.[34] Since British writers of the period liked to represent France as a place of literary and political excess, it is a fine irony that their newspapers flaunted the salacious material denied to their novels and, despite the lurid repute of French fiction, less prominent in Gallic than in British journalism.[35] Leckie also demonstrates how novelists in Britain found ways to deal with adultery in respectable fiction, ranging from Caroline Norton and Mary Elizabeth Braddon in the 1860s to Henry James and Ford Madox Ford into the next century. Nevertheless, perhaps in part because of divorce court journalism, the subject of wifely adultery remained taboo. As Leckie acknowledges, Norton's heroine in *Lost and Saved* (1863) is not an adulteress but the victim of a sham marriage, and in *The Doctor's Wife* (1864) Braddon rewrites *Madame Bovary* without the adultery. James and Ford go further, but, by showing how they adopt the viewpoint of the betrayed party and exploit unreliable narrators, Leckie's analysis makes it plain that they construct adultery in a quite different way from the nineteenth-century Continental tradition. While journalism was allowed surprising licence, British novelists had to deal with the subject of adultery through tact and indirection, and wifely adultery long remained virtually off limits.

In this way, while the tradition of libertine writing in France encouraged adultery fiction, Protestant evangelicalism – abetted by fears of French social instability – militated against its production in Britain. However, British socio-political and literary history of the Restoration and early eighteenth century suggests another part of the explanation. Chapters 4 to 6 of this book argue that the first English novel, Aphra Behn's *Love-Letters Between a Nobleman and His Sister* (1684–7), is a novel of adultery; that it helped begin a tradition of adultery fiction in Britain, much of it written by women; and that, from around 1740, this tradition was slowly expunged. Study of early British adultery fiction reveals that it differs radically from that of nineteenth-century Continental Europe, especially in that the writers who contributed to it, especially the women, questioned the double standard of sexual morality and asserted women's entitlement not only to a degree of personal independence but to sexual pleasure. Though the social and historical factors behind this movement are complex, it is not a coincidence that it began after the two English Revolutions, the one that set up a Commonwealth until the Restoration, and the other that dethroned James II. During this period the rights of the subject in relation to State and family were extensively discussed, notably by John Locke; and, towards its end, the rights of the female subject were forcefully raised by Mary Astell and others.[36] Early British adultery fiction served a number of aims, including political propaganda and social satire, but it also provided a means for questioning accepted codes of sexual conduct that, especially in the hands of women writers, could seek to redress the balance of moral judgement in favour of women. Yet, as feminist literary historians have shown, and as Chapters 5 and 6 of this book confirm from the history of later eighteenth-century adultery fiction in Britain, a backlash ensued. This intensified from about 1740, though it began rather earlier, and its effects were similar to those rationalized by Kant and Hegel. In other words, women were confined to a private sphere, defined by marriage and family, in which they were bereft of political and even many legal rights but invested with moral responsibilities.

It is significant that in France a similar backlash had already taken place in the early eighteenth century. Joan DeJean has argued convincingly that women played the key role in inaugurating the novel in France but that its subject matter led to its partial suppression. Two parts of DeJean's case are especially relevant. The first is her dual claim that, by virtue of its treatment of marriage, an early narrative by Lafayette, *The Princesse de Montpensier* (1662), 'can be said to usher in a new era in French women's writing'; and that, since literary history places Lafayette at the origin of the novel, 'the modern novel is thereby defined as the novel of adultery'.[37] The parallel with the tradition begun in Britain by Aphra Behn's *Love-Letters*, and its later suppression, is striking; but its full implications can only be gauged if a key distinction is drawn. Crucially, none of Lafayette's fiction, any more than Behn's or that of her successors in Britain, resembles the nineteenth-century novel of adultery. Adultery does not even take place in *The Princesse de Montpensier* or *The Princesse de Clèves*; instead, as DeJean shows, the pivotal issues of both are arranged marriages and female claims to independence. *The Comtesse de Tende*, a narrative attributed to Lafayette but not published till long after her death, may seem an exception in that it tells a story of actual adultery. Here too, however, the focus is on marriages of convenience. The story highlights the suffering not only of lover and wife, who both die, but of the wife's friend whom her lover marries for her wealth and position; and it points out the prior infidelity of the Comtesse's husband who lives on to a ripe old age.[38]

Secondly, DeJean also discusses the memoir-novels written by women in the period after the publication of *The Princesse de Clèves* and quickly suppressed by French literary history. Although these too are not fictions of adultery, their subject matter is close to that of Aphra Behn and her successors, which they influenced: 'Adultery, legal separation, illegitimate births, even custody battles – any cause for public scandal is dwelled on in loving detail'.[39] DeJean points out that, in the same period, 'French legal theorists loyal to the State had argued in a series of treatises in favour of the contract theory of marriage'. The object of such arguments was 'to give the State the authority necessary to take control over marital disputes away from ecclesiastical courts in favour of secular courts'; but it produced 'an unexpected side-effect: it encouraged private individuals to consider the possibility that unhappy unions could be terminated'.[40] Some of the people to consider such a possibility were women, and some of them wrote about it in memoir-novels, which met an outraged response from the many who feared 'woman answering to no one, woman as "legal adventuress"'.[41] The result was a campaign, spearheaded in literature by Boileau, to prevent women 'from using the novel as a public forum for such dangerous ideas as a wife's equality with her husband'.[42]

The cultural and ideological conflict recounted by DeJean had the same unhappy ending for those who supported increased rights for women as the parallel conflict in Britain that it anticipated. Its importance is that it laid the ground for a new form of misogyny, in which woman's role in public life, including in writing and publishing, was closely restricted, and her sexuality was subject not only to tight control but to a kind of redefinition that, in Britain, sought to deny her entitlement to sexual pleasure. Ironically, while in Britain this form of misogyny halted writing by women that explored sexual and marital relations from a viewpoint relatively sympathetic to them, a related form, reinforced in Continental Europe by philosophers such as Kant and Hegel, helped give rise in the following century to the novel of wifely adultery. The history of adultery fiction in France and Britain thus emphasizes again how essential it is to distinguish between different kinds of adultery text. Early adultery fiction, mainly female-authored and by no means centred on the adultery of wives, is concerned above all with problems that arise from marriage as an institution constraining women's social and affective aspirations; while nineteenth-century adultery fiction, written almost exclusively by men, is concerned much more with the role of the wife and its potential for social disruption.

From this point of view, the novel of wifely adultery should be considered not only as a literary genre but as part of the history of misogyny. The following chapters attempt to contribute to that history, first by considering works by two of the main theorists of adultery fiction, then by detailed analyses of examples from the long eighteenth century in Britain and later nineteenth-century France. `

2

Tony Tanner: *Adultery in the Novel*

Adultery in the Novel is only the first part of what Tanner intended as an even larger project, which he never completed. In the Preface, he outlines his enterprise as follows: 'a kind of prolonged prologue (or preliminary discourse) to the discussion of what I take to be one of the most important features of the development of the novel as we know it, or knew it' (xii).[1] This feature is 'the role played by the transgressive act of adultery in fiction' (xi). Since the book runs to nearly 400 pages, the word 'prolonged' is no understatement; and it is a prologue in three main ways. First, it sets out a range of ideas on the subject in a lengthy general introduction. Second, two of the three novels to which Tanner devotes entire chapters, Rousseau's *Julie, or the New Heloise* and Goethe's *Elective Affinities*, are not strictly speaking novels of adultery. In *Julie* the transgressive act is pre-marital fornication, though adultery is certainly threatened; in *Elective Affinities* it consists not in actual but imaginary adultery. Tanner argues that both are highly significant as precursors of the novel of adultery, but the only such novel he analyses at length is the third and last of his exemplary texts, *Madame Bovary*. Third, *Adultery in the Novel* is deliberately speculative and exploratory. Tanner calls it 'an exercise in reading', and he explains at the outset that, in order to open up a topic of such scope and complexity, he was obliged to bypass much of the secondary literature on his three texts and even 'many of the standard procedures of literary/ historical criticism' (xi). His approach is therefore eclectic, though much influenced by the Freudian-Lacanian and deconstructionist thinking that was becoming prominent at the time of writing in the late 1970s, and also drawing, especially in the Introduction, on the history of ideas and on structural anthropology.

Because of the exploratory character of the work, Tanner's Introduction does not take the form of a consecutive argument but consists of a series of discrete though loosely connected sections.

These set out a number of leading ideas, or working propositions, the most important of which I will try to summarize. First, marriage is the fundamental institution not only of nineteenth-century bourgeois society but of bourgeois society itself, and – as Tanner's formulations tend to slip from the specific to the universal – even of society in general (15–16, 28–9, 80–1, 85). Second, given the pivotal importance of marriage, adultery poses the most radical threat to social stability and continuity (17, 66). Third, this threat is all the stronger because marriage is not only analogous to but connected with the various other conventional systems on which society depends, especially language (53, 84–5). Fourth, the novel is an inherently transgressive form (3), and the novel of adultery shows this defining characteristic to the full. The reason for this is that, by portraying the breakdown of the key structure, marriage, it implies the instability of all the other conventional structures (84). Fifth, the novel of adultery wanes as marriage declines in importance, and this movement goes hand in hand with the rise of modernist literature and the alienation of the modernist writer from society and the reading public (13–14, 15, 85–6).

The scope and ambition of Tanner's project involved a number of risks, the most obvious of which is over-generalization. He tends in particular not only to slip from specific to universal in discussing the importance of marriage, but to speak of 'bourgeois society' as if it were everywhere one and the same. This slippage is related to two further problems. One is that *Adultery in the Novel* pays little regard to history: the history, for instance, of the legal and other institutions governing marriage and adultery, which differed – as in various ways they still do – from one nation to another. A case in point is the statement that, 'up to the end of the eighteenth century, adultery was an offense that could be, and still was, prosecuted in a court of law', and that in the nineteenth century the offence 'remained in the books' though it was 'never publicly prosecuted' (14). Though Tanner does not indicate to which country he refers, this appears to confuse with a law against adultery the English procedure of an action for so-called 'criminal conversation', by which a betrayed husband could seek to recover damages from his wife's lover. Such an action became a precondition for divorce, and husbands could and did make use of it until well into the nineteenth century, when it was abolished by the Matrimonial Causes Act of 1857; as Lawrence Stone has shown, adultery itself had been quietly decriminalized two centuries previously.[2] Elsewhere in Europe the laws were different, including in Scotland where 'notour' or persistent adultery remained a criminal offence. To give two other examples, under the Napoleonic Civil Code adultery was a crime punishable by imprisonment for an erring wife and her lover, who could also be fined, though only by a fine for an erring husband; and in Spain, except for a brief period under the Republic in the 1930s, it ceased to be a criminal offence only in 1978.[3]

The second problem is that the view of adultery Tanner proposes is essentially patriarchal, even though he recognizes that the novel of adultery focuses almost exclusively on adulterous women (13). This can hardly have been his intention, but it follows in part from his selection of sources, fictional and non-fictional alike, and in part from preconceptions to which no amount of acumen or erudition can give total immunity. The philosophical sources he uses to explore questions about marriage and adultery – chiefly works by Maine, Locke, Rousseau and Vico – are all written from positions that are in different ways patriarchal if not also, there are grounds for arguing, misogynistic.[4] Thus, when Tanner declares that 'Adultery threatens all family bonds' (29), he is not stating a truth universally accepted but an ideological maxim. Indeed, the entry on adultery in Larousse's *Grand dictionnaire universel du dix-neuvième siècle* contains versions of the maxim from different ends of the political spectrum: '*Adultery* is the ruin of the family and of society', by the abbé Louis Bautain, and '*Adultery* is a crime which contains in itself all others', by the socialist Pierre-Joseph Proudhon.[5] In the same way, *Julie, or the New Heloise* endorses an enlightened paternalism, *Elective Affinities* confines its two leading female characters to roles of renunciation, and *Madame Bovary* cannot help bearing the marks of Flaubert's misogynism, despite his theory and practice of artistic impersonality.[6] Since, until recently, the Western canon consisted mainly of works not only written but chosen by men, it has been difficult to avoid or even to be aware of patriarchal or masculinist assumptions; and alternative ideas of marriage and adultery have too often stayed hidden from view. For this reason the term 'novel of adultery' has been allowed to define a type of fiction almost invariably concerned only with the adultery of wives.

Though Tanner's Introduction has these and other shortcomings, the sheer scope of his project made some of them difficult and some impossible to avoid. Despite this, however, he raises so many critical questions about the theme and its possible implications, and his readings of the novels he discusses in detail are so provocative, that anyone studying adultery in literature is likely to be in his debt. That is the justification for the present chapter, which concentrates chiefly on his analyses of *Julie* and *Elective Affinities*. Both novels are of special interest because they predate the novel of wifely adultery while addressing cognate themes. Both also deserve to be much better known than they are currently outside their countries of origin – *Julie* not least because it was so influential in its own period, *Elective Affinities* because it raises such radical questions about marriage, sexual desire, and infidelity.

What made Rousseau's novel notorious in his own time, and for at least 200 years afterwards, was the love affair between the heroine Julie and her tutor St. Preux. Although much of the text is taken up with Julie's life after she marries her father's choice of husband, Monsieur de Wolmar, her last letter to some extent undercuts the exemplary role she plays as wife and mother by declaring her passion for her lover unextinguishable. Many contemporary readers found this apparent volte-face disturbing, as Nicola J. Watson has shown in discussing English responses to the novel.[7] The most striking feature in Tanner's reading of *Julie* is, therefore, that it focuses not on the novel's explicit concern about the heroine's sexual relations with the hero, but with what he suggests is its unadmitted yet palpable interest in her relations with her father the Baron d'Étange and her cousin Claire. Presenting St. Preux as passive and impotent, Tanner argues that the truly powerful love relationship in the novel is between Julie and her father, and that this is later subsumed into a quasi-incestuous arrangement in which Julie brings everyone she loves – husband, father, cousin, even former lover – under the same roof.

In focusing on the father, Tanner's interpretation opens up a key issue in *Julie* to which previous critics had paid inadequate attention. The interpretation is open, nevertheless, to various objections. In particular, it makes uneven and misleading use of psychoanalytical theory; it takes insufficient account of the novel's historical and ideological contexts; and the close reading on which it depends is at times arbitrary and selective. These three objections may be illustrated from a letter that Tanner rightly cites as pivotal, in which Julie relates to Claire her father's violent reaction on discovering she is in love with St. Preux. First, referring to Julie's account of how her father lost his temper and struck her and her mother repeatedly, Tanner claims: 'the attack could hardly be more sexual, albeit specific inadmissible incestuous lust has been translated, or distorted, into a violent anger that is permitted to the father simply because he is the father' (124). This assertion carries little if any weight, because Tanner gives no textual evidence to support it, apparently relying solely on the assumption that anger here signifies lust. Instead, he refers to a psychoanalytical concept in which the father and mother copulating form a 'combined object' in the eyes of the child (124); though, confusingly, he switches point of view to suggest that in this case the combined object is Julie and her mother in the eyes of the father. Second, moving to the sequence in which, ashamed of his violence, her father took Julie on his knees, Tanner observes 'a distinctly postcoital silence and exhaustion' (124), and then declares: 'here the physical detailing is so excitedly minute in a way that is so absent from Julie's letters to St. Preux that it seems to me permissible to perceive the scene and the attendant emotions it aroused in terms of barely controlled incest' (126). Although Tanner quotes from Julie's letter at length, he again offers no serious textual evidence for his sexualized reading. Instead, he omits material that does not favour it. In one case this emphasizes Julie's concern for her relationship with her lover rather than her father; in the other the mother's delight that father and daughter are reconciled – a delight that would be hard to understand if the scene played out in her presence had the sexual character Tanner gives it.[8]

What must be said in favour of Tanner's discussion of the scene is that it calls attention to emotions and actions of such violence as to demand explanation and even to invite psychoanalytical exegesis. However, a convincing reading needs not only to provide proper textual evidence, but also to take full account of what is at issue both in the scene and in its surrounding context. For example, while Tanner is correct to remark that the episode contains physical detail absent from Julie's letters to St. Preux, there is no ground for his epithet 'excitedly minute', and the novel's epistolary form offers a different explanation for the discrepancy from the Freudian one he proposes. *Julie* is written entirely in letters – a fact Tanner mentions but to which he pays little attention – and Rousseau suited each letter carefully both to correspondent and addressee. Since Julie, St. Preux and Claire all devote themselves to virtue, it is scarcely plausible that any of the letters between them would contain sensuous detail; but there is no reason why Julie should omit the physical facts either of her father's attack or of the affection each displays in its aftermath. The moment that seems most to invite Freudian interpretation is the one when Julie describes her father's behaviour after he has taken her on his knees:

> a certain gravity he dared not lay aside, a certain mortification he dared not overcome placed between a father and his daughter the sort of charming embarrassment that modesty and love lend to lovers; meanwhile a tender mother, overwhelmed with joy, secretly devoured a sight so sweet. (I.lxiii.144; 119)[9]

Here it is the comparison relating father and daughter to lovers that calls out for explanation. Indeed, as Peggy Kamuf has observed, the novel's editors in the Pléiade series reveal how sensitive a topic this is by trying to cover it up.[10] On the most literal level, it could be argued that the simile is by no means implausible from one young girl writing to another within a culture that valued filial affection highly, and that the innocence with which the remark is made tends to discount an erotic dimension. If, however, the simile is read in Freudian terms, what needs to be asked is whose fantasy is at stake. Since it is Julie who is writing, it might seem natural to suggest, with Tanner, that it is the character's. Indeed, Tanner does not hesitate to infer from a previous letter by Julie (I.liii) that 'the root fantasy is of being stabbed by her father herself', claiming: 'That is the dreaded/desired penetration' (121). One problem with this inference is that, as Janet Todd and Christine Roulston have suggested, the father's attack on his daughter is closer to rape than to any form of consensual incest.[11] Another is Tanner's use of a crude model of psychoanalytical criticism that addresses the character rather than the text. Instead, the proper question to ask is what might have been at issue for Rousseau in writing Julie's letter and in imagining the scene it describes. While, within Tanner's terms of reference, Julie's account of her father's behaviour could be read as implying suppressed desire on his part rather than hers, the key fantasy that requires attention is authorial, ideological, and cultural. Tanner's interpretation succeeds in establishing that the novel underscores the power of the father. It also suggests, more debatably, that the source of that power lies in sexual desire that culture requires to be repressed. What it leaves out are other sources of the father's power, and Rousseau's own agency in figuring them. These questions may be tackled by considering the larger role played both by the scene itself and by the father in the rest of the novel.

First, the immediate result of the scene is to cause Julie to miscarry. Although Tanner notes this, it is also necessary to register a further effect: the collapse of Julie's hope to use her pregnancy as a way of persuading her father to let her marry St. Preux. Second, and more important, is the impact of the father's violence – all the more shocking in a book that, according to the imaginary critic in the second Preface, contains 'Not a single evil deed' (8; 573). The scene is not only a turning point in the action, but a defining moment in the presentation of the Baron as father and aristocrat. In attacking his daughter, and then marrying her to a nobleman closer to his own age than hers, the Baron attempts to reaffirm patriarchy and aristocracy. At the same time, however, and by exposing his own reactionary failings, he brings home what Rousseau saw as the need to regenerate marriage, family and social order.

By associating what he calls 'the name of the father' with the Baron d'Étange, Tanner blurs a crucial distinction with Wolmar, the novel's other father-figure. Wolmar's relation to Julie and St. Preux is almost entirely paternalistic, and his role is to exemplify an enlightened, benevolent and therefore – it is suggested – proper form of authority. If this seems to state the obvious, it is far from plain in Tanner's reading, which not only emphasizes Étange over Wolmar, but diminishes the latter's role in creating the new order at Clarens by diverting almost exclusive responsibility to Julie. What lies behind that emphasis is Tanner's insistence on locating the heroine as the origin of a quasi-incestuous household in which everyone of importance to her lives together. But the attribution of 'a dream of total incest' to Julie (114) is misleading, because it is not strictly speaking her dream, or even Wolmar's. Quoting a later remark by Tanner on the subject (170), Christine Roulston assigns the metaphor of incest to Rousseau, for whom, she says, 'the incest model seems to be a way of controlling desire, insofar as the incest taboo is greater than the adultery taboo. In this sense, the avoidance of adultery can be maintained through the avoidance of incest.'[12] By attributing a dream of incest to Julie, Tanner risks implying that female desire is inherently transgressive. Roulston places the motif where it belongs, for it is the novel that assumes that female desire is transgressive and that it must therefore be subjected.

Despite such problems as these in the way Tanner interprets the novel, his account of the new family order that Julie and Wolmar establish shows at its best his ability to produce cogent and far-reaching propositions about fiction, culture and history. Five such propositions are especially significant. In order of appearance in his chapter, these are as follows: first, while the father is pre-eminent in *Julie*, the decline and disintegration of paternal power is an essential feature of novels of adultery (137); second, Rousseau's blueprint of a new way of life at Clarens is 'a high-bourgeois dream' closely resembling the one adumbrated by Richardson in *Pamela* (150); third, the same blueprint also anticipates ways of family life that would dominate bourgeois society over much of nineteenth-century Europe (159); fourth, a key factor in that life is the wife's supposed unemployment, which aroused fears that she might be tempted into adultery (160); fifth, *Julie* heralds orthodox nineteenth-century bourgeois attitudes to adultery (167). Subject to varying degrees of modification, each of these propositions has a critical role to play in any theory of the novel of adultery.

Taking them one by one, it is, first of all, a striking fact that with one exception there is no canonical novel of adultery in which the adulteress's father has more than a marginal part. In most cases he is simply dead, as in Eça's *Cousin Bazilio*, Tolstoy's *Anna Karenina*, Fontane's *L'Adultera*, Alas's *La Regenta* and Galdós's *Fortunata and Jacinta*. Where he survives, as he does for a while in *Madame Bovary*, and throughout *Effi Briest*, he is a benign, almost avuncular, presence who carries no hint of the authority or menace of Julie's father or indeed, in Samuel Richardson's novel, Clarissa's. The exception is Jacobsen's *Marie Grubbe*, an historical novel in which Marie's father represents the patriarchal, even feudal, order against which the individualistic heroine rebels. This is a far cry from Rousseau, but *Julie* anticipates the several novels of wifely adultery that conflate the father, minus his terrible power, with the husband. Though this type of father does not appear in the more ironic examples of the form, such as *Madame Bovary*, *Cousin Bazilio*, or *Fortunata and Jacinta*, the husbands of Anna Karenina, Melanie van der Straaten, Ana Ozores and Effi Briest are all not only old enough to have fathered their wives but treat them with a greater or lesser measure of partly well-meaning but largely impotent paternalism. The eclipse or disappearance of the father in the novel of wifely adultery is connected with the social, economic and ideological changes that conditioned the structure of the bourgeois family and, in particular, its classic nuclear form. According to the nuclear model, it is not the senior male of an extended family who holds most power but the husband, who may or may not be a father. It is, precisely, the husband's authority that is challenged in the novel of wifely adultery.

Second, Tanner's comparison of the 'almost pathologically mechanical orderliness at Clarens with the regularity maintained in the house of Pamela and Mr. B. after their marriage' (151, note 9) does not merely confirm that Rousseau had learned from Richardson. More important, it points to the parallel if not quite contemporaneous projects of two middle-class writers to push aside what they saw as the degenerate institutions of a decayed aristocracy and install superior codes of morality and behaviour. The success of those projects, carried forward of course by many others as well as by the two novelists, is borne out by the extent to which bourgeois family life in nineteenth-century Europe followed similar patterns. As Tanner puts it, in her domestic rituals 'Julie is anticipating how countless middle-class Victorian and bourgeois families will survive, through a compromise whereby obligatory duty is made palatable by regressive fantasy, and regressive fantasy is justified by accomplished duty' (159). He cites the cult of the child and what he calls the 'desperate retrospective eclecticism' of much nineteenth-century art and architecture as examples.

In the fourth proposition identified above, Tanner claims that 'Julie's picture of her maternal bliss also bespeaks the kind of unemployment that was to beset many later bourgeois mothers', and that it is this that helps explain 'why adultery becomes a paradigm for a large number of problems in nineteenth-century society and thus a key subject for novelists' (160). The case is more complex than this formulation can encompass. On the one hand, the idea of wives turning to adultery through lack of anything meaningful to do is borne out by most of the canonical examples: *Madame Bovary* above all, but also *Cousin Bazilio*, *Anna Karenina*, *La Regenta*, and *Effi Briest*. On the other hand, each of these cases signifies differently because it is determined by a distinct cultural and ideological context. For example, the idleness of Emma Bovary, fed by fantasies from her reading, differs from that of Anna Karenina, leading an aristocratic social life that Tolstoy despised, and from that of Effi Briest, married while still effectively a child, and neglected by her husband. More important still, perception or ascription must not be taken for fact. While Balzac's *Physiology of Marriage* argues that the leisure it attributes to the bourgeois wife creates all too many opportunities for her adultery, its exaggerated alarm on the subject suggests that such a danger was at least as much a projection of male fears as a social reality.[13] Balzac's casual attitude to male adultery is the other side of those fears.

Finally, there is Tanner's claim that Julie's arguments against St. Preux's proposal that the two could still be lovers after her marriage 'announce and define what is to be the orthodox bourgeois attitude to adultery' (167). Distinguishing between tolerance for adultery in eighteenth-century aristocratic society and its rejection by the new bourgeoisie, Tanner remarks:

> where there were other rules and relationships and sanctions holding society together, the idle class, or part of it, could afford to consider adultery a kind of game without endangering the structure of society. The matter is very different when we move into the bourgeois era and its novels, for then adultery is anything but a game – it is invariably a prelude to tragedy, if that word may be applied to any experience in the nineteenth-century novel. (166–7)

Here, and subject to two important qualifications, Tanner points to a fundamental difference between attitudes to adultery in eighteenth- and nineteenth-century European fiction and society. The first qualification is that for most nineteenth-century writers only wifely adultery was a matter of such extraordinary concern; the second, that some – among them Sand, Jacobsen, and Fontane – questioned the received ideas of the time about adultery, male and female.[14] Tanner is right to indicate a difference, and to connect it with the rise of the bourgeoisie; but it is complicated greatly by divergences rooted in social rank, national culture, and attitudes to gender and sexuality. These divergences are epitomized by the several versions of marriage that the novel offers.

At one extreme is the marriage of the Neapolitan marchioness who, true to cultural stereotype, takes affairs for granted and leads Milord Edward into inadvertent adultery by pretending she is single. At the other is the ideal Milord Edward advocates of marriage for mutual love. In between are two other kinds: that of Julie's parents, in which the father, 'Long inconstant and philandering, [. . .] lavished his youthful flames on a thousand objects less worthy of pleasing than his virtuous companion' (III.vii.265; 237); and that of Claire and her husband, founded on mutual respect and companionship. By the time he was writing the novel, Rousseau had established himself as 'the declared official enemy of adultery', according to the Pléiade editors.[15] This enmity was closely linked with his criticism of a decadent aristocracy in France and its arbitrary power. So, when Milord Edward argues with Julie's father in favour of marriage for love, an authorial footnote asks whether it is any wonder that women in France, 'tyrannized by the laws', 'so grievously avenge themselves through their morals' (II.ii.158–9 [p. 159]; 134).

In *Julie* Rousseau conveys an assumption, widely held in France and England at the period, that marriage for rank or fortune among the aristocracy often went hand in hand with tolerance for adultery. Writing from exile in Paris, St. Preux paints a picture of fashionable licence and asks: 'Besides, how can one expect from either party a more honest outcome of a bond about which the heart was not consulted?' (II.xxi.222; 194). Despite his criticism of aristocratic adultery, it is this view that lies behind his proposal that he and Julie could still be lovers after her marriage to Wolmar: in other words, he takes such a liaison as justified by prior and mutual love. Rousseau responds to St. Preux's proposal in a footnote of arch irony that Tanner oddly reads as equivocal (III.xvi.277; 248; Tanner, 167). A Protestant and a Swiss, his own position was more austere. The novel expresses disapproval not only of rank and fortune as bases for marriage, but of erotic passion too. Since it takes Julie's sexual transgression more seriously than that of St. Preux, its attack on adultery is grounded not only in a critique of aristocratic decadence but in a type of misogynism that would also underlie the dominant nineteenth-century constructions of female adultery. It is therefore a masterstroke on Rousseau's part – though one he adopted from Richardson – to have Julie defend marriage as sacred and repudiate adultery. Although her diatribe may be recuperated as 'Julie's way of dealing with her fear of adultery',[16] she adds rhetorical credence to his didactic case, and all the more because she is an already fallen member of the sex he believed to be weaker.

Julie's letter rebutting St. Preux's proposal defines marriage as 'the public and sacred faith [. . .] without which nothing can subsist in the legitimate order of human affairs' (III.xviii.296; 265). She therefore argues that to seduce a wife is a sin; nevertheless, she reserves her most vehement denunciation for the adulteress:

> How many falsehoods, how many lies, how many double-dealings to cover up a criminal traffic, to betray a husband,

corrupt servants, deceive the public! What a scandal for
accomplices! What an example for children! What becomes of
their education amidst so much attention given to gratifying
criminal passions with impunity? What becomes of the peace of
the household and the union of its heads? (III.xviii.297; 266)

In her next letter she goes on to reject 'the idea that love is essential
to a happy marriage', declaring that 'honesty, virtue, certain
conformities, less of status and age than of character and humor,
suffice between husband and wife' (III.xx.306; 274). It is this that
accounts for the plan she forms with her cousin Claire to marry the
latter's daughter to her elder son: a union not on the aristocratic
model, governed by rank and wealth, but on a bourgeois code of
enlightened affection and sobriety. If, however, such a plan evokes
Tanner's attribution to Julie of a dream of 'total incest', the
authorial design is quite different. *Julie* attempts nothing less than
to suppress female desire in the interests of motherhood and the
patriarchal family. In this way the novel once more foreshadows
developments in the nineteenth century. As Catherine Belsey
remarks when discussing Victorian marriage, 'One way of ensuring
the continuity of perfect concord in a marriage of true minds is the
suppression of female desire. [. . .] Companionate marriage
becomes in effect a renunciation of desire.'[17]
    In her chapter on the novel, Peggy Kamuf explains that, like the
original Heloise,

> Julie is positioned at the juncture of one social order which can no
> longer sustain its claim to legitimate power and another which
> must succeed to the claim without violence, that is, legitimately.
> In *Julie*, this articulation is worked out through Julie's passage from
> her father's archaic law of aristocratic privilege to the renewed
> order of an enlightened Wolmar, a passage that marks the
> intermediate term of her passion for St. Preux as disorder. (103)

The bourgeois attack on adultery in this way constitutes a claim not
only to moral but to social legitimacy, because it is designed to
exclude the birth of adulterine children. Kamuf shows how much
was at stake by arguing that the wife's ability to produce a child in
secret with another man than her husband 'exposes the arbitrary
prerogative of the father and thus of the conventions which protect
that prerogative'. She goes on to infer that for the emerging

bourgeois patriarchy it was necessary 'both that the sterile conventions of the extinguishing order be renewed in a natural relation and that the woman's duplicity – the potential for falsifying this "natural" link – be itself exposed, brought to the surface and made visible' (105).

Although Kamuf refers to Tanner only in her endnotes, and does not engage directly with his arguments, she provides a more convincing reading of the episode in which Julie's father strikes her and then takes her on his knees. First, she suggests that, 'by attacking his daughter, M. d'Étange denies the natural link which the convention of his authority is meant to guarantee: the father's attachment for the child he knows is legitimately his' (107). Second, she puts a very different construction from Tanner's on Julie's comparison with the awkwardness of two lovers. The point she underlines is Julie's remark that only her innocence, which she has lost to St. Preux, was missing from the scene:

> The acknowledgment of a discrepancy between filial affection and an erotic embrace – between a father and a lover – makes Julie guilty of a desire that does not correspond exactly to her father's. In effect, Julie knows (guiltily) that the 'natural union' of father and child – this 'natural scene' – is produced by a lie, the child's lie that she too desires only the father.
>
> The crime, therefore, is in the knowledge that the father's law rests on the lie by which the child pretends to be 'his', the product of his desire alone. (111)[18]

Far from attributing incestuous desire to Julie, as Tanner does on the questionable premises identified above, Kamuf proposes that the scene discloses the subversive difference of female desire that it is part of the novel's mission to suppress.

The critical and theoretical force of Kamuf's essay shows how far the psychoanalytical/deconstructionist approach pioneered by Tanner can lead – in this case from a feminist position. However, that approach does not altogether accommodate the element of dialogue within the novel itself. This is built into its epistolary form, and it is reproduced in the prefatory discussion that Rousseau stages between himself (albeit not as author) and an imaginary critic. It also often breaks out in the footnotes – at different points approving, scathing, irritated, or ironical – with which he peppered it. In obvious ways *Julie* is a programmatic work, laying out a blueprint for a new social order. But at the same time it is divided against itself, nowhere more than in Julie's confession in her final letter – not headed 'From Madame de Wolmar', like all her correspondence after her marriage, but 'From Julie' – that she cannot overcome her love for St. Preux. While this can be read, with Kamuf, as the author's reminder of irremediable female duplicity, it may also represent an implicit admission that the utopian project to which so much of the book is devoted is sterile.[19]

No one has expressed more trenchantly than Susan Moller Okin the nature and effect of the impasse in which Rousseau's thinking not only in *Julie* but in all his mature work locks women: 'The ancient two-fold demands made of woman – that she be both the inspiration of romantic, sexual love, and the guardian of marital fidelity – are seen at their most tragic in Rousseau.'[20] Okin reinforces her point by discussing *Émile et Sophie, ou les solitaires*, the unfinished sequel to *Émile* (1762), in which the marriage between Émile and Sophie breaks down as a result of the latter's adultery. Such an outcome is in keeping with the nineteenth-century novel of adultery that, Tanner convincingly argues, *Julie* prefigures, even though in one key respect the sequel points beyond it.[21] It also confirms once more the double standard of sexual morality that he does not emphasize sufficiently.

Tanner also presents Goethe's *Elective Affinities* as a precursor of the nineteenth-century novel of adultery. He begins his chapter on it by quoting Thomas Mann, who called it 'that novel of the mystic dominance of nature over human psychology', and 'the most daring and trenchant novel about adultery that the moral culture of the Occident ever produced'.[22] The second of these remarks is a paradox, as Tanner indicates, because none of the four main figures in *Elective Affinities* commits adultery. Nevertheless, the moral and imaginative tenacity with which Goethe treated the problems of love, marriage and fidelity powerfully supports Mann's claim.

As H. G. Barnes has declared, *Elective Affinities* 'cannot be said to enjoy the recognition which an incomparably written work, yielding profound insights into the human heart, might be expected to command. Its impact on European literature seems minimal when compared with the prestige enjoyed by some English, French, or Russian novels.'[23] This assertion is as valid at the start of the twenty-first century as it was in 1967, when it was published, so

Tanner showed characteristic discernment in giving Goethe's novel a central place in his study. More debatable, however, are the terms in which he sought to justify Mann's remark: 'if you take adultery in its larger sense of an improper conjunction, or the bringing together of things that law decrees should remain apart, then the novel does indeed explore this problem at every level as it occurs within bourgeois society' (179). Leaving aside the exaggeration 'at every level', there are two main difficulties with this claim. First, it is too abstract; second, the social order portrayed is not bourgeois, nor does Tanner succeed in demonstrating that it prefigures a bourgeois society of the future.

If psychoanalysis takes pride of place in Tanner's reading of *Julie*, structuralism dominates his discussion of *Elective Affinities*. In the final part of his chapter on Goethe's novel, Tanner returns to the role of the father, which occupies so much of his chapter on Rousseau's. Most of the discussion, however, expands on various other ideas he had developed in his Introduction: in particular, the notion that systems of relationship function in the same way as language, and that the novel points to the potential for crisis in the social as in the linguistic order. Arguing, for example, that a preoccupation with the themes and the activities of taxonomy and categorization pervades *Elective Affinities*, he writes:

> just as things have first to be separated to make identification and meaning and orientation in the world possible, and then to be related by certain laws so that the experienced world does not fall apart into monadic fragments; so individuals have first to be separated by family, class, tribe, etc., and then to be related by laws decreeing the class of the marriageable as distinct from the unmarriageable. This indeed is why marriage and language are so intimately connected, as the structuralists have taught us to recognize. In being so clear on all these matters, what Goethe's novel invites is, not further interpretation – which would indeed be redundant – but a recognition of certain conditions that effectively determine how social and passional relations can be *thought about*. (221; Tanner's emphasis)

However, interesting though this view is, and despite his apparent disclaimer, Tanner cannot avoid offering his own interpretation. This interpretation stems from the structuralist thinking to which he refers; and its principal limitation is a failure to take account of historical and textual specificity. The result is not only the false assumption that the novel depicts bourgeois social life, but, as with *Julie*, a disregard both for the novel's historical context and its form.

The social order depicted in *Elective Affinities* is that of the minor nobility and gentry. Of the four main characters, Eduard is styled in the first sentence as 'a wealthy baron' (I.i.3; 242); Charlotte is of similar rank, having previously served as a lady-in-waiting (I.xi.75; 318); the Captain is a soldier by profession, though not in current service; and Ottilie, Charlotte's orphaned niece, is her dependant.[24] Eduard and Charlotte live at leisure on a landed estate, selling part of it when they want to raise money; and among the various characters who visit them are the Count and the Baroness, higher up in the aristocracy; the interfering Mittler, a former cleric and a self-taught legal expert who lives on the income of an estate bought from his winnings in a lottery; and two professional men, the Assistant and the Architect. Unlike St. Preux, not one of these figures shows links with the bourgeoisie; and, though Goethe's novel is implicitly critical of the aristocracy, it is not easy to find in it the bourgeois ideological tendencies that are manifest in *Julie*.[25]

Instead of prefiguring a new middle-class order, in an important sense *Elective Affinities* looks backwards and outwards rather than forward. For example, the various activities depicted in the novel of planning, reducing to order, tidying up and repressing are not intrinsically bourgeois, as Tanner assumes. What they represent in their historical context is a sustained interrogation of attitudes and practices spread by the Enlightenment, and rehearsed unavailingly in the novel by a fading minor aristocracy. As John Winkelman has argued, the novel is not set in an historical vacuum, but during a period of the Napoleonic Wars that was especially critical for Germany.[26] Responding to the crisis, the novel asks questions not only about the decadent German nobility, but about many of the ideas, ideals and hopes central to contemporary European civilization. Yet, while challenging Enlightenment culture, *Elective Affinities* by no means abandons Enlightenment values of enquiry. The result is a probing, sceptical novel, ironic and lyrical by turns, that offers no comfort to bourgeois or other pieties.[27] It is therefore easy to appreciate why the novel's most recent English translator has called it 'a chilling, in some ways a repellent book' (xx); but it is not necessary to share this assessment to understand why a text that is so morally and intellectually disturbing has suffered the neglect pointed out by Barnes.

Despite the unnecessary abstraction of Tanner's approach, it is the distinction of his reading of *Elective Affinities* to recognize the radical nature of its questioning about marriage, sexual desire and adultery. For example, in discussing the scene in which Eduard, Charlotte and the Captain debate the significance of the term that gives the novel its title, he remarks that the word

> poses a potential paradox, since *Verwandtschaften* are the family relationships, i.e., the ones you do not, in fact, and cannot choose [*wählen*]. Goethe's use of the word [. . .] points exactly to the paradox of marriage – that it is notionally a voluntary nonblood relationship that immediately becomes a binding blood relationship. (208–9)

This insight shifts attention from the original chemical sense of the term, which has preoccupied nearly all of the novel's critics, to its social implications – the point being that only in marrying is it possible to choose one's kin. That choice made, Tanner continues, the novel asks what happens when further affinities supervene:

> The problem – once you move from the inanimate world dominated by natural laws and enter the social one in which law, custom, and choice are all operative in deciding 'divorces' and combinations – is that there is no control in advance on what may precipitate attraction or repulsion. [. . .] Charlotte wants to get beyond allegory, playing with the resemblances between the inanimate and the human realm, and to hold onto the uniquely human meaning of the words 'kinship by choice.' But the very phrase contains a paradox and potential disintegration, for what may be combined by kinship may be separated by choice. (209)

It is this problem that the novel's notorious pivotal episode casts into relief. Here Eduard and Charlotte, the married couple at its centre, have sex while each is thinking of another with whom they are in love: Eduard of Ottilie, Charlotte of the Captain. As Tanner argues, what is so unsettling about this episode is its suggestion 'not just that married sexual activity may effectively be adulterous sexual activity but that it may not in fact be possible to tell – or to keep – them apart' (191).

Tanner is right to emphasize how fully the novel succeeds in dramatizing the conflict between marital obligation and sexual desire and in exploring some of the most searching implications of that conflict. In going on to claim, however, that the novel's most impressive achievement is to lay bare and to problematize the systems of meaning that determine how patterns of relationship are to be understood, he misses a key point and bypasses two important opportunities.

The key point missed is the novel's form. Although Goethe called *Elective Affinities* a novel in his subtitle, he began it as a *Novelle*; and, as critics have often recognized, the text draws many of its qualities from this specifically German tradition.[28] Just as Tanner says little of *Julie* as an epistolary novel, so he does not acknowledge the significance of the *Novelle* for *Elective Affinities*. Instead, he treats it as if it differed little from what he loosely calls the 'bourgeois novel'. In drawing attention, for instance, to 'the level of generality, verging on allegory, on which the book is conducted' (184), he refers to a central feature of the *Novelle* form, but apparently without recognizing that this is what it is. The result is that he gives disproportionate emphasis to qualities that are intrinsic to the form rather than peculiar to Goethe's novel. A case in point is his remark that the 'larger irony' of *Elective Affinities* is that 'the participants are largely unaware to what extent they are, as it were, the victims and servitors of the very language of signs, formulae, figures of speech with which they are amusing or enlightening themselves. In ways they cannot perceive, they are their own experiment' (211). Within the tradition of the *Novelle*, there is nothing remarkable about this kind of irony and stylization – including the raising by the characters of the very moral, social and philosophical questions with which the work as a whole engages. Applying the structuralist notion of language as a kind of prison-house, Tanner goes on to assert that 'the property owners become paradoxically owned by the metaphors they play with, or by the redundancy of signs and projections that they make use of during their leisure hours. In so doing, they effectively help to create the situations and patterns in which their unused energies will find formal expression' (213). In a way characteristic of structuralism, this gives signs and language determining power, overlooking their functions and referents. Though such a perspective has its interest, it ignores what the novel does with the conventions of the *Novelle*, a form virtually designed for the raising of radical questions.

The first opportunity Tanner passes by is that of pursuing the links between *Elective Affinities* and *Julie*. These are significant, not least because one novel was written in the heyday and the other at the close of the Enlightenment; and, given that he discusses them in consecutive chapters, it is odd that he does not compare them. The links are close enough to suggest that the later work in part rewrites its predecessor. First, while both novels present attempts by the characters to create a kind of country-estate utopia, in Goethe's the attempt is both less ambitious than in Rousseau's yet more destructive in its failure. Second, while *Julie* does not overtly suggest either that its social prescriptions are flawed or that human desire is beyond ordering, *Elective Affinities* neither commits itself to a position on marriage or adultery nor implies that, at least in the given social order, there is any way of containing or managing desire except through death. Third, while both novels show great interest in education, Goethe's, again unlike Rousseau's, avoids prescribing any system, although it allows the Assistant to expound his views and shows two very different outcomes of education in Ottilie and Charlotte's daughter Luciane. But perhaps the most interesting link between the two texts is the death by water in which each culminates. Whereas Julie saves her younger son from drowning but dies in the aftermath, in *Elective Affinities* the son of Eduard and Charlotte is drowned as a result of Ottilie's haste, confusion and distress after Eduard has revealed that he was born from what was imaginatively if not physically an act of 'double adultery' (II.xiii.206; 455). The death of the child in *Elective Affinities*, as well as, ultimately, that of Ottilie herself, points to the starker implications of Goethe's novel. *Elective Affinities* is more directly ironic, critical and interrogative than *Julie*, written as it was during a period in which Enlightenment aspirations seemed to have failed, and lacking the confidence that Rousseau could affirm as a member of the rising bourgeoisie. At the same time, these are the qualities that prevented it from influencing the fiction of its own century.

The second opportunity Tanner forgoes is that of distinguishing between Goethe's novel and later fiction of adultery. In terming the act of imaginary infidelity between Eduard and Charlotte 'nonadulterous adultery', Tanner underlines its essential paradox more effectively than those who, like H. G. Barnes, have adopted the phrase 'spiritual adultery'.[29] However, his approach does not accommodate the several important differences between the construction of marital infidelity in *Elective Affinities* and in nearly all nineteenth-century adultery fiction. The most obvious of these is the proposition the episode incorporates that adultery may be defined in terms of psychological as much as of physical betrayal. This is not only to endorse Christ's admonition, 'That whosoever looketh on a woman to lust after her hath committed adultery with her already in his heart' (Matthew 5:28), but to give it literal embodiment, for the baby born from this virtual adultery resembles not his mother or father but the Captain and Ottilie.[30] Furthermore, the episode also suggests that both partners in the act of adultery are equally guilty, whereas almost all nineteenth-century European adultery fiction not only neglects adultery by men, married or not, but is based on betrayal of husband by wife. Despite the influence of the double standard, this is consistent both with Christian precept and with the Protestant doctrines in which Goethe had been brought up. Because original Christian principles had become blurred by secular institutions and practice, such implications are all the more arresting.

Nevertheless, the episode also contains a suggestion that runs counter both to Christian teaching and to traditional moral values: that adultery may consist in sexual relations not only between a husband or wife and another person, married or not, but between the husband or wife themselves when they are in love with someone else. Goethe compounds the problem by involving both spouses in this virtual double adultery. He advances his suggestion not discursively but through the paradoxical language in which he refers to Eduard and Charlotte's intercourse and its aftermath:

> In the dim light of the lamp inner attraction asserted, imagination asserted, their rights over the real. Eduard held only Ottilie in his arms; before Charlotte's soul the Captain hovered nearer or further; and so, miraculously enough, the absent and the present enticingly and blissfully wove themselves together.
>
> And yet the present does not let itself be robbed of its monstrous right. They spent a part of the night in all kinds of talk and pleasantries that were all the freer because unhappily the heart took no part in them. But, when Eduard awoke the next morning in the bosom of his wife, the day seemed to look in upon him ominously, the sun seemed to him to be lighting up a crime; he crept from her side, and, peculiarly enough, when she awoke she found herself alone. (I.xi.78–9, TM; 321)

What is remarkable about this account is its claim that both 'inner attraction' (*die innre Neigung*) and 'the present' (*die Gegenwart*) have rights (*ihre Rechte; ihr ungeheures Recht*). While adulterous desires may prevail over 'the real', so that husband and wife make love in fantasy not with each other but with the objects of those desires, their married relation can reassert itself afterwards in all its easy familiarity. Goethe's phrasing is ambiguous in that it offers opposite definitions of the crime that Eduard imagines is coming to light. On the one hand, it might be supposed that the crime consists in effectual betrayal of the marriage. Yet it is the present that the narrator terms 'monstrous' (*ungeheures*), presumably because it contrasts so jarringly with the blissful fantasy husband and wife have just enjoyed. For, while both have betrayed their marriage in imagination, they have also betrayed their true emotional unions in fact. The novel restates the paradox when Eduard, seeing for the first time the child born of sex without love between him and his wife, exclaims to Ottilie:

> Shall I frighten your pure soul with the unhappy thought that a man and wife, estranged, in their embraces may defile a legal union by their real living desires? Or since we have come so far, since my relationship with Charlotte must be brought to an end, since you will be mine, why should I not say it? And I will, though it is harsh: this child was begotten and conceived in a double adultery! It severs me from my wife and my wife from me when it ought to have united us. May it be a witness against me, and may those beautiful eyes tell yours that in the arms of another woman I belonged to you, and may you feel, Ottilie, truly feel, that only in your arms can I expiate that error, that crime. (II.xiii.206–7, 455)

Again there is no question, even for Eduard, that both he and Charlotte have sinned morally and psychologically against their marriage. Yet, at the same time, he also gives weight to what he terms 'their real living desires', and he claims that he can only expiate the crime by honouring those desires through union with Ottilie.

Tanner represents this central contradiction more accurately than those who, like H. G. Barnes, assume that the sin it embodies is against marriage, or those who, like H. Jane Plenderleith, assume that it is against love and/or against the self.[31] At the same time, however, he tends to mystify it by suggesting, for instance, that Eduard's use of the word 'crime' (I.xi.79; 321) implies 'that law can engender criminality, or, to put it more extremely and worryingly, it implies the possibility that the legal may incomprehensibly turn into its supposed opposite and become the very thing it was formulated to prohibit and exclude' (195). This rephrases his earlier remark, in the Introduction, that 'contracts *create* transgressions' (11); and it is equally specious because, in attributing all power to the system, it omits – or denies – human choice and agency. Instead, in *Elective Affinities* Goethe presented some of the most painful truths involved in marital infidelity; and at the heart of that presentation is the fact that adultery involves more than one betrayal. It is in this way that the novel justifies Thomas Mann's remark, and, in doing so, goes beyond all subsequent nineteenth-century fiction in its exploration of adultery.

There are two further respects in which *Elective Affinities* presses its enquiry into the problems of marital infidelity. First, it places a child at the centre of the action as it develops. The son born to Charlotte and Eduard from their act of 'nonadulterous adultery', neither adulterine nor wholly legitimate, helps define and set in relief the conflicts that infidelity creates, especially through his death. Charlotte, whose adulterous desires are less strong than her husband's, responds to her pregnancy by re-dedicating herself to her marriage, but for Eduard the child proves that the marriage is false. After the child's death, on the other hand, Charlotte tells the Major (as the Captain has become) that she agrees to Eduard's proposal for a divorce; and the Major himself cannot regret the death, envisaging 'Ottilie with her own child in her arms as the best possible compensation for what she had caused Eduard to lose', and 'a son in his own lap who would be the image of himself with more right than the one who had died' (II.xiv.213; 461). Only Ottilie cannot accept the death, declaring: 'In a terrible fashion God has opened my eyes to the crime in which I am caught up' (II.xiv.214; 463), and promising to atone for it. In this way, and with frightening economy, the novel sets out a range of responses not only to a child born to a marriage without love, but to a child who is in a sense adulterine, and not only to the birth of such a child but to his death. Only *Anna Karenina*, among later nineteenth-century novels, handles the problems raised for spouses and lover by legitimate and adulterine children with comparable insight.

Elective Affinities offers a possible solution for its quartet of mismatched and unmatched characters through the availability of divorce, and this is the second respect in which the novel extends its enquiry. Though the married pair do not take this path, any more than they commit adultery, the novel marks it out for them in two ways. First, both have already been married, and only the deaths of their former spouses have enabled them to marry again. The Count expresses the point with typical cynicism: 'In their case Death did willingly what the courts, when it is left to them, do very unwillingly' (I.x.69; 311). Second, the Count and the Baroness, who are conducting a semi-clandestine affair, themselves wish to escape unhappy marriages. For the Baroness divorce is possible, but not for the Count; however, on their reappearance several chapters later the Count's wife has just died and they are to marry as soon as it is decent. Goethe uses the introduction of the Count and the Baroness to dramatize opposite opinions on marriage and divorce. On the one hand, Mittler puts the traditional view, departing in dudgeon before the Count and Baroness arrive. On the other, they take the free-and-easy line often associated at this period with the aristocracy, though the Count also flirts with the radical ideas that marriages should last only for five years, and should become indissoluble only when one of the spouses has been married three times. The novel sets these and other positions at issue, offering little evidence that would enable Goethe's own stance to be determined. Later nineteenth-century novels of adultery that deal with divorce take a position either against it, like *Anna Karenina*, or for it, like Fontane's *L'Adultera*. The distinction of Goethe's novel is to present the issue dispassionately.

Without including the physical act of adultery, *Elective Affinities* shows a deeper insight into issues of marital infidelity than nearly all later nineteenth-century fiction. It not only presents in subtle yet sharp definition the conflict between marriage and adulterous desire, but moots divorce as a possible solution, and embodies the conflict in the shape of a child who is effectively killed as a result. What made it difficult for Goethe's successors to learn from his novel was the growing restriction of thinking about marriage and adultery imposed by bourgeois culture. That culture was not as all-embracing as Tanner assumes, and fortunately it did not encumber Goethe. Writing in a small aristocratic court, within a continuing Enlightenment tradition of unfettered enquiry, and in a country where divorce had been long established, he was able to raise questions that nineteenth-century ideology too often blocked.

Yet there is one important respect in which the assumptions behind Goethe's novel are in accord with those behind the new ideology that was emerging, and indeed behind *Julie* that had helped announce them. Although, unlike the novel of wifely adultery, *Elective Affinities* by no means portrays women as the weaker sex, it gives Charlotte and Ottilie roles that conform not only to the doctrine of separate spheres but to an ideal of passive and even saintly resignation. At the start, Goethe has Charlotte distinguish between concerns that she identifies as typically male and female:

> Men attend more to particular things and to the present, and rightly, since they are called upon to act and to influence events. Women, on the other hand, with an equal rightness attend more to the things that hang together in life, since a woman's fate and the fate of her family depend on such things hanging together and it is up to her to see to it that they do. (I.i.6; 245)

In accordance with this generalization, Eduard is more active and indeed impulsive, while Charlotte is calm and restrained, keeping the welfare of others in view. When she, an excellent musician, accompanies her less practised husband in a duet, the narrator calls her 'a good conductor and a shrewd housewife' (I.ii.17; 257) for the carefulness of the balance she keeps between his irregularities and the demands of the music; and her response to the Captain's embrace is to reciprocate only in part and to repeat her wedding vows on going back to her room. The narrator hints that the reason for this reaction is her sense that, following her night with Eduard, she may be pregnant: 'she was seized by a curious apprehension, a joyous and anxious trembling, which resolved itself into a woman's most sacred hopes and longings' (I.xii.84; 326). Ottilie takes much further this care for significant others. When she plays music with Eduard, she not only adapts her manner to his but creates of it 'something whole and alive' that has its own truth (I.viii.55; 297), and later even her handwriting becomes indistinguishable from his when she completes a task of copying he has begun.

However, Ottilie's role is figured still more clearly in the *tableau vivant* designed by the Architect in which he casts her as the Virgin Mary, holding the baby Jesus in a traditional Nativity scene. This accords with the narrator's remarks that 'her whole disposition was towards the house and domestic matters' (I.viii.54; 296); that she looks after Eduard with loving care; and that, after the baby is born, 'she became as good as a mother to the growing boy, or rather she became another sort of mother' (II.xi.197; 445). One of the aphorisms in Ottilie's diary reads: 'Voluntary dependence is the finest condition, and how would that be possible without love?' (II.v.151; 397). But if part of her role is devotion to others – so that, for example, she is prepared to give up Eduard to Charlotte following the birth of their baby – another part is an equally self-denying sense of moral duty. After the child is drowned while in her care, she tells Charlotte: 'God has opened my eyes to the crime in which I am caught up' (II.xiv.214; 463), and she can forgive herself only on the condition of 'complete renunciation' (II.xv.216; 464). It is not necessary to assume that Goethe endorses Ottilie's response to the events that enfold her any more than he endorses the educational theories of the Assistant. However, while those theories advocate the increasingly dominant doctrine of separate spheres – 'Educate the boys for service and the girls for motherhood' (II.vii.164; 410), as the Assistant puts it – Ottilie embodies a code of female virtue and moral exemplariness that Comte and Michelet, among others, would develop, and that is the other side of the wilful, passionate and erring figure of the wife in later nineteenth-century fiction of adultery. In this respect *Elective Affinities* anticipates the tradition that would follow, though in a way that is much less misogynistic.

In the final section of his chapter Tanner takes up this aspect of the novel by commenting on the figure of the father. He suggests that the novel presents this figure not in the form of Eduard, its only actual father, but symbolically, in the three *tableaux vivants* in which Charlotte's daughter Luciane plays a leading role. These, he argues, present 'a glossary of archetypes of male power' (229); with one of them, 'The Paternal Admonition', signifying that in the new bourgeois home obedience will be enforced not by physical power but by 'conscience' (228). However, it is possible to read the *tableaux* quite differently. First, as H. B. Nisbet and Hans Reiss have pointed out, the task of interpreting them is complicated by the fact that 'Goethe himself is known to have considered such *tableaux* aesthetically illegitimate since they rested on a confusion between art and life'.[32] Indeed, the fact that it is the egotistical and attention-seeking Luciane who stars in them itself suggests that they should be read with caution.

Second, although the print entitled 'The Paternal Admonition' was used in the eighteenth century for the moral edification of young ladies, the painting on which it is based, by the seventeenth-century Dutch artist Gerard Ter Borch, is actually a brothel scene.

Drawing attention to this fact, Susan Sirc argues that Goethe's presentation of the *tableau* suggests he may have known the picture's true meaning, and that he may therefore be 'treating the whole "tableau" with sophisticated irony'.[33] If this is so, it is consistent with the questions raised by the novel about Eduard's quasi-paternal relationship with Ottilie. H. Jane Plenderleith, who discusses these matters, points to the 'aspects of control, power and exploitation' that the relationship shows, and so puts a quite different construction upon it.[34] Again, then, the novel seems not to prefigure the emergent bourgeois order so much as to hold up established beliefs and practices for examination. In this case the beliefs and practices are those of patriarchy. Since the nineteenth-century novel of adultery is an essentially patriarchal form, it is not surprising that none of its practitioners drew on *Elective Affinities*. As I have shown elsewhere, only George Sand, in *Jacques* (1834), took up Goethe's novel, though she did so to support the giving way of a failed marriage to a successful one.[35]

Tanner ends his chapter by returning to the idea that the characters are trapped in the signifying systems through which they live: 'they all inhabit a present that is full of "pictures" and re-presentations of the past in many forms. In striving for uniqueness and difference, they are unavoidably and inextricably involved in repetition and similarity' (231). Unlike the many insights of Tanner's discussion, this does little justice to the complexities of Goethe's novel, but it anticipates the approach of his next chapter, on *Madame Bovary*.

Because of his structuralist interest in language, and because of the novel's extraordinary textuality, *Madame Bovary* is the novel with which Tanner's approach works best. His chapter on the novel is the climax of his book – indeed, at 67,000 or so words, it is long enough to be a book in itself. It is therefore a paradox that, of the four main chapters in *Adultery in the Novel*, the one on *Madame Bovary* contributes least to the question of how adultery fiction might be theorized. The chief reason for this is that it focuses not so much on adultery as on textuality.

Like Roland Barthes,[36] Tanner argues that 'The interest has moved conclusively, in Flaubert, from the referends to the referring – from world to text' (302). One of the problems this approach produces is that the sole evidence offered is textual – though

Tanner does not hesitate to cite a range of prominent theorists. When, for example, he declares that 'Flaubert's whole book makes us aware in a new way that the crisis in marriage is also, and not by metaphor but by identity, a crisis in language' (363), he offers no evidence other than that of the text that there was a crisis of either kind. In particular, the proposition that Flaubert was in some way telling the truth about French society – even about bourgeois society in general – is simply taken for granted, or, rather, finessed through commentary on the intricacies of the text.

Tanner's concern with the textual and the linguistic takes him so far that he presents Emma Bovary as a victim not of bourgeois society or of patriarchy but of language itself. After a brief introduction, the first four sections of his chapter deal with some of the men who, he says, 'make up the male context within which she must articulate her life, or have it shaped and defined for her' (235): her husband Charles; the tax-collector Binet; her first lover, Rodolphe; and the pharmacist Homais; and he goes on to deal with three more in the seventh section: her second lover, Léon; the draper and moneylender Lheureux; and the blind beggar. Tanner argues that the novel begins by presenting Charles Bovary's first admission to school in order to dramatize 'the enculturation process' (240), and, more specifically, 'the various stages involved in the entry into language' (244); and that the crisis of language it depicts is represented by Binet's meaningless duplication, Rodolphe's failure to distinguish, Homais's empty but tyrannical labelling, and a whole set of 'degenerative displacements or transformations' (285) such as various forms of fetishism. However, although he portrays bourgeois society as a kind of box that denies difference, like the one that destroys Hippolyte's leg (282), and although he suggests that Lheureux's office, Homais's Capharnaum and Binet's workshop are all 'bourgeois interiors that in different ways serve to intensify the impossibility of Emma's life' (298), he claims that the true villain is language. For him, 'Emma is caught and lost, caressed and violated, created and destroyed in and by the language into which she is born – a signal victim of the privileged discourses of the time' (312).

There are several serious difficulties with such an argument. First, Tanner repeatedly refers to adultery as if it had the same meaning irrespective of gender or marital status, even though he recognizes in his Introduction that nineteenth-century novels focus 'almost inevitably' on 'the adulterous *woman*' (13), and even though that woman is always a wife. In light of this fact, the large claims he proposes for the significance of adultery require modification, at the very least, in order to take account of the gender biases in law, society, ideology, and (arguably) language. Second, if it is the case that Emma Bovary is a victim of language – rather than, say, of law, society, or ideology – it is difficult to explain why the novel has to be about her rather than anyone else. Tanner raises this question, without recognizing its consequences for his argument, by suggesting that '"duplicity" is latent in the very nature of the phenomenon of language' (335), so that, for instance, 'punning can be seen as a kind of verbal adultery' (324); and by stating:

> Emma is not a unique but an exemplary case. She is inserted into a syntagmatic relationship [marriage], but her whole being tends to think and feel in (increasingly confused) associative constellations. Both of these modes of establishing relations are inherent in the language, indeed in *la condition linguistique.* (365)

Third, although Tanner asserts that 'The triumph of adultery is the destruction of difference', on the same page he acknowledges that 'Marriage as [Flaubert] perceived and depicted it simply offered a different mode of reification and dehumanization' (367). This leaves unanswered, and unanswerable, the question why Flaubert chose to write about adultery – wifely adultery – rather than marriage.

A further implication in his argument that Tanner seems not to recognize concerns the figure of the father. Presenting the doctor Larivière as a symbolic reminder of that figure, he suggests that 'the number and variety of foot and leg ailments and weaknesses' in the novel points to a 'decline in potency and decisive authority in the Father', and that this 'is inextricably linked with the increasing instability of marriage, and with the growing uncertainty about its status and "binding" power' (322). This is not just to imply but to state a cause-and-effect relation between the decline of patriarchy and the rise of marital instability, as signified by (wifely) adultery. In this case it is especially relevant that, once more, Tanner offers no evidence apart from the text of Flaubert's novel that marriage was increasingly insecure. If the masculine foot and leg ailments to which he refers will bear the Freudian reading he presupposes, in which they represent a crippling of the phallus, then the novel would appear to endorse not merely patriarchy but misogynism. This would be in keeping with the dominant construction of wifely adultery at this period in France, as articulated by Hippolyte Lucas in his essay on the adulterous woman, and by the entry on adultery in Larousse's *Grand dictionnaire universel du dix-neuvième siècle*.[37] That Tanner does not recognize the implication is consistent both with his failure to deal adequately with the double standard inherent in almost all adultery fiction and with his reliance, in exploring questions concerning marriage and adultery, on philosophical sources written from patriarchal if not downright misogynistic positions.[38] Although he brings out the patriarchal nature of the name 'Madame Bovary' (236, 305–7, 312), he appears to assume that the novel simply depicts the ideology the name inscribes, even perhaps questions it, rather than implicitly sustaining it. Similarly, his convincing demonstration of how Emma 'is "morselized" by Charles's eye and by Flaubert's text' (351) stops short of exploring what might be at issue in the sexual, masculinist bias it indicates.

While an interesting essay on Flaubert's novel, Tanner's chapter on *Madame Bovary* therefore has little of direct relevance to contribute to a theory of adultery fiction. Its highlights are its inspired explanation of why the novel begins with Charles Bovary's admission to school, its attention to how Emma is presented, in particular her 'morselization', and its detailed and often ingenious demonstration of the novel's textuality. But – and not least because it offers no comparisons – it certainly does not sustain its claim that *Madame Bovary* is 'the most important and far-reaching novel of adultery in Western literature' (235). Such a value judgement might carry weight if Tanner were able to prove that there was a crisis in marriage and in language in mid-nineteenth-century France, that this double crisis had implications for bourgeois society in general, and that the novel represents it critically. The fact that he succeeds in proving none of these things takes nothing away from Flaubert's novel: *Madame Bovary* remains a superb achievement that not only survives but triumphantly rewards repeated re-reading. Instead, as the main focus of Tanner's discussion suggests, the novel's value lies not so much in what it has to say about adultery – in that respect *Elective Affinities* goes much further, not least because Goethe imposes no sexual double standard – as in its endlessly inventive and provocative use of language.

3

Children and Childlessness in the Novel of Wifely Adultery

Given the importance of matters of inheritance and legitimacy in the novel of wifely adultery, it is not surprising that two of the most interesting critical approaches to this kind of fiction have focused on questions raised by the transgressive woman's childbearing. As I have indicated in Chapter 1, one of the main tenets by which the double standard of sexual morality was rationalized in eighteenth- and nineteenth-century Europe was that of legitimate inheritance. On the grounds of rights to inheritance and the continuance of the male line, it was generally held that the wife should not have sexual contact with any man but her husband, in case offspring conceived outside the marriage might covertly supplant his own. On such grounds alone, and leaving aside what may underlie them,[1] much is at stake in the role of children in the fiction of wifely adultery. The aim of this chapter is twofold. First, through reference to a range of examples, mostly novels of wifely adultery but also several that border on or foreshadow the form, it analyses patterns both of childbearing and childlessness. Second, it considers and evaluates two previous treatments of the question from approaches that are in several respects quite different. My approach is the one I employ throughout the book. It is formalist, historical, and comparativist, being based on the analytical comparison of novelistic texts on the same theme and produced in the same historical period, but within several different national traditions and ideologies.

The two previous discussions of the question are by Naomi Segal and Loralee MacPike. Segal's approach is based on Freudian psychoanalytical theory and its modern recensions, especially those influenced by feminism, and it takes special account of authorship and gender.[2] Her main contentions may be summarized as follows. First, the adulteress's child is positioned either in a 'patrilinear' or in a 'matrilinear' structure (8). Second, in 'patrilinear' texts, a son enables the transfer of the wife 'from one paternal chain to another' (10), so that 'the author-protagonist-narrator remains inside a protective patrilinear structure' (192). Third, in 'matrilinear' texts, a daughter marks the sin and, in Freudian terms, the inadequacy of the mother; but, though the mother dies, she offers 'a portrait in negative of the potential dispensability of male authorship' (192). A fourth claim, following on from the third, is that, 'in male-authored texts, bad women have daughters' (115). This is a complex thesis, but Tony Williams highlights one of its leading emphases when he says that, according to Segal, in nineteenth-century male-authored novels the woman who commits adultery has 'a difficult relationship with a daughter, who, by virtue of the fact that she is female, is both reproof and punishment', whereas 'the wife whose adultery is forestalled is typically locked in a closer relationship with a sick son'.[3] Segal's approach is of special interest here because it produces a thesis about adultery fiction that can function as a test case for the application of a particular theoretical paradigm, in this case one based on psychoanalysis. However, as I have pointed out in Chapter 1, not all the texts considered by Segal are novels of adultery. For her, the presence of 'adulterous desire' (61) is enough to generate the fictional patterns she finds.

MacPike's approach is quite different from Segal's, and its focus is not confined to questions of adultery.[4] Her subject is the representation in nineteenth-century fiction of the childbearing of so-called fallen women, and her approach one that combines feminism with comparative literary history. MacPike's study, published eight years before Segal's, anticipates it in some respects by arguing that writers of the period distinguish between lawful and transgressive sexuality through their portrayal of childbearing, and that the issue of inheritance is crucial. However, she considers a wider range of texts, including novels by women as well as men, and she offers an historical perspective on the whole question.

There are many potential reproductive patterns in novels of wifely adultery. At one end of the spectrum, the wife conceives neither with husband nor lover; at the other, she conceives with both. Between these extremes, she may produce either legitimate or adulterine children; and the legitimate offspring may be born either before or after her adultery. Two further questions are highly

character has five children, in the following order: a daughter and a son with her husband; and a son, a daughter and a further son with her lover. The love affair is conducted for many years in parallel with the marriage; it is tolerated by the husband, who is himself promiscuous; and, perhaps for this reason but also in conformity with the laws of the period, the lover's children are treated as his own.[8] It is this toleration of adultery within marriage that largely serves to distinguish *A Woman of Thirty* from the classic novel of wifely adultery.

However, in the attention it gives to offspring in an adulterous marriage, *A Woman of Thirty* comes much closer to the emergent form. Balzac's melodramatic plot highlights the significance of such children only too glaringly. First, in an episode with the none-too-subtle title 'The Finger of God', the elder adulterine son, his mother's favourite child, is drowned after a malicious push from his legitimate but slighted sister. Second, in an episode several years on, the same sister elopes on the spur of the moment with an escaping murderer, later marrying him and accompanying him on his career as a pirate. She briefly meets her father again when her husband captures the ship on which he is sailing; and she is reunited equally briefly with her mother after her husband has been killed and when she and her own daughter are dying of poverty and malnutrition. Third, the novel ends with an episode in which the adulterous wife discovers, just before she dies, that the daughter she has had with her lover has begun an affair that is not only adulterous but incestuous, since the daughter has fallen, in ignorance of her parentage, for her mother's lover's legitimate son.

There are several implications to the story of the woman of thirty. The most blatant is that the crimes of the adulteress are likely to be punished – in this case, even to the third generation. Another, more interesting, implication has been noted by Loralee MacPike in a general remark on the adulteress's child: 'Good women bear sons, bad women daughters who cannot carry on the male line, thus ensuring that negative qualities in the parents (particularly the mother) will not be part of the moral '"genealogical continuity"' (57).[9] Referring to *A Woman of Thirty*, MacPike also points out that the drowning of the adulterine son negates 'any possibility of paternal succession through illegitimacy'. While Julie d'Aiglemont has sons as well as daughters, it is true that even the legitimate son does not survive long into adulthood, and that the second adulterine son also dies young. There is, however, a third possible implication in her story, and one that sits contradictorily with the first two: that part of the problem is with marriage. Despite having married for love, against the wishes of her father,[10] Julie not only cannot love her husband but cannot love the children she has with him. This implication is consistent with the libertine side of a highly paradoxical text in which extra-marital affairs are tolerated, and in which the woman of thirty is celebrated as an object of male desire.[11] On the one hand, therefore, *A Woman of Thirty* heralds the classic novel of wifely adultery through the theme of maternal guilt and the questions of succession and inheritance underlined by MacPike. On the other, its libertine and sub-erotic elements recall the older traditions out of which the new form partly developed.

The second work by Balzac to anticipate the classic novel of wifely adultery is *The Muse of the Department* (1843). Here, the problem of the wife's preference for adulterine children does not arise, because she has no children with her husband. However, the children she has with her lover lack any role in the narrative except as pawns in transactions of property and succession. As in *A Woman of Thirty*, the husband tolerates his wife's adultery, even though she leaves him and his provincial estate for several years and lives in Paris with her lover. The reason for this extraordinary forbearance is that his ambitions of territorial expansion and social advancement require children he can claim as his own to inherit his lands and titles.[12] This text, at least, shows none of the anxieties about inheritance – either moral or material – emphasized by MacPike. But, in contrast with the husband, there are few if any compensations for the wife. Although she dumps her lover, who has exploited her shamelessly, Balzac gives her no alternative but to return to a loveless marriage in which, forced to renounce her aspirations as a writer (she is the muse of the novel's title), she can only devote herself to her children and to charity.

There is a single key respect in which the full-fledged novel of wifely adultery differs from these examples by Balzac. It is that, in nearly all examples of the form, wifely adultery is intolerable, leading not only to marital breakdown but to the humiliation of both partners and usually also to the death of the wife. *A Woman of Thirty*, for all its contradictions, anticipates the new form in the role it gives to children; *The Muse of the Department* in showing how female aspirations may find an outlet in adultery. While, in the latter case, Balzac has the wife's adultery produce no fatal outcome, he gives her ambitions no other scope. Instead, undermining

husband she does not love, and is unable to love the daughter she has with her lover. Indeed, there is even a sense in which the converse is true for her husband: Karenin's relation to his son is cool and overbearing, though dutiful; whereas he feels for a while a deep emotional bond to his wife's adulterine daughter. The fact that the two parents bond with children of the opposite sex is psychologically interesting in itself. But there are also ways of explaining this bonding that pull against psychoanalytical models. First, the novel suggests that Anna channels into her relation with her son the need for loving that is not met by her marriage. Second, Anna not only nearly dies in bearing her daughter, but pregnancy and childbirth come to represent for her the danger of losing Vronsky through the loss of what she believes binds him to her, her looks. Third, under Russian law the husband had rights over all children born to his wife, adulterine or otherwise, while the marriage still continued; and, as the novel makes clear, marriage could not be ended easily.[16] From Anna's point of view, her daughter therefore constitutes an obstacle to her happiness with Vronsky. Yet it does not follow from this that, by giving access to Anna's perspective, Tolstoy invites sympathy for her. Instead, she is plainly defined as a bad mother in the episode when Dolly visits her in the country (VI.xvii–xxiv); and, in the sequences presenting the feelings of her son, the focus is poignantly on his sense of bewilderment and betrayal. In accordance with MacPike's paradigm, this son is available at the end as a line for inheritance; whereas, because of her sex, the adulterine child, though she survives and is adopted by Karenin, is not. All this suggests how deeply the novel is rooted in conservative, patriarchal ideology. Fundamentally, Anna's children function as part of a case against wifely adultery. One main part of that case is Tolstoy's wonderfully convincing presentation of her son's point of view.

Although *Madame Bovary* and *Anna Karenina* are often considered as typical novels of adultery, not all examples from the tradition endow the adulterous wife with children. Neither Luiza, in Eça de Queirós's *Cousin Bazilio*, nor Ana, in Alas's *La Regenta*, has a child, whether with husband or lover; and in each case this raises a different set of questions.

Cousin Bazilio has often been described as a Portuguese adaptation of *Madame Bovary*,[17] but there is little in common between the character and situation of Eça's heroine and those of Flaubert's. In particular, Luiza is not only childless, but she is also on the whole contented with her husband of three years when she enters her affair; and her seducer is her former fiancé, who had broken their engagement when his father's business had failed. The childlessness of Jorge and Luiza is constructed by Eça not to imply that the marriage is empty, but to produce a space that adultery all too easily fills. No sooner does Jorge go away, for the first time since their marriage, and no sooner does Bazilio choose his opportunity, than Luiza quickly succumbs. In these respects as in others, Eça follows the example not so much of *Madame Bovary* as of the emerging Naturalist movement.[18] In accordance with Naturalist thinking, he has Luiza follow the line of least resistance when occasion beckons and she is physically aroused. But the novel also shows both Jorge and Luiza regretting their failure to have children; and, in its presentation of sexual licence in Lisbon society, it indicates a widespread sterility and corruption. The fact that both themes reappear in *La Regenta* suggests that Iberia produced its own version of adultery fiction in which childbearing – or, in these cases, childlessness – plays a different role from elsewhere.

Alas's novel contrasts both with Eça's and with other novels of wifely adultery in that the heroine's affair begins very late in the action, in the gap before the penultimate chapter.[19] Her childlessness is explained by her husband's impotence; and no pregnancy follows the affair, which comes to light very quickly. Like *Cousin Bazilio*, therefore, *La Regenta* addresses quite different issues from those I have identified in *Madame Bovary* and *Anna Karenina*. Two of the most important of these are conflict between the clerical and the secular establishment, and, in one of the parallels between Alas's novel and Eça's, an all-pervasive corruption and decadence. The power of the Church is in part personified by Don Fermín De Pas, canon theologian of the cathedral, that of the secular state by the seducer, Don Alvaro Mesía; and it is the struggle for Ana between these two that delays her surrender to Mesía for so long. But the motives of De Pas in his relations with Ana are little less ignoble than those of her seducer. His object is not her spiritual good, but her moral submission, both as a demonstration of his social power and as hollow compensation for the fact that his position precludes him from becoming her lover.

La Regenta imagines sexual desire as characteristically blocked, misdirected or perverted. Ana's childlessness in her marriage, and

of wifely adultery. *Marie Grubbe* points instead to a code of fatalistic individualism, consistent not only with a Protestant culture but with the theories of Darwin that Jacobsen had translated into Danish.[21] Jacobsen identified the key values of this code when he declared his abiding interest in 'the struggle of one or more human beings for existence, that is their struggle against the existing order of things for their right to exist in their own way'.[22] For him, a woman or a man could be justified in forming relationships according to sexual preference, irrespective of any need to produce offspring and even when, like Marie, she crossed class boundaries. Marie's childlessness is part of her emancipation – though this is limited by the hardship and abuse which, thanks to Jacobsen's assumptions about female sexuality,[23] she accepts from her beloved third husband.

What largely enables a measure of emancipation for Jacobsen's heroine is a fact that has too often escaped notice in discussions of novels of adultery – the availability or otherwise of divorce.[24] While there was no provision for divorce in France between 1816 and 1884, or in Spain until 1932, and while divorce was difficult to obtain in pre-Revolutionary Russia, Marie Grubbe is entitled not only to end her marriages legally but to remarry twice. Divorce was available in various Protestant countries, including Denmark, from as early as the sixteenth century,[25] and its established if sometimes threatened acceptance is a key influence on adultery fiction from Protestant cultures. This emphasizes once more how important it is for the critic to take proper account of cultural specificity, a point further reinforced by Theodor Fontane's three novels of adultery.

Fontane's first such work, *L'Adultera* (1882), is unique in the canon of nineteenth-century adultery fiction in that it ends happily. Published only four years after the final part of *Anna Karenina*, it follows Tolstoy's novel in giving its heroine offspring both from marriage and from adultery, but diverges radically in allowing her divorce, remarriage to her lover, and gradual acceptance by society. *L'Adultera* does not sidestep the problems posed to an adulterous wife by her children, but neither does it suggest that they are beyond remedy. First, it allows its heroine, Melanie, clarity and courage in facing a potentially disastrous conflict of loyalties. Invited by her husband to look at their children as she leaves them for the last time, she refuses; and she later explains this apparently callous response when she says: 'If you run away from your marriage for no other reason than because you love another man, then you give up your right to play the tender mother' (XX.111; 122).[26] The bitter consequences of this renunciation are shown when Melanie's older daughter rejects her in hatred, but she does not crumble. Second, the novel permits Melanie to bear an adulterine daughter who, exceptionally among narratives of adultery, not only survives but becomes the core of a new and better marriage. This outcome is all the more pertinent because the daughter's name, Aninette, recalls that of Anna Karenina's daughter, Ani. Third, like Jacobsen, Fontane gives his heroine a distinctively Protestant code of self-determination. What enables Melanie to leave husband and children to live with another man is her conviction that her first marriage was a lie: 'I must start a new life and find in him what was missing from my old life, and that is truth' (XVI.92; 102). Melanie also resembles Marie Grubbe in her acceptance of the consequences, which at first are damaging though her position eventually improves.

Fontane's second novel of adultery, *Beyond Recall* (1891), is unique in the nineteenth-century canon in a quite different way from *L'Adultera* in that its action turns not on female but on male adultery. While children play a part in this novel too, it is of much slighter thematic importance. The daughter and son of Helmut and Christine von Holk are adolescents, born in the earlier, happier years of a marriage that has sunk into difficulty; and no child results from the fleeting affair their father has during a long absence from home. Because Fontane sets only the first eight and the last brief three of the novel's thirty-four chapters in the family home, he gives limited opportunities for the children to figure strongly. However, the conflicting views expressed by the parents about their children's education is an early sign not only of tension between them but of different codes of values. In this way son and daughter are significant not in what they do or in what happens to them, but in what they show about their parents' marriage; and Fontane broadens this function by using the daughter, Asta, as a kind of Jamesian reflector. In the opening chapters he gives Asta a subsidiary but an appreciable role in the conversations through which, characteristically, he develops the themes of his novel; and what she especially reflects are the differences between her parents and the troubles they forebode. However, unique as the novel may be in turning on male adultery, it is revealing in that, unlike novels of wifely adultery, it shows no consequences falling on the children – even though, despite a reconciliation between husband and wife,

root in Britain.[29] Not only was *East Lynne* written by a woman, but it is centred on wifely adultery; as a bestseller of its day that has only recently begun to interest critics, all it lacks is canonical status. Wood took every precaution to avoid offence to her readers, permitting almost no attention to adultery as such and constructing a plot that offers to explain though not to excuse her heroine's behaviour. The most implausible part of that plot not only punishes the adulteress through her children, but also, against the moralizing grain, invites sympathy.

Isabel Vane has three children with her husband before she leaves him for another man; she bears a son to her lover after he has left her in turn; and, following her divorce, disfigurement and reported death in an accident, she returns incognito to her former home, where her husband has remarried, to act as governess to her own children and those of the new wife. Here she endures not only the family's attempt to expunge her memory, including the renaming of the daughter christened after her, but the slow expiry of her elder son from consumption. Wood goes further still in condemning Isabel to silence as she witnesses her former husband's intimacy with his new wife, and as she sees her own children given second place by their stepmother. Such emotional torture is all too obvious retribution; yet, because it is so extreme, and because, throughout the novel, Isabel has almost no freedom of action, she emerges at the end not as a villainess but almost as a martyr. Lyn Pykett and E. Ann Kaplan have shown how, in other areas of its plot, *East Lynne* demonstrates the powerlessness of a young wife and mother and the emotional and domestic pressures to which she is exposed.[30] In these ways the novel offers a subtext about women's oppression that takes it in a quite different direction from the classic novel of wifely adultery. It is a striking paradox that in Britain, with its moral and institutional taboos on writing about sexual matters, it was a woman who produced a bestselling novel of wifely adultery, even though she took care to provoke no blushes and to spare no fictive punishment. Even more striking, however, is that Ellen Wood's treatment of an adultery plot allowed her to highlight afflictions suffered by women in the home.

East Lynne is consistent with MacPike's paradigm in that Isabel's first child is a daughter, against the expectations of her husband, and in that two of her male offspring die: not only her adulterine son, but also the elder son she has with her husband. It is further consistent in that, unlike Isabel, the second wife bears her husband a son before a daughter. However, Isabel's third son, named after the father, survives; and this means that her part in the line of inheritance can continue. More interesting still is that Wood makes her heroine a good mother. In this respect Isabel is contrasted both with her cousin by marriage, Lady Mount Severn, who is selfish and insensitive, and, more subtly, with her husband's second wife, who prefers her husband to her children and who tends to manage rather than care for her children.[31] Wood also has her heroine influence her nephew, son to Lady Mount Severn, powerfully and for the good. These emphases bear out another part of MacPike's argument, that 'a bad woman's love of her son [may] redeem her' (64); so again the effect is to mitigate, even challenge, stereotypes of the adulterous wife.

Like most of the other novels discussed in this chapter, *East Lynne* conforms better to MacPike's view than to Segal's of the relation in nineteenth-century fiction between childbearing and transgressive female sexuality. There are two main reasons for this. First, Segal's approach, unlike MacPike's, largely excludes issues of culture, history and ideology. Second, even if all Segal's readings of her chosen texts were equally convincing, the range of her examples is limited. MacPike's approach is stronger because it considers the question of childbearing within the general context of attitudes to transgressive female sexuality, including those of female writers as well as male, and because it sets that context in an historical framework. In particular, MacPike offers an explanation for the fact that it was in the nineteenth century that childbearing came to have the meanings studied by her and by Segal. Drawing on Foucault's *History of Sexuality*,[32] she argues that the medicine, psychiatry and economics of the period created a new discourse of sexuality that was all the more highly charged because 'sexuality determined inheritance' (56), and that gave it a kind of symbolic potential it had not possessed in the previous century. Such a thesis is in keeping with the arguments set out in Chapter 1 of this book about the role of inheritance and legitimacy in the novel of wifely adultery. It is also supported by the fact that the adultery fictions of the long eighteenth century discussed in the next three chapters give the childbearing of transgressive women none of the symbolic value it has in nineteenth-century fiction. In these texts, many of which are by women, pregnancy and childbearing may act as consequences of

Part II
Circumtexts

both the upper and the lower classes took a remarkably relaxed and permissive attitude to sexual behaviour. It is possible, but not proven, that the lower-middle classes did not share in this cultural change, continuing to cherish Puritan and then Methodist values throughout the century without a break. It seems certain that the more pious of the Anglican upper bourgeoisie and gentry were also unaffected by the change. [. . .] For those who did not share the religious convictions of these respectable, God-fearing middle ranks, however, the eighteenth century was a period of extraordinary sexual tolerance.[4]

Although Stone's selection and interpretation of evidence has not gone unquestioned,[5] and although, as the next chapter will show, attitudes markedly hardened in the 1740s, there is no dispute that the Restoration and the first few decades of the century was a period of unusual sexual licence both in word and deed, at least among the aristocracy and upper bourgeoisie. As Stone observes, 'sexual promiscuity became a hallmark of fashion at court and in high political circles',[6] and a whole ideology of libertinism flourished, most pungently in the work of Rochester.[7] Not only did Restoration comedy make fornication and adultery its stock in trade. When political turmoil hampered theatrical production in the early 1680s, the popularity of French amatory fictions such as *Les Lettres portugaises* (1669) and *La Princesse de Clèves* (1678), both recently translated into English,[8] paved the way for a new sexual-ization of narrative.

The basic conditions for the emergence of amatory fiction in Britain were, therefore, a culture of tolerated sexual licence in the upper classes, especially the court; the open expression, publication and dramatization of libertine thinking; and the adoption of a tradition already well established in France of narratives revolving not only on love but sexual scandal.[9] The constraints on theatrical production during the early 1680s were the catalyst. It was at this time that Aphra Behn (1640–89), her livelihood as a dramatist threatened,[10] turned to other literary forms, especially narrative, publishing *Love-Letters Between a Nobleman and his Sister* in three parts between 1684 and 1687. Reprinted in its complete form in 1693, four years after Behn's death, it had, according to Janet Todd, become 'the epitome of erotic fiction' by the beginning of the eighteenth century, with at least six further editions appearing between 1708 and 1765 (Introduction, xv).[11] At the same time, like much of Behn's other work, the novel was written not only to supply the author with an income but to comment, from a broadly Tory perspective, on the turbulent politics of the period. All the leading characters are closely based on contemporary figures, and the action tracks critical events that took place up to the middle of the decade, including the Rye House Plot of 1682, and, three years later, the death of Charles II, his succession by James II, and Monmouth's abortive Rebellion. Behn's central male character, Philander, standing for Forde, Lord Grey of Werke, provides the chief connection between politics and love. It is he who elopes with Silvia (Lady Henrietta Berkeley), takes part in the conspiracy and invasion that represent the Rye House Plot and Monmouth's Rebellion, and commits various other infidelities. But *Love-Letters* is no less a novel because its characters are based on contemporaries and its action on actual events. Although the links are transparent, Behn added figures and incidents of her own devising, and, as Warren Chernaik has pointed out, 'the pulsations of feeling charted in the exchange of letters are entirely authorial inventions'.[12]

The fact that *Love-Letters* was written by a woman, and that it reflects directly on the key political events of the time, are not the only respects in which it differs from most adultery fiction of the nineteenth century. A third disparity is the narrative form, which is exclusively epistolary in the first part and partly so in the other two; and a fourth is the adoption at various points in the action of a comic and even farcical perspective such as is often found in Behn's plays. These differences are significant: the first because, unlike the impersonal voice in most novels of wifely adultery, the mixture of voices, as Janet Todd has observed, calls narrative authority in question (xxx–xxxii); the second in a similar way because it invites a response that is not uniformly serious and that is capable of critical disengagement. However, the most striking contrast with later fiction of adultery concerns the equivocal status given in the novel to marriage.

In nineteenth-century adultery fiction, the key sexual transgression was most often to be single adultery by a married woman with an unmarried man. Behn's novel implies a quite different set of values, because it begins from single adultery by a married man with an unmarried woman who is, moreover, his sister-in-law. Philander's initial offence is therefore not only adultery but, according to the kinship rules of the period, incest.[13] The picture is complicated further by another three factors. First, Philander tries to justify his

with whom, when the First Play was ended, he could Discourse with of useful things of State, as well as Love; and improve in both the Noble Mysteries, by her Charming Conversation' (335). Although Hermione is accused of manipulating him, although his fellow conspirators criticize him for uxoriousness, and although the narrator remarks that 'Love had unman'd his great Soul' (434), it is a measure of Behn's critique of upper-class matrimony that the only marriage in the novel grounded on mutual support and affection is bigamous. Marriage by arrangement or imperative is therefore one of the factors that give different meanings to adultery in Behn's novel from those it would carry in the nineteenth century.

A second key factor is the ideology of libertinism. While Behn's work consistently attacks arranged and forced marriages, the attitude it implies towards libertinism is more complex and open to argument. What complicates the display of libertine ideology and behaviour in *Love-Letters* is the fact that Silvia takes over from Philander the role of its main representative. Early in the novel Philander draws on standard libertine arguments in his campaign to seduce Silvia, for example when he attempts to justify incest not only with a sister-in-law but in general:

> No tyes of blood forbid my Passion; and what's a Ceremony impos'd on man by custome? [. . .] let us love like the first race of men, nearest allied to God, promiscuously they lov'd, and possess'd, Father and Daughter, Brother and Sister met, and reap'd the joys of Love without controul, and counted it Religious coupling, and 'twas encourag'd too by Heav'n itself. (11–12)

Claiming that a wife is a woman 'whom we Wed for interest and necessity' (18), he declares that he objects not to his wife's adultery but to her insincerity: 'I adore the Wife, that when the heart is gone, boldly and nobly pursues the Conqueror, and generously owns the Whore, – Not poorly adds the nautious sin of Jilting to't: That I cou'd have born, at least commended; but this can never Pardon.' For her part, Silvia learns the lesson only too well, delivering later in the novel what she describes as *'an invective against Marriage'* in which, for example, she calls it 'a trick, a wise device of Priests, no more', and asks 'who is't loves less than those that marry?' (112, 111). Regarding marriage in such a light, the two make no bones about resorting to it as a legal expedient when Silvia marries Philander's gentleman.

In Part Two of the novel, however, pregnant and virtually abandoned by Philander, Silvia has a harder lesson to learn: if marriage is no guarantee of love, neither is fornication or adultery. Philander shows no compunction about brushing aside all obstacles in his path to sexual gratification and then moving on. Hence the striking parallels between his marriage and his affairs with Silvia and Calista: in each case he enjoys the woman, elopes with her, and leaves her either with a child or pregnant. In Part Three, already wiser by experience, Silvia hears the theory behind such practices from Don Alonzo, a young man she meets while herself in male dress. One of the main articles of the libertine's creed, illustrated serially by Philander, is that 'enjoyment' declines after 'possession'. Thus Don Alonzo celebrates 'Gay Inconstancy, and the Blessing of Variety' (388), boasting: 'I never repeat any thing with Pleasure' (392). Silvia, having already discovered how to play off against each other the attentions of several different men, including not only Philander and Octavio but Brilljard and Octavio's amorous uncle, is able to turn the tables on her new acquaintance, not only converting him to a constant lover but finally ruining him. Like Miranda in Behn's novella *The Fair Jilt* (1688), she becomes a female libertine; and though, like Miranda, she is criticized by the narrator, she survives and even prospers. The novel's last words on her are that she 'was forced to remove for new Prey, and daily makes considerable Conquests where e'er she shows the Charmer' (439).

One of the crucial questions raised by *Love-Letters* is therefore how to regard the libertinism not only of Philander but Silvia. It is complicated by the fact that Philander is responsible for Silvia's corruption, as he implicitly admits when he exclaims: 'Oh what an excellent thing a perfect Woman is, e're man has taught her Arts to keep her Empire, by being himself inconstant?' (236). The remark is all the more telling because it is applied not to Silvia but to his next victim, Calista, and because of what might be termed the domino theory of sexual transgression, 'That where the sacred Laws of Honour are once invaded, Love makes the easier Conquest' (267). But the novel also shows what compels a woman to learn 'Arts to keep her Empire' through its portrayal, in Part Two, of Silvia's slow and painful realization that the man for whom she has deserted her family, and whom she still loves, is betraying her, especially when the money he has left her starts to run out. On the one hand, the narrator does not hesitate to criticize both characters directly, as when she remarks of Silvia that 'she had this wretched Prudence,

Nobleman and his Sister illustrates what would be lost to British novelists, male or female, from the middle of the eighteenth century to the start of the twentieth: the freedom to deal at all frankly with sex, or to combine with such playful knowingness amatory and political themes.

Delarivier Manley (*c.* 1674–1724) is the second of the three female authors from the period notorious for sexually scandalous fiction. Manley's narratives are more acutely partisan than *Love-Letters Between a Nobleman and his Sister*. As Paula McDowell has shown, she was 'among the first English authors self-consciously to devote herself to propaganda as a livelihood', and she developed her political narratives from two established models: 'the largely aristocratic French tradition of "feminocentric" fiction used as a tool of social and political satire, and the long-standing tradition of middling British women's polemical political activism through print'.[23] The relations in Manley's narratives between the historical and the invented, and between the amatory – indeed erotic – and the political, are complex and difficult to interpret. In the first case, McDowell is right to argue that 'Manley was writing propaganda, and the power of propaganda, like the power of "gossip", cannot be measured in terms of quantifiable "truth".'[24] In the second, as Catherine Gallagher has said of an erotic passage from Manley's most famous book, *Secret Memoirs from the New Atalantis* (1709), her narrative frequently 'works on two levels: it can be enjoyed as mere story, suspending the referential issue, or as defamation'.[25]

Events of Manley's lifetime offered a great deal of scandalous material. According to Lawrence Stone, discussing the Calvert divorce case of 1698–1710,

> There is a peculiarly brutal and exploitative quality about gender relations in the period 1680 to 1720 [. . .]. Violence, perjury, rape, and obsessive promiscuous sexuality are the hallmark of this age, when gender relations were on the turn, when women were at last beginning to assert themselves, and when contractual theories were starting to spread even into domestic relations, modifying the patriarchal power of parents and friends and raising the aspirations for the happiness of children.[26]

Stone's case studies bear out most of this statement amply, though it misleadingly suggests that women had not asserted themselves successfully in earlier times (during the English Revolution, for instance), and overlooks the constraints on female behaviour that would strengthen during the eighteenth century. Exploiting the turbulence of its period, the *New Atalantis* contains many examples of sexual corruption in its virulent attack on the Whig ministry. The attack was effective enough to help bring down the ministry in the year after first publication, but the continuing demand for Manley's book, which went through several reprints until as late as 1736, suggests that it had more to offer than topical scandal.[27] Indeed, though McDowell claims that it was Manley's success as a propagandist rather than her 'sexual themes and behaviour' that provoked attacks from male contemporaries,[28] it was her reputation as a writer of licentious narratives whose own morals did not bear inspection that put her beyond the pale a generation later. What is at issue in the present discussion is neither the truth nor the licence of Manley's narratives, but the attitudes they convey towards sexual morality in general, and male and female adultery in particular. The webs of topical and scandalous reference in her narratives are often extremely intricate, and it is beyond the scope of this book to do more than identify, where relevant, the historical figures who play a part in them.

In contrast to the novel of wifely adultery, it is generally men, not women, whom Manley's narratives construct as the most dangerous threats to social and sexual order. Indeed, Manley almost goes so far as to define men by their capacity for infidelity. One of her male characters in the *New Atalantis* explains the problem only too clearly in advising one of the many female victims: "tis one of the *Arcana*'s of Nature, not yet found out, why our Sex cool and neglect yours, after possession, and never, if we can avoid it (and have our Senses about us) chuse our selves Wives from those who have most obliged us' (I, 416; 80).[29] The point is underlined when the narrator reveals that, though true, the advice is given for self-interested reasons. Not for nothing, then, does the narrator later refer to men as 'the troublesome Sex' (I, 576; 154). Indeed, one of the other female characters finds in her reading a lesson that her own experience, and the book as a whole, suggests may actually be true: 'that to be entirely Happy, one ought never to think of the faithless Sex' (I, 341; 38).

Manley's narratives also contain a number of female characters who are guilty of sexual and other iniquity, and Ros Ballaster has

Manley attributes chiefly to her Whig targets, though she also has more room than he suggests for various examples of female vice and malevolence. It is therefore not surprising that she constructs adultery only as one among other temptations and dangers for women, and not necessarily the most significant. The *New Atalantis* contains many almost casual examples of male and female sexual sin, and often seems to take male adultery virtually for granted. The dozen or so stories given at length all involve rape or seduction, and all lead to betrayal. Only two, however, pivot on adultery; and in both cases the female partners play a quite different role from that of the adulterous heroine in fiction a century later.

The first main adultery story in the *New Atalantis* has two plots. Its critical difference from the scenario that typifies the novel of wifely adultery is that in both plots it is not the woman but the man who is married. Hernando Volpone, wedded by his father 'to a Wife he hated' (I, 485; 115), prevents an apparently suitable marriage for his ward Louisa in order to seduce her. He succeeds only by dint of a false marriage ceremony, after which she bears a child and lives with him openly until he infects both her and his wife with venereal disease, and Louisa dies of grief at his infidelity. In the parallel plot, Hernando's brother Mosco, married to his father's former mistress, is already tiring of his lover Zara. Despairing, she drowns in circumstances suspicious enough to bring him to trial, though not conviction, for her murder. While in both plots the adulteress comes to grief through deception and betrayal, the most interesting link between them is the theme of polygamy – though polygyny would be the more accurate term. Polygamy was much touted at the period, and not only by libertines;[33] Manley, who herself claimed to have been tricked into a bigamous marriage,[34] demonstrates its dangers for women. In the first plot, Hernando succeeds in seducing Louisa not so much because she loves him but because he is able to convince her that polygyny is natural and lawful. In the second, Zara, who belongs to a dissenting sect, is 'of an Opinion that Cohabitation makes a Marriage' (I, 502; 123), and she not only accepts Mosco's false assurances that he will leave his wife to live with her but tries to lure him away by offering money. It is for this reason, and because Zara makes the first advances, that the narrator withholds the sympathy she extends to Louisa, attributing Zara's death to 'Divine Vengeance' for having bestowed 'her guilty Affections upon a

Person marry'd to another' (I, 516; 130). Both men, however, escape serious damage, with Mosco left 'at full liberty to pursue, without controul, his Amours and his Ambition', and Hernando becoming '*Grand President*' (Lord Chancellor) and remarrying (I, 517; 130).

At an earlier point in the *New Atalantis*, Astrea, Goddess of Justice, remarks that 'Men may regain their Reputations, tho' after a Complication of Vices, *Cowardice, Robbery, Adultery, Bribery* and *Murder*, but a Woman once departed from the Road of Virtue, is made incapable of a return' (I, 355–6; 45). The placing of 'adultery' in this list of iniquities is as telling as the use of the verb 'made'; and Manley's keen awareness of the double standard of sexual morality, sharpened by personal experience,[35] also marks the narrative's other principal adultery story. So explicit a judgement never occurs in novels of wifely adultery, however clearly they show the double standard in action. The other adultery story, that of Diana, Countess of Bedamore, contrasts strongly in three further ways with nineteenth-century adultery fiction.

First, both Diana and her lover are married: she to a valetudinarian much older than herself; her seducer, Don Tomasio, to a woman he does not love with whom he has been yoked 'for Conveniency' while both were still in their teens (I, 752; 242). Second, the two scenes of Diana's seduction are as erotic as any among Manley's narratives. This is all the more striking not only because, as Tony Tanner has observed, the act of adultery is almost always elided in canonical nineteenth-century fiction,[36] but because, unlike most of the stories in the *New Atalantis*, the only other one about adultery is devoid of erotic content. In the scenes of Diana's seduction, Manley presents what novelists a century later would only be able to hint at obliquely: the power of female sexual desire and the pleasure of its gratification. Third, after the couple's inevitable discovery and Diana's betrayal, the narrator invites the reader's forgiveness when she remarks: 'it was impossible for any Eye to have seen a Beauty dazzling, as hers, in such Distress, without wishing to acquit her of her Fault' (I, 768; 250). Though Manley qualifies her judgement with the word 'wishing', so explicit a plea for an adulterous heroine rarely if ever occurs in nineteenth-century fiction. Indeed, while the phrasing gives Diana's beauty as much weight as her suffering, the complexities of the story suggest that other factors inviting forgiveness are her need for physical satisfaction and her exploitation by her lover, who not only deserts her but later blames her in court for running away with him.

Manley endorses her plea by underlining the betrayed husband's sympathy and tenderness to his wife, whose penitence nevertheless forces her into seclusion.

Manley's next book, *Memoirs of Europe* (1710), further develops the perspectives on sexual attitudes and behaviour presented in the *New Atalantis*. Like its predecessor, it also mixes sexual and political corruption; but, although often regarded as a sequel, it differs in several respects.[37] First, unlike the *New Atalantis*, where the chief narrators and auditors in the narrative frame are female and divine, in *Memoirs of Europe* all are mortals, and most of them are men. Second, while most of the narrative deals with sex and politics in England, parts of it recount not only the military campaign of Horatio (Charles Mordaunt, Earl of Peterborough) in Spain but also political and sexual episodes elsewhere on the Continent. Third, the narrative structure is more complex, involving a variety of narrators and a group of narratees among whom a different figure in each volume receives special attention. Pointing out that the dedicatee and the main narratee of the first volume are male, while those of the second are female, Ros Ballaster has argued that this 'differentiation of texts by sex' indicates some variation of subject matter.[38] However, although the Preface to Volume 2 claims that, 'The Entertainment being to a Lady, there's not so much of the Politick, as in the first Part, more of the Gay' (II, 383–4), both volumes combine stories of politics and sex and, indeed, often interweave the two. The more significant difference involves the kinds of sexual stories told; and the links between the stories and the main narratees are more complex than Ballaster suggests.

In Volume 1, the main narratee is Horatio, and the pretext for the stories is in part to console him for the death of his wife, in part to inform him about events in Constantinople (England) in his absence. In Volume 2 the main narratee is Ethelinda (the Countess of Königsmark), and the pretext is chiefly, as Ballaster says, 'to divert her thoughts from her onetime lover, Prince Theodorick (Charles XII of Sweden)'.[39] Questioning the charge of loose construction often levelled at Manley's narratives,[40] Paula McDowell has pointed out that 'Both the *New Atalantis* and its sequel *Memoirs of Europe* are structured as a series of conversations, in which the usual fare of the marketplace, street, or alehouse, "news mongering and . . . gossip about current topics", is discussed in the privacy of a small group.'[41] In *Memoirs of Europe*, however, Manley gave the stories and discussion of its courtly participants a greater measure of thematic unity. Addressed chiefly to Horatio, the first volume styles him as a model husband as well as a brave and victorious general, and presents, as examples of contemporary iniquity, stories of suffering female virtue and male oppression. As in the *New Atalantis*, the focus is less on female adultery than on male; less on adultery than on seduction and betrayal by men. Merovius, the first main narrator, sounds the keynote early when he declares: 'it was ever my Opinion, that he who debauches a young Creature, is a *Villain*, and in a great measure the Author of all those Follies she afterwards becomes guilty of' (II, 54).[42] Not only does his own conduct honour the same principle in the first story he tells, but he gives a glowing account of the virtue of women in Sarmatia (Poland), the country to which he is an envoy, and this is borne out by his second principal narrative, related to him by a female slave. Unlike several of the victims in the *New Atalantis*, the slave's mistress, Honoria, refuses to have sex before marriage despite the arguments and promises of the man she loves. Since he is a prince, he is designed for a marriage of equivalent rank, and she ends by committing suicide in grief at his duplicity.

Most of the adultery narratives in the first volume of *Memoirs of Europe* follow a similar pattern. One of the male figures, Count Alarick, has the husband of a woman he fancies killed by ruffians, though she had refused him, and in another affair he escapes with his life while the husband he has cuckolded cuts his lover in pieces. But these adventures are merely preludes to a longer narrative in which Annagild, Princess of Dacia, is wronged both by Alarick and by the husband she has just married. Alarick's pursuit, despite her attempts to rebuff him, conspires with the jealous reaction of her husband's mistress to expose her to an entirely false charge of adultery. Afterwards husband and mistress repair to 'a House of Pleasure' (II, 165), while she is kept as 'a sort of Royal Prisoner at large' (II, 167). In this case, however, the narrative frame suggests that would-be seducers will not always escape, for Alarick's story is told by the Count de St Gironne who is conducting him to an undisclosed fate in another country. Another element of the frame further emphasizes Manley's proto-feminist message, for St Gironne expresses misogynistic prejudices that his own story plainly undermines, and that his two male auditors question.

Manley's narrative strategy in the first volume of *Memoirs of Europe* is dual: to contrast not only the attitudes of her male narrators, but the cultures on which they comment; and to arrange most of the stories of any length on a scale of ascending iniquity. Thus, while Merovius, the first main narrator, is favourably disposed towards women, and describes a country in which they are celebrated for modesty and virtue, the misogynist St Gironne reports on the vice of Constantinople, effectively ruled by the dowager Empress Irene. Again, however, St Gironne's attitudes are undermined by his own narrative. First, as Ros Ballaster expresses it, Irene is one of those women in Manley's work 'who imitate the "masculine" practice of exploiting and victimizing the innocent', and the narrative invites condemnation of this 'cynical rehearsal of masculine power moves'.[43] Second, even St Gironne's catalogue of sexual and other corruption in the court of Constantinople contains examples of female virtue. Theodecta, forced by Irene into a bigamous marriage with the Emperor, refuses to abandon her religious principles; and Porcia, widowed after never complaining of her rigid treatment in an arranged marriage to an elderly man, refuses to remarry so as 'no more to inslave herself' (I, 276).

Manley ends the first volume of *Memoirs of Europe* by reverting to Merovius for two adultery stories from Sarmatia. In the first, a husband goes on a 'ten Years loose Pilgrimage' (II, 327) of sexual exploitation, and rejects his forgiving wife on his return because her physical attractions have vanished, albeit through grief at his absence. When their elder son protests at his cruel reproofs, he kills him on the spot. The second story hinges on wifely adultery, but in a way that reinforces Manley's critique of male sexual licence. Its two main characters, Ismena and Iuvius Iagello, are members of families locked in a bitter feud. Iuvius can have access to Ismena only by taking advantage of her stepmother Gonneril's desire for him. Unfortunately he does so all too fully, not only by having sex with her but by delaying his escape to make love with Ismena after the couple have been married in secret. The result is discovery thanks to Gonneril's jealousy, and the narrator does not hesitate to point a didactic message: 'Poor *Iagello* lost his Life for his weak Compliance with her base Desires, tho' done in order to a lawful Happiness. Heaven did not approve the Deceit, however vertuous was the Cause, but punish'd him for the guilty Effects' (II, 352–3). So heavy a punishment is startling for a sin that contemporaries might have laughed off as virile opportunism, but Gonneril comes off even worse. As a further example of a woman who manipulates others for her own gratification, she is 'convicted of notorious Adulteries' (II, 354), fails her trial by ordeal and burns to death.

Volume II of *Memoirs of Europe* has a closer thematic consistency than Volume I because it is tailored more directly to the situation of its main narratee. As a later story explains, Ethelinda is in love with Theodorick, but has been sent away to Saxony to prevent her from marrying him. There she is courted by the Prince, Beraldus, who cannot marry her legally because of his 'Marriage of State' to a religious devotee (II, 604). Although, despite pressure from her father, Ethelinda refuses the marriage 'with the Left Hand' that Beraldus proposes instead (II, 610), Theodorick repudiates her and will not see her again. The three main stories in the first two Books of Volume I, and the discussion and further anecdotes they provoke, offer contrasts and analogues to Ethelinda's position. All three also turn on wifely adultery.

The opening two stories contrast most sharply with Ethelinda's by presenting an exploited and an accommodating husband respectively. In the first, Thais marries the unsuspecting Clodius at her lover's suggestion in order to screen their affair. Having run through much of her husband's money, she accepts an offer from Cicero (Lord John Somers, one of the most powerful Whigs of the period) to live with him as his mistress, leaving her husband in debtor's prison. What compounds the offence is that Clodius has introduced Cicero to Thais, lent him money, and sent Thais to him for help. Boosting her attack on a leading Whig minister, Manley has her narrator exclaim: 'That she was the Wife of an injur'd Friend! a Friend who passionately lov'd her, and had tenderly oblig'd him, rather heightened his Desires' (II, 471). However, this moral outburst is at odds with the viewpoint of the prospective mistress, presented less than two pages earlier:

> *Thais* was pleased, or rather charm'd with the Magnificence of *Cicero*, and tho' he was much older and not so handsome as *Clodius*, yet a Lover seldom fails of getting the Advantage over a Husband in the Opinion of the Mistress: Those unabated Ardors! that extremity of Fire! height of Rapture! keenness of Embrace! all deadned by long and sure Possession, shews one so much to the Advantage of the other, that it is no wonder they get the preference. (II, 469–70)

The generalization comes close to justifying Thais's affair, if not her desertion of her husband, which finally leads to his disappearance at Cicero's instigation. It is especially striking that Manley does not vilify the adulteress but offers to explain her betrayal, concentrating the satire on her powerful and unscrupulous lover.

The second story goes even further in palliating wifely adultery, and partly through its setting in France. In this case the narrator is female, and she begins by describing the free and easy manners of the French aristocracy:

> Nor does a marry'd Woman scruple to receive the publick Addresses of a Lover, which the Husband is so far from giving himself any pain at, that he looks on it as a Merit in his Wife, as if she could not be Lovely without Adorers, and consequently not deserving his Passion; tho' he does not fail to repay that Adoration in kind to some other Beauty: Thus the eternal round is Loving and being Beloved; yet all esteem'd Innocent, 'till some publick Indiscretion forces 'em to see what they would unwillingly believe. (II, 500–1)

Cornutus, sent to France as an ambassador, falls in with the custom of the country with the result that his wife Arethusa has an affair with the young courtier Endymion. The conduct and outcome of the affair are remarkable for several reasons. First, it is presented more for its erotic than its scandalous impact, even though the three figures represented – the Duke and Duchess of Manchester, and Lord Grafton – were well known. Second, although the affair becomes common knowledge, no one tells the deceived husband, partly from a sense that he has invited his betrayal, but also because 'there was not any that had so much Malice to *Arethusa*' (II, 532). Third, and most significant, the narrator congratulates husband and wife on their prudent handling of potential disaster after Cornutus finds Arethusa in bed with her lover. Cornutus decides to accept Arethusa's implausible explanation on condition that she blames her maid and sees no more of Endymion. Although the narrator is the maid in question, although she has lost her position as a result, and although she criticizes Arethusa for lying, she nevertheless expresses admiration:

> Wou'd not all Mankind marry, continu'd *Charlot*, were they sure of a Wife with so much address as my Lady? If the married People are but of Intelligence, they may for ever secure each other; Lord *Cornutus* preserv'd *Arethusa*'s Fame, she in return prevented him from risquing his Life; she manag'd him to the

Envy of all her Sex, that is, he lov'd her, did not care to make an ostentatious squander of his own Person and Valour, and therefore wou'd be manag'd. He redoubled his Affection, now fully convinced of her Merit, since she had Adorers. (II, 547)

The fourth unusual feature of the story is that, despite a name that draws attention to his betrayal, Cornutus is not treated with the contempt often fastened on cuckolds. Indeed, a brief inset story about an insanely jealous husband, placed between the beginning of the affair and its discovery, invites the reader to weigh an extreme alternative against trust and tolerance (II, 532–6).

Along with this inset episode, the story of Cornutus and Arethusa introduces a series of narratives and discussions pivoting on male jealousy. Although there are few direct parallels, the theme is relevant to Ethelinda's position as a mistress, and to her rejection by Theodorick. The third main story in Volume II offers a further variation. Erminia has married Rufus, whom she does not love, because he is wealthy and unobjectionable. She preserves her virtue through a 'Cold, and Uninterprizing' temper (II, 560) until she falls passionately for Silanus. When she finally grants her lover a rendezvous, he keeps her so long that her husband not only has time to find them but reaches such a pitch of fury as to kill Silanus on the spot. Although Erminia is only too penitent, and although Rufus takes her back, he is fatally unhinged by the jealousy that has overtaken him, and that he has never experienced previously. Yet the episode is presented in such a way as to develop its potential neither for scandal nor for moral or prudential lesson. Instead, the narrator half excuses Erminia's falling in love with a man not her husband when he exclaims: 'the God of Love does not long permit a *vacuum*!' (II, 560). Then, replying to Ethelinda's question about how Erminia has led her life after losing her husband, he declares: 'with Honour, Madam, if your Highness will not rank your self on the side of those Inhumans, that pretend there is no return to Vertue [. . .] when a Lady has once deviated from her Path' (II, 573). Without condoning Erminia's lapse directly, Manley fashions her story in such a way as to encourage a sympathy, understanding and tolerance rarely extended in other periods to female adultery.

The final book in the second volume of *Memoirs of Europe* returns to politics in Britain. It contains little further amatory intrigue, except in a coda that pokes fun at Manley's old enemy Steele, has the opera singer Catherine Tofts summarize scandalous passages from her career, and accuses two of the Duke and Duchess of Marlborough's daughters, and two of their female cousins, of secret enthusiastic prostitution. For the next few years Manley was to become even more closely involved in Tory propaganda, working for the Secretary of State Robert Harley and, for a time, with Jonathan Swift, succeeding him as editor of the *Examiner*, to which she contributed several issues.[44] In 1714, however, after George I's accession and the appointment of an entirely Whig ministry, her career as a political writer suddenly stopped. In her fictionalized autobiography *The Adventures of Rivella*, published in the same year, she represents herself as declaring that from then on she would 'write of Pleasure and Entertainment only', agreeing with the male narrator 'that Politicks is not the Business of a Woman' (II, 853). Paula McDowell argues that these statements were given tongue in cheek, and that a letter of the same date as the Preface to *Rivella*, in which Manley offered her services as a propagandist to Harley and sketched 'her plans for another full-length political allegory along the lines of the *New Atalantis*', indicates that she had no intention of changing tack. The explanation for Manley's virtual silence as a political writer after 1714 is probably to be found in the increasing success of the campaign against what Addison, in 1711, had styled as 'Party-Rage in Women'.[45] As McDowell puts it, 'Periodicals like the *Tatler* and *Spectator* contributed to the conceptual reconsignment of "the Fair Sex" either to a polite public or to a private sphere reconceptualized as a safe haven from the realm of state affairs and especially the new party politics.'[46] The career of Eliza Haywood (1693–1756), Manley's successor as leading writer of scandal fiction, demonstrates how during the next thirty or so years women writers found themselves increasingly precluded from dealing not only with political but sexual topics.

Ros Ballaster has provided so accurate and succinct an account of the differences between Haywood's scandal narratives and Manley's that it is convenient to quote from it at length:

> It is significant that, unlike Manley, Haywood did not indulge in any form of political journalism. She produced three novels that owe clear debts to the scandal fiction of Manley, even echoing the latter's famous title of the *New Atalantis*, but the seduction/

betrayal motif was now exploited for the purposes of a more general moralism and Haywood betrays no interest in direct political intervention or allegiance to other opposition figures or forces. Haywood's targets in the two scandal novels of the 1720s are not leading politicians but court figures and private individuals. These novels show none of the 'insider's' knowledge that made Manley's work so threatening to the Whig politicians who brought her to trial and the stories are presented as moral exempla. The over-arching structure of a Tory ideology remains in place, but the mercenary self-interest Manley had identified as the defining characteristic of the male Whig politician is now identified with court culture in general and contrasted with the pleasures of country retirement.[47]

Ballaster also explains how Haywood's third scandal narrative, *The Adventures of Eovaai* (1736), was unable, because of the changes in governmental and ideological structures that had taken place, 'to reproduce the political instrumentality of Manley's scandal fiction during the reign of Queen Anne'.[48]

Haywood's first and most successful scandal narrative, *Memoirs of a Certain Island Adjacent to the Kingdom of Utopia* (1724–5), is of interest to this study for two reasons. As a scandal chronicle in the mould of the *New Atalantis*, it presents a panorama of sexual transgression ranging from fornication to adultery (male and female), prostitution, incest and homosexuality. Like Manley's narratives, it was also written and published during a period in which the freer codes of conduct associated with the Restoration were beginning to tighten, especially for women. *Memoirs of a Certain Island* is based on the lives of various of Haywood's contemporaries, most still living and many identified more or less explicitly by a Key printed at the end of each of the two volumes. As with Manley's narratives, it must be read with due awareness of its genre: not only chronicle, but scandal. It is often difficult to determine how far Haywood stretched attestable fact, especially in cases where she was clearly movitated by personal animus – as with Flirtillaria (the wife of George Hill) and Gloatitia (Martha Fowke Sansom). Nevertheless, although it would be wrong to read the book either as a series of biographical sketches or as fiction, it provides an interesting if uneven picture of how a woman writer of the 1720s saw the relation between female adultery and other forms of sexual transgression.

Haywood built the chief message of *Memoirs of a Certain Island* into its narrative structure. Although the structure is for the most part episodic, the assorted stories are framed as an anatomy of iniquity and betrayal displayed by the God of Love to a young male traveller. The villains of the piece are not only Lust, an impostor who frequently succeeds in impersonating honourable Love, but also financial self-interest. One of Haywood's targets is accordingly marriage for financial or social advantage; but her criticism is also more specific. At the heart of corruption she places the Enchanted Well, an obvious allegory for the South Sea Bubble, showing its destruction at the end of her first volume. In this way, through their often infamous content, the *Memoirs* both emphasize love as the proper basis for marriage and attack the impact on personal and family lives of early speculative capitalism.

Like Manley's scandal narratives, Haywood's contrasts most sharply with the nineteenth-century novel of wifely adultery in its failure, or refusal, either to discriminate significantly between male and female sexual sin or to define adultery by married women as the most meaningful form of marital infidelity. Indeed, although the sequence of episodes seems at times almost random, some are clearly arranged to demonstrate sexual and other misconduct on the part of both sexes. The opening two stories involve serial male followed by serial wifely adultery. Although the first is entitled 'The History of Graciana', it quickly gives way to an exposure of the seducer and betrayer Romanus, then to a separate narrative in which Flirtillaria repeatedly cheats her over-trusting husband (I, 14–33; I, 33–43).[49] Yet adultery is presented as the most heinous sin neither for the male nor the female transgressor; it is one among a range of offences, not all of them sexual. Instead, the deepest iniquity is betrayal itself, especially for motives of self-interest, and almost irrespective of marriage. Some of the more complex episodes show a chain of treachery and, at times, of retribution. For instance, Clarismonda becomes the instrument of her husband's punishment after he jilts his fiancée in order to marry her. Hating him so much that she cannot bear his embraces, she takes a soldier for her lover; but she in turn is requited, albeit unawares, by his preference for a mistress from his own class (I, 49–55). More melodramatic is the story of Count Montreville, who debauches Martasinda, then leaves her; for her response of suicide is repeated by his own mother, victim of another act of betrayal (I, 265–71). In this case none of the liaisons is adulterous, and the main transgressors are male.

The values embedded in Haywood's narrative in some ways hark back to an earlier code of gallantry. For example, one of her male characters declares: 'there is no such thing in nature, as a Lover who can restrain the Impatience of Desire, when Hope receives Encouragement from the Object of his Passion' (I, 250); and Cupid himself says of one of the female characters, in love with the man who besieges her: 'Cold Chastity may for a while defend the Fort, but soon the icy Rock dissolves, and leaves the Passage free' (II, 53). Each figure is led into adultery, with disastrous consequences, but in both cases the narrator blames tempter more than tempted, and for the same reason: neither acted under Cupid's influence. If both a man and a woman may be excused in part by the force of genuine passion, Haywood reasserts a more conventional double standard elsewhere, as when Cupid remarks: 'my Influence never yet led the bold Ruffian to *ravish* what he wish'd to enjoy, nor gave the Woman confidence to *own*, unask'd, the secret Fire which burn'd within her Breast' (I, 264). It follows that, for her, "tis scarce possible to be a Man without being inconstant and ingrateful' (I, 54); while women are defined as 'a Sex, which is indeed the purest part of the Creation while with Sin untainted, but when once corrupted, and oversway'd by Passion, the very worst and most irreclaimable' (II, 201). The first of these statements could equally have been made by Manley; but the second could not. Manley's awareness of the double standard was keener; and, as one of her male narrators in *Memoirs of Europe* suggests, she did not assume that a woman who succumbed to sexual temptation would be unable to restrain herself in future.[50] The difference of attitudes points to the increasing acceptance of a new ideology of femininity in the 1720s, even on the part of a writer such as Haywood.

Although Cupid claims that 'Adultery and Incest are grown common Crimes, and scarce wear any other Name than that of venial Transgressions' (I, 155), he reserves his strongest censure for male and female homosexuality (I, 156–7; II, 94). Yet the main target of Haywood's narrative is not what she terms 'unlawful Blendings' (I, 157), but inconstancy; and not even adultery, but treason to heterosexual love. According to Cupid, it is constancy that distinguishes him from his shadow, Lust: "tis by my *Unchangeableness* alone I am proved the *God*' (I, 112). Because *Memoirs of a Certain Island* applies this standard both to male and female behaviour, even while discriminating between men and women in other respects, the code of sexual morality it promotes is distinctly more equitable than that of the nineteenth-century novel of wifely adultery.

Before Haywood undertook her first scandal chronicle with *Memoirs of a Certain Island*, she had already established herself as a successful writer of fiction. William H. McBurney has pointed out that, in terms of book sales, her first novel, *Love in Excess; or, The Fatal Enquiry* (1719–20), shares with *Robinson Crusoe* and *Gulliver's Travels* 'the distinction of being the most popular English fiction of the eighteenth century before *Pamela'*.[51] Equally significant, as William B. Warner has shown, Haywood was the first prolific writer of romantic formula fiction.[52] According to Cheryl Turner, 'The level and consistency of her output in the 1720s was unequalled by any other woman throughout the century, although it is worth noting that many of Haywood's works consisted of 100 pages or less'.[53] Haywood's stock in trade was less adultery than the threat or the reality, specifically for women, of seduction, rape or forced marriage. Her first novel illustrates her characteristic attitudes clearly.

In several ways *Love in Excess* anticipates *Memoirs of a Certain Island* in its figuring of sexual transgression. Here also the leading offences are ambition and inconstancy, both especially on the part of men; and again, too, sexual desire unredeemed by love. The main plot charts a sentimental education for its hero, D'Elmont. At first inspiring love but never feeling it, he causes one woman to enter a convent in despair and marries another, Alovisa, from self-interest, only to fall for a third, Melliora, entrusted to his care soon after his marriage by her dying father. While this is clearly Love's revenge, the rest of the novel allows D'Elmont to reform by proving himself a model of persistence and (just) fidelity. On the way he encounters two less tardy examples of male constancy, one given by his own brother, the other by Melliora's. D'Elmont also meets standard cases of male depravity, including a friend who tries to seduce the jealous Alovisa by promising to reveal the identity of the woman he loves, and a Marquess who abducts Melliora from the convent in which she has taken refuge. These men, too, are corrected by Haywood's plot: one killed as a result of his attempt at seduction, the other, disappointed in his designs on Melliora, reclaimed for marriage to the fiancée he had rejected.

Although the action of *Love in Excess* revolves round D'Elmont, the female characters play more interesting roles. The action is set in motion when Alovisa flirts with him incognito; and it is resolved by Melliora who, having staged a scene of recognition with her brother and her guardian D'Elmont, exploits patriarchal convention wittily by having them choose the latter as her husband. Other female characters provide further contrasts, especially Melantha, who has sex with D'Elmont in the guise of Melliora; Ciamara, a rich young Italian widow who tries and fails to seduce him; and Violetta, who falls in love with him but suffers and dies in silence.

Haywood presents a narrower spectrum of sexual transgression in her amatory fiction than in her scandal chronicle: there is no homosexuality, incest, rape, or seduction, though the latter two are both threatened; and, because the novel is less about having sex than achieving the right kind of marriage, adultery plays only a marginal role. However, the terms in which Haywood constructs the novel's single act of adultery contrast significantly with those typical of nineteenth-century adultery fiction. It is the man who is married rather than the woman; it is the woman who controls the event rather than the man; and, although she becomes pregnant, she does not suffer. What explains this unusual scenario is that the woman, Melantha, not only substitutes herself for Melliora, whom D'Elmont has plotted to seduce, but marries another man shortly afterwards, and, as the narrator laconically puts it, has 'the good fortune not to be suspected by her husband, though she brought him a child in seven months after her wedding' (160).[54] These words, and their positioning at the end of the novel's second part, imply that Haywood was, at least on occasion, prepared to condone the kind of sexual opportunism traditionally conceded only to men. Indeed, as David Oakleaf suggests, the fact that Haywood does not specify the sex of the adulterine child may have been provocative at a time when patrilineal anxieties were strong (Introduction, 19).

Although Melantha fails to escape scot-free, in that she has to cover for her pregnancy by marrying, her example is also provocative in that she seems an exception to the novel's normal rule of disavowing, even punishing, pursuit of sexual desire without love. In this respect Haywood appears to allow female initiative to compromise her novel's amatory ethics. The rest of her story, however, adheres to a fundamental principle declared by the narrator in an outspoken address beginning with the statement: 'When love once becomes in our power, it ceases to be worthy of that name; no man really possest with it, *can* be master of his actions; and whatever effects it may enforce, are no more to be condemned, than poverty, sickness, deformity, or any other misfortune incident to humane nature' (185–6). Although the novel shows that male transgressions in the name of love are treated more tolerantly, it makes clear that this principle applies to women as well as to men; and Haywood tempers her appeal by having those of her characters who fall in love do so only once. It follows that the most serious wrongs the novel identifies are wrongs against love: those of 'inconstancy, or ingratitude' (186). In this way D'Elmont is not to be judged too harshly for pursuing Melliora, with whom he falls in love after his misguided marriage – indeed, conveniently for him, the novel kills his wife off halfway through. What he must do is prove his constancy not to marriage but to love. The key differences between Haywood's ideas of sexual infidelity and those that dominate the novel of wifely adultery are therefore that inconstancy is more a problem than adultery, and that it is more a problem with men than with women. Haywood also draws attention to the dangers of marrying for self-interest, and, for a woman, of taking the initiative in expressing desire for a man. Outside pornographic fiction, the kind of tolerance she shows for transgression motivated by passion would be unusual in English fiction only 20 years later; and from a female writer it would have been wholly inadmissible.

As the following chapter will show, a reaction against amatory fiction began as early as the 1720s, the time of Haywood's greatest success. William B. Warner has argued that Defoe took a typically equivocal part in the reaction with *Roxana* (1724);[55] certainly, along with *Moll Flanders* (1722), the novel offers a quite different perspective on sexual transgression.

First, as their title pages suggest, neither work gives special emphasis to adultery. Moll is advertised as having been 'Twelve Year a *Whore*, five times a *Wife* (whereof once to her own Brother)', but also 'Twelve Year a *Thief*'; whereas Roxana is styled as '*The Fortunate Mistress*'.[56] Instead, both women pursue careers of serial quasi-monogamy: although they commit not only adultery but bigamy, and in Moll's case incest, none ever betrays a husband or a lover with whom she is living for another man. Roxana, whose life is less convoluted than Moll's, provides the clearer illustration. Her first husband deserts her when he becomes bankrupt, and she takes up with her landlord to avoid destitution. Since he has been deserted by his wife, who has been unfaithful, the liaison is doubly adulterous, but it functions in all respects like a marriage, including the procreation of children, until the man is murdered. According to Lawrence Stone, in the eighteenth century bigamy 'seems to have been both easy and common' among the less well off, and 'more or less permanent desertion was also regarded as morally dissolving the marriage'.[57] Thus both Moll and Roxana are fictional examples of a then familiar phenomenon.

Second, however, the two novels are more concerned with prostitution than adultery. Moll supports herself as a mistress, and then as an occasional prostitute, after she discovers that her second (and bigamous) marriage is incestuous. While never descending to casual prostitution, Roxana is mistress successively to a German Prince, a Dutch merchant, a lover (presumably royal) in England whose identity is kept secret, and an English lord, before reuniting with her merchant whom she finally marries. Although the ideological tendencies of Defoe's fiction are complex and require careful interpretation, *Roxana* turns on two main concerns: the role of a woman as an independent economic agent, and the resulting impact on the family. Maintaining her independence by exploiting her sexuality, Roxana finds all too late that she cannot escape the ties that bind her to her servant Amy and to her daughter Susan, whom Amy eventually murders.

In arguing that *Roxana* is Defoe's attempt 'to reform the novel of amorous intrigue', Warner cites not only the stock professions of moral intent in the so-called editor's Preface, but also the double voice of the narrative, in which Roxana's older self judges her younger one.[58] Though he rightly points out that the narrative is hardly erotic, he neglects Defoe's distinctive obsession with finance that fills the gap. Unlike the work of Aubin and Rowe, *Roxana* does not refer directly enough to the novel of amorous intrigue to offer a more conventionally moral alternative; neither, like Richardson's *Pamela*, does it attempt to neutralize and replace it. Instead, it and *Moll Flanders* exploit the themes of seduction, adultery and prostitution as a way of representing the moral and other hazards of economic individualism.for a woman. Like other male writers of the period, Defoe for the most part left fictions about female sexual transgression to the other sex. Two exceptions are John Cleland's *Memoirs of a Woman of Pleasure* (1748–9; more often known as *Fanny Hill*) and Tobias Smollett's *The Adventures of Peregrine Pickle* (1751).

As Peter Sabor has suggested, *Fanny Hill* responds to Henry Fielding's *Shamela* (1741) as well as to the work that Fielding parodied, Samuel Richardson's *Pamela* (1740–1).[59] Cleland's interest is not in transgression as such, but in uninhibited sexuality, so he has his female narrator express not only her delight in sexual pleasure but her joy in marriage. However, after suffering prosecution (albeit unsuccessful) for obscenity, Cleland produced an expurgated version and then, more significantly, changed narrative gender for his next novel, *Memoirs of a Coxcomb* (1751). Not only does *Memoirs of a Coxcomb* attempt less to arouse than to reform, but, in the new climate of moral improvement,[60] its account of a journey to happy marriage after a series of sexual adventures is much more acceptable from a male narrator.

Peregrine Pickle is more complex, for, although the narrator is impersonal and the hero is male, it contains an inner narrative of about 50,000 words entitled 'Memoirs of a Lady of Quality' that is an apology for the life of Frances Anne, Viscountess Vane.[61] The question of authorship remains undetermined, though it seems likely that, as G. S. Rousseau puts it, 'Smollett edited and revised Lady Vane's memoirs without changing their contents'.[62] As Rousseau also observes, the inclusion of the Memoirs 'has long been recognized as the reason for the novel's initial popularity'.[63] Several scandalous memoirs by women appeared around 1750, including those by Laetitia Pilkington, Teresia Constantia Phillips, and Charlotte Charke;[64] and Lionel Kelly has suggested that Lady Vane may have found encouragement from the first two, which preceded her own.[65] However, one reason why 'Memoirs of a Lady of Quality' is remarkable is that, unlike the others, it appears in the course of a novel – and one written by a man. As Jerry C. Beasley has noted, the insertion of Lady Vane's autobiography into a work of fiction 'blurs distinctions between the actual and the imagined, the objective and the subjective'.[66] But the memoir is of special interest to the present discussion for the same reason that made it notorious in the 1750s: the subject's repeated adultery.

By her own account, Lady Vane owed the many vicissitudes of her life to two crushing misfortunes. After an early and blissfully happy marriage, her husband fell ill and died, leaving her 'an unprovided widow' (449); she then yielded to the importunity of family and friends in marrying William Holles, Viscount Vane – a match as disastrous emotionally and sexually as it was propitious materially. Considering herself 'absolved of all matrimonial ties' (456) by her utter incompatibility with a husband who was not only impotent but whose conduct was often arbitrary and ludicrous, she embarked on a series of affairs, escaping at intervals from the marital home only to find herself obliged to return by arguments of friends or shortage of money. Lady Vane is careful to emphasize that she was faithful to each of her lovers. Of her first affair she claims: 'I had never offended, but in loving too well' (470); of her second, that she held it 'as sacred as any nuptial tie, and much more binding than a forced or unnatural marriage' (485). Though she pays conventional respect to 'virtue, modesty and honour' when she first feels adulterous desire (454), she accuses herself of 'a real act of ingratitude' on one of the occasions when she yields to persuasion in returning to her husband, commenting: 'So little is the world qualified to judge of private affairs!' (486). In this way Lady Vane proposes sexual ethics that recall those of Behn, Manley and Haywood. Indeed, her energy and independence, if not her claims to fidelity, evoke Silvia in *Love-Letters Between a Nobleman and his Sister*. But contemporaries did not hesitate to draw the same parallels on other grounds. In a letter to Sarah Chapone, Samuel Richardson classed Lady Vane with her sister memoirists and their predecessors – who, he pronounced, seem innocent in comparison:

> Mrs. Pilkington, Constantia Phillips, Lady V. (who will soon appear, profaning the Word *Love*, and presuming to attempt to clear her *Heart*, and to find gentle Fault only with her *Head*, in the Perpetration of the highest Acts of Infidelity) what a Set of Wretches, wishing to perpetuate their Infamy, have we – to make the Behn's, the Manley's, and the Haywood's look white.[67]

Smollett, on the other hand, must have thought differently. James L. Clifford is probably right to suggest that from his point of view Lady Vane's error 'had not been criminal sensuality, but rather a daring nonconformity which flouted the rules of society' (xxvi). It quickly became clear, however, that such a view was held only by a minority. Although the Memoirs gave *Peregrine Pickle* its early popularity, the criticism they attracted, along with other incidents that contemporaries found too racy, harmed the novel's reputation and signalled that novelists should avoid such material in future.

The reaction to *Peregrine Pickle* illustrates the changes in codes of behaviour and taste that were already becoming widely accepted by mid-century. In response, Smollett expurgated his novel for its second edition in 1758. True to picaresque tradition, Peregrine is anything but a saint; but in his revised form he is less of a sinner.

For instance, Smollett entirely removed a section beginning with Peregrine and his companion laying 'close siege to every buxom country damsel that fell in their way' (166), had a married woman rebuff rather than gratify Peregrine's first attempt on her virtue, and cut a whole chapter (LXVI) involving an intrigue with a nun, along with an episode in which Peregrine enjoys a lady's favours in place of her lover.[68] Even so, the hero's amorous and other exploits place in a flattering light those of his compeer Tom Jones. While Tom is seduced by Molly Seagrim, and succumbs to coquetry with Mrs Waters, to importunity with Lady Bellaston, even in his revised form Peregrine attempts and commits both seduction and adultery; furthermore, in sharp contrast to Tom's treatment of Sophia, he attempts to rape the woman he later marries. Smollett learned the lesson in his later fiction, which includes no material likely to give as much offence. In the case of the Memoirs, however, he could have atoned only by cutting them completely. If, as seems likely, he sympathized with Lady Vane, he probably found such a step unpalatable. Besides, the style of the Memoirs is not salacious, and they had not only helped sales but he may have been paid for inserting them. The main changes to this part of the text – probably made, as Clifford says, 'at her ladyship's request' (xix) – are therefore aimed at enhancing her character by emphasizing the romance of her first marriage, her generosity, and the strength of her reasons for leaving her first lover after he had first abandoned and then come back to her.

If Lady Vane sought to insulate her Memoirs by embedding them in a fictional context, she failed to disarm criticism. A characteristic later comment is Anna Laetitia Barbauld's: that they 'can only now raise astonishment at the assurance which could give such a life without compunction'.[69] More important, in publishing under his own name a tale of serial wifely adultery Smollett set an example that no one was eager to follow. Indeed, with this one equivocal exception, scarcely any serious male novelist in Britain after Defoe dealt with female adultery until Hardy and Meredith; and only a few – including Henry Fielding in *Amelia* – paid attention to adultery by men. Confined to a subordinate role in a novel centred on male social and sexual aggression, 'Memoirs of a Lady of Quality' marks out the marginal space to which female sexual nonconformity would increasingly be relegated.

5

Ideology of Femininity and Criminal Conversation: 1728-71

During the period in which Manley and Haywood were writing, and while their narratives and Behn's continued both popular and profitable, a reaction was already under way. One of its earliest and best-known manifestations was in the theatre – the arena in which Restoration licence was most public and blatant. Though not the first attack of its kind, Jeremy Collier's *Short View of the Immorality and Profaneness of the English Stage* (1698) had a rapid impact not only on the professional lives of dramatists and players but on the character of drama itself. In its immediate aftermath Congreve and D'Urfey were prosecuted, and a group of actors, including Thomas Betterton and Anne Bracegirdle, were fined.[1] Then, from about the turn of the century, the licentious dialogue and dramatic action stigmatized by Collier and others were on the wane. New forms, such as the periodical essay, and developing ones, such as the conduct book, appealed to a wider audience than the theatre, and began to disseminate politer standards of speech and behaviour. Along with the novel, they gained further importance after the Stage Licensing Act of 1737 limited the number of London theatres and subjected all plays to effective pre-production censorship.

It is beyond the scope of this book to consider at any length the various forces that produced such changes. Nevertheless, three broad factors in the cultural transformation of eighteenth-century Britain may be distinguished. First, the power and prestige of those in the middle ranks of society expanded further. Second, especially through the impact of Methodism, radical Protestant thinking came to influence attitudes and behaviour far beyond the nonconformist enclaves from which it spread. Third, women from the middle ranks played an increasingly significant role, both as active and symbolic bearers of new ideological values. The first and the third of these factors are identified by Jane Spencer when she observes: 'The increasing separation of home from workplace in the late seventeenth century laid the foundations for a new bourgeois ideology of femininity, according to which women were very separate, special creatures.'[2] This new ideology is illustrated by Steele, writing in the *Spectator*, when he tells his female readers that 'the utmost of a Woman's Character is contained in Domestick Life; she is Blameable or Praise-worthy according as her carriage affects the House of her Father or her Husband. All she has to do in this World, is contained within the Duties of a Daughter, a Sister, a Wife, and a Mother.'[3] Such a view had far-reaching implications for women who wrote, as Spencer shows for the novelists. Specifically, as Jeslyn Medoff puts it, women who sought to follow in the footsteps of Behn

> would have to make conscious decisions about accepting, rejecting or refashioning her precedents, not only in style and subject matter but in the personae of their writings, in the personae they, as authors, would assume in public (in formal letters, prefaces, dedications and the like), and in the way they tried to control their reputations as women, which were essentially inseparable from their reputations as writers.[4]

Needless to add, however, the new ideology did not affect women alone. The *Spectator* was in the vanguard of a campaign to spread new standards of polite culture among a general reading public, as Samuel Johnson recognized later in the century when he wrote that it and its predecessor the *Tatler* 'continue to be among the first books by which both sexes are initiated in the elegances of knowledge'.[5] At the same time, as Terry Eagleton has argued, '"feminine" values relegated by the sexual division of labour to the private realm [were] now returning to transvaluate the ruling ideologies themselves'.[6] This is the source of what Eagleton calls 'a deep-seated "feminization" of values throughout the eighteenth century that is closely allied with the emergence of the bourgeoisie',[7] and in which the morality of Protestant Dissent played a leading role. Indeed, Nancy Armstrong goes so far as to suggest that 'the Puritan revolution, which failed to seize political control through force as well as polemical writing, in fact succeeded in the eighteenth century sentimental fiction that delegates control to the female'.[8]

A writer who represents all three configurations of middle rank, Protestant nonconformity and female virtue is Elizabeth Rowe (1674–1737). The daughter of a prosperous clothier, brought up in a tradition of Presbyterian Dissent, Rowe was widely read and influential until well into the nineteenth century, especially for her series of imaginary epistles, *Friendship in Death* (1728) and *Letters Moral and Entertaining* (1728, 1731, 1732). Rowe sought to advance moral awareness and restraint through graceful examples of polite correspondence, some of which turn to quite different effects the kind of scenario exploited by Behn, Manley and Haywood. Among the hundred or so letters of the complete collection, some are about seduction, and 13 about adultery or its avoidance. Rowe limits her concern to relationships in which only one of the parties is married. For her, male sexual transgression is as sinful as female, and the married and unmarried partners bear equal guilt. This principle of equity, unusual at the time and for long afterwards, is reflected in her evenhanded attribution of marital status. Three of the seven stories of adultery involve wives, and three husbands (in the remaining case it is unclear which party is married); similarly, in two of the four stories of adultery avoided the woman is married, and in two the man. There is also one letter exhorting a single man not to commit adultery, and one counter-adultery story written in the voice of an unmarried woman.

Rowe's stories of adultery are powerful warnings, and they allow no pleas in mitigation. For instance, the very first of the *Letters Moral and Entertaining* presents Philario, married by his father at the age of twelve to a girl of ten 'only to secure her vast fortune to his family' (I.i.1).[9] Philario falls in love with Amasia and seduces her, but his forced marriage is not allowed to extenuate his violation of trust. Having succumbed to a fatal illness, she writes him a piercing letter of reproach in which she appeals to him to use in prayer for her forgiveness the same eloquence that betrayed her. A later letter (X) in the same series presents a different Amasia, who has seduced its writer, Celadon, despite his obligations to her husband. Here it is the man who falls ill and reproaches the woman for her treachery. Two further stories highlight other evils adultery brings. In Letter XVIII of Part II of *Letters Moral and Entertaining*, a wife writes from her deathbed to her sister confessing that, through a single act of infidelity, her elder son is another man's; she asks for her husband to be told, so that he may correct the injustice of a will leaving all his estate to the same son, neglecting four other children.

Letter XV of Part III presents a woman 'cut off from human society' by the pregnancy that resulted from her affair with a married man (III.xv.206). Kept by him in the country, and unable to break with him despite his callousness towards her, she bitterly regrets the absence of any provision for her daughter and the appalling example she has set her.

The stories of adultery avoided are equally uncompromising. The two that occur in Part I are from a woman and a man respectively, both unmarried; they are also complementary in other respects. Silvia explains to her friend Belinda that she has left for the country to avoid the tempting company of a handsome Frenchman; Herminius tells his sister how a seduction he had planned has brought him to reform. In Silvia's case, unlike those of heroines in scandal fiction, literature does not undermine but encourages morality. She quotes verse to bolster her weakening virtue, and she regains self-control when the wife of the man she loves refers to an exemplary story in romance (I.iii.19–20). Herminius returns from a tour of Europe during which he has had at least one affair to find his beloved Cleora married to a man who, he confesses, demands his respect and obligation. Having decided all the same to seduce her, he is brought to recognize his conduct as absurd not only by her calmly impervious responses, but by her 'modesty [. . .] truth and justice' (I.vii.42).

It is scarcely a coincidence that Rowe borrows Silvia's name from Behn's most famous heroine. In both letters, as elsewhere in the collection, characters whose names and situations evoke romantic and amatory fiction act improving roles. But Rowe by no means underestimates the difficulties of resisting temptation. Part II contains a further letter from Silvia (V) in which she tells her friend she was wrong to think her battle won. A single visit from the man she loves has shown her that she has not conquered her passion, and that her ideas of a romantic death are an illusion. Rowe strengthens her didactic message by refusing to minimize the struggle and pain required to resist temptation. A further letter in the same Part (VII) strikes a similar note. Teraminta, in an arranged though affectionate marriage, just stops short of adultery with her husband's man of business, but they cannot conquer their passion and her lover is devastated by her death. While in this case the woman holds off from the final step, Letter IV in Part III tells how a man draws back from the brink. Again, Rowe neither defers to the double standard, nor endorses the conventional idea that male sexual desire is too urgent to be resisted. Though the *Letters* are transparently didactic, they do not merit John J. Richetti's charges of crudity and artistic ineptitude.[10] Rowe's style is lucid, alert and intelligent; her piety is not complacent; and her ability to mime the discourses she opposes anticipates Richardson's in the next generation.

Although the 1720s marked the zenith of Eliza Haywood's success with novels of amorous intrigue and scandal fiction, Penelope Aubin (1679–1731) had already mounted a more direct and less subtle challenge than Rowe's. Her seven novels, published between 1721 and 1729, fused moral homily and romantic adventure, and proved sufficiently attractive to warrant a collected edition in 1739 and reprints into the earlier nineteenth century.[11] As William B. Warner has remarked, three elements of Aubin's novels 'give them a distinctly English, bourgeois, Protestant cast':

> First, her narratives are guided by a particularly insistent doctrine of providential rewards, whereby 'strange' and wonderful 'accidents' guarantee final happiness to the virtuous. Second, she purifies her heroines of the sort of erotic desire so explicitly present in Behn, Manley, and Haywood. Finally, her novels make the heroine's literal physical virginity the indispensable criterion of virtue.[12]

The second and third of these elements look forward to Richardson's *Pamela*, which was to exert so powerful an influence not only on the later development of the novel in Britain but on its status as a literary form. Jane Spencer has pointed out that Richardson admired Rowe, printed her fiction, and may have written the preface to the collected edition of Aubin's novels published in 1739, shortly before he began work on *Pamela*.[13] The crucial changes he initiated were to displace the romantic adventures of Aubin's fiction into domestic life, and, moving beyond the upper-class settings favoured by Aubin and Rowe, to establish class itself as a key subject and motive of fiction. If, however, as Spencer also observes, Aubin's example 'turned the tide in favour of moralized fiction',[14] it was Richardson who brought it to a flood by producing novels that first incorporated and then took over all the essential functions of conduct literature.

In *Desire and Domestic Fiction*, Nancy Armstrong claims not only that Richardson 'deployed the strategies of conduct-book literature within fiction', but also that he 'contained the strategies of the most deleterious fiction – a tale of seduction – within the framework of a conduct book'.[15] Although the paradox is convincing, it blurs two crucial distinctions, already present in Richardson's fiction, that gained extra importance in the following century. These concern gender and marital status. Novels of amatory intrigue before Richardson dealt with illicit sex before, during, and indeed after marriage; and they did not valorize female chastity to the same extent. His versions of the seduction narrative narrowed it sharply. First, the attempt at seduction fails; second, its target is female; third, she is still unmarried; fourth, and perhaps most crucial, any sexual desire on her part is erased. Richardson switched the focus to feminine virtue and its testing in the period of courtship, suppressing problems both of female desire and of marital conflict.

In blurring the distinctions of gender and marital status, Armstrong's formulation also begs the question of what kind of seduction narrative might be considered 'most deleterious'. If Richardson drew the teeth of the seduction narrative by having it succumb to feminine virtue, his example also had several further effects. One of these was in literary history, for, as Jane Spencer has pointed out, although the novel of seduction was first developed by female novelists, in whose hands it could 'make a strong attack on the double standard that demanded chastity of women, but not of men', the writers of the seduction novels best known today were male.[16] This reflects the extent to which Richardson and, later, Defoe became established as founders of the English novel. Again, as Spencer also indicates, later male novelists who handled plots of seduction idealized female innocence to promote a conservative and sentimental message, as Goldsmith did in *The Vicar of Wakefield* (1766) and Mackenzie in *The Man of Feeling* (1771). In these cases, seduction succeeds (though, in *The Vicar*, via a false marriage that is later revealed to be valid); but a further question is the greater value given to a virgin's chastity than a wife's. As the previous chapter has shown, women's amatory fiction earlier in the century was able to encompass all kinds of sexual transgression. If Richardson's example helped narrow this to the loss of virginity, British novelists of the following century would be able to treat such a theme only within tight limitations, and they would find themselves all but precluded from dealing with the sexual fall of a wife. In the wake of Richardson, female novelists followed his lead, building on his assimilation of conduct literature into fiction, but they did not shrink from representing problems within marriage, including adultery. They wrote, however, under increasing constraints. Sixty years later, these would consign adultery to the margins altogether.

Two anonymous narratives, published with the same title in 1743 and 1744, suggest how attitudes to the representation of wifely adultery were changing. Significantly, both are *romans à clef*. The first, *The Fair Adultress: or, the Treacherous Brother*, looks back in part to an older tradition, that of amatory fiction. It is set in Cyprus, styled as 'that amorous Island' (5);[17] most of the characters, such as St. Amour, Bellflour, and Mallamour, bear the type names of romance; all the main figures, except for the adulterous couple, are idealized; and, though none of the narrative is erotic, some of it is mildly salacious – as when the maid Eliza is knocked over by accident, 'exposing her bare Limbs to the Servants' (20), or when the narrator comments on the sight through a telescope of a couple making love. On the other hand, *The Fair Adultress* also displays the moralistic emphasis promoted most recently and most influentially by Richardson. Not only is its plot one of wifely adultery detected and repented, but it ends with the narrator in a platonic liaison with the maid Eliza who has helped in the discovery. The most blatant evidence of a pious drift that sits oddly with the story's other trappings occurs when the narrator finds Eliza weeding in her garden. Leaning heavily on emblems that Richardson had just exploited in *Pamela*, Eliza does not hesitate to point out the traditional allegorical application: 'The Pulse and Flowers put me on thinking on the Soul. The Weeds upon our Errors. Our Vices, like the Weeds, grow rank and fast, that will not let our Virtues (the Pulse and Flowers) flourish, till the loath-some Weeds are forc'd away' (44).[18] The narrator waxes equally sanctimonious in response: 'O Virtue! lovely Virtue! how beautiful thou art! [. . .] Virtue is rewarded in this World: Even the Vicious revere it, and stand in awe at its Innocence and Brightness' (45). The echo of *Pamela*'s notorious subtitle *Virtue Rewarded* is unlikely to be accidental.

What is also symptomatic about *The Fair Adultress* is its implicit and sometimes explicit misogynism. Although two of its female characters are virtuous – Eliza and the narrator's addressee, his married sister – the story begins by telling how the adulteress's mother had tricked her father into marriage after he had kept her as his mistress, and how, after her marriage, she had been rumoured to have had other affairs. The tone of this introduction is knowing and mildly licentious, and it can have no other function but to point up what the main narrative suggests is female cunning and excess. Furthermore, not only is that narrative centred on the adultery of a wife, but her partner is her brother-in-law; and, in keeping with the double standard of sexual morality, it pays little attention to him despite his guilt and his violent and capricious behaviour. It is the adulteress whom the narrator calls 'wicked' (9) and 'evil' (10), and even Eliza refers to her as 'that insatiate Woman' (35). These are all pointers to changing attitudes that would deepen the stigmas on female sexual transgression.

However, it is also significant that *The Fair Adultress* is probably based on a recent case of marital breakdown in Ireland. In 1761, among a collection of trial reports entitled *Adultery Anatomized*, were published 'The Proceedings of a Remarkable Trial for Criminal Conversation, in which the Right Honourable the Lord Viscount B––D, of the Kingdom of Ireland was plaintiff, against his own Brother The Hon. R–––D Defendant'.[19] The compiler states that the trial was held in Ireland, where all those concerned lived, and that the proceedings had never been printed but had come to him in manuscript. There are enough similarities between report and novel to support identification. The two not only turn on the unusual fact of adultery between wife and brother-in-law, but in both the adultery is exposed to the husband by a letter that goes astray, the adulterer is also married, the wife's servant claims that she knew about the affair only when it was too late to stop it, and the story ends with the wife confined to her husband's home and the brother-in-law in effective exile overseas. It is clear from the initials and other details given in the trial report that the aggrieved husband was Robert Rochfort, created Viscount Belfield in 1751 and Earl of Belvidere in 1756; and that the accused wife was Mary, daughter of Viscount Molesworth, whom he had married in 1736.[20] A further link is the similarity between the husband's title until 1751, Baron Belfield, and Count Bellflour, the name the novel gives him. According to the trial report, Belfield dropped proceedings against his brother when the latter agreed to leave the country for good, but renewed them when, some years later, he returned. The result was that he was awarded £20,000 in damages and his brother was imprisoned for debt (223); while he was able to confine his unhappy wife for the remaining 30 years that she lived at Gaulston Park, his subordinate country seat.[21] These developments are not reflected in the novel, because they took place after its publication in 1743.

Unlike its predecessor, *The Fair Adulteress* of 1744 advertises in its subtitle that it is *'Founded on Real Facts'*.[22] The facts to which it refers involve the Duke of Beaufort's successful prosecution of Lord Talbot of Hensol for adultery with his wife Frances, after which he divorced her by Act of Parliament in 1744.[23] Lawrence Stone, who provides a case study of the marriage and its failure, argues that the Beaufort story

> illustrates the intolerable strains placed upon marriage in England in the mid-eighteenth century when the old practice of choice of a spouse based almost exclusively on considerations of financial and political advantage was now having to compete with the new ideal of free choice by those involved, based on settled affection.

He concludes that 'The almost inevitable result was adultery by one or both sexes.'[24] Not surprisingly, the novel conveys a less balanced view. Though one of its several narrators declares that the courtship of husband and wife 'was founded upon the same Basis as most modern ones are. He wanted to be Master of her Fortune,' he completes his sentence by alleging that the bride 'was stark-mad to get from her worse than *Egyptian* bondage, as she call'd it, and take her full Swing of Pleasure' (121). This statement turns on two distortions of the case recounted by Stone – both of which are significant in themselves and, at the same time, are characteristic elements in the developing construction of wifely adultery. First, as Stone makes clear, 'prudential calculations of power and money' must have played a part on both sides in promoting a marriage uniting two of the wealthiest noble families in England.[25] These motives the novel reduces and simplifies to produce a stereotype of a grasping, impotent lord whose age, in the same way, it exaggerates. Beaufort was not twice as old as his wife, as the writer claims, but only four years her senior; and he is named 'Don Dandin' in mocking allusion to the famous line in Molière's eponymous play ('You asked for it, Georges Dandin'). Second, although Stone indicates that the marriage was showing signs of strain before it had lasted a decade, he cites no evidence to support the novel's portrayal of the Duchess as driven from the start by pursuit of sexual gratification.

The Fair Adulteress follows its namesake of 1743 by contrasting female sexual licence with an example of virtue and purity. Naming its heroine none too subtly Libertina, it does not stop at exposing her affair with Talbot (Philocell), but alleges that she also had liaisons with her mother's footman and her gardener; and it presents her mother, Frances Scudamore (Laura), in an almost equally derogatory light as a rival for the footman's affections. The counter-example is Talbot's wife, Mary (Asteria), who is portrayed as an unfortunate and undeserving victim. Indeed the novel heightens the pathos of the betrayed wife through its narrative structure: it begins by showing her abandoned in the country, exposed to scandal that she has done nothing to merit; and later not only displays her as a pattern wife but gives her a role as one of the story's narrators. The glaring contrast between domestic virtue and sexual profligacy is clearly designed both to promote the ideology of femininity and to check what the novel presents as dangerous female independence. It is in keeping with these aims that it smears Viscountess Scudamore, whom one of the narrators rightly describes as 'amongst the most distinguished of the Femmes Scavantes' (29), apparently on the ground that 'Wit and Gaiety are most commonly inseparable Companions' (32); and that it criticizes the Duchess's marriage settlement for keeping most of her wealth out of her husband's hands. This 'pernicious Custom', claims the same narrator, 'renders the Matrimonial Union a state of perpetual Jarring and Discontent by leaving the Wife independant of her Husband, who grows less careful of her Conduct that she would otherwise be, because she knows that if she suffers for any Failing, it can be only in Reputation, and not Substance' (31–2).

The second *Fair Adulteress* further resembles its predecessor by combining moral attitudes with exploitation of the story's salacious potential. Though it begins by declaring that 'Scandal is of use to the Public, as it prevents the too great Increase of wanton Amours, and is therefore an Antidote to Lust' (21), it does not hesitate to offer several Haywoodesque scenes, as when Libertina is saved by the footman from drowning but not from leaving 'all her lovely Limbs expos'd to his eager Grasp' (51), when the two are surprised in near *flagrante delicto*, and when she receives her future husband in an all too revealing undress. This contradiction typifies the literature of criminal conversation that would become established 30 years later and which is discussed at the end of this chapter. If the two narratives point forward to that tradition, their moralizing also suggests some of the obstacles novelists might face if they tried to deal with sexual transgression. At the same time, both assert the defence that they are based on fact, the first through its claim to be based on original letters (iii), the second through its subtitle and plain allusions to a scandal to which Beaufort's divorce had given uncomfortable publicity.

By the middle of the century, as Donald Thomas declares in his history of English literary censorship, 'Puritanism had become the cry for a reformation of manners, no longer confined to Puritans in the political or theological sense and, therefore, a much more powerful force.'[26] As a result, it became more difficult to publish openly any material that would be seen as licentious, although, according to Peter Wagner, the stream of such publications 'took some time to peter out, until it disappeared into an underground'.[27] Janet Todd has defined the consequences for women writers, further confined by the ideology of femininity:

> The new writer had to conform to the age's ideal of womanhood, whatever the individual reality seemed to be. She had to be virtuous and domestic, writing either from financial necessity, unsupported by the proper guardians of femininity such as husband or father, or from a desire to teach virtue to the unformed. The work she wrote was not presented aggressively to the public as an artful piece desiring to overwhelm the reader and give fame to the author. Instead it was a response to misfortune that had thrown the woman into the unusual necessity of providing financially for herself and her dependants. She would write and earn money while filling as before every possible domestic duty.[28]

No writer illustrates better the shift that had taken place by mid-century than Eliza Haywood.

Haywood's *The History of Miss Betsy Thoughtless* (1751) registers very clearly the changes that were to affect the construction and representation of sexuality in British literature until near the end of the nineteenth century. As Beth Fowkes Tobin has observed, in the 1740s, following the success of her amatory and scandal fiction 20 years earlier, 'Haywood redefined herself as a writer of moral essays and improving novels' (Introduction, xv–xvi).[29] In that decade, for instance, she published *The Female Spectator*, 'generally regarded as the first periodical directly aimed at a female readership to have been edited by a woman';[30] and also two novels, *The Fortunate Foundlings* (1744) and *Life's Progress Through the Passions* (1748), both of which show the influence of Richardson and Henry Fielding. What makes *Betsy Thoughtless* especially significant is the extent to which it represents a reshaping of Haywood's previous fiction along lines drawn by Richardson's *Pamela*.

As Jane Spencer has demonstrated, *Betsy Thoughtless* played a leading role in establishing a type of novel in which a young woman learns how to behave not only with virtue but discretion.[31] The plot of the reformed coquette, further developed by Frances Burney in *Evelina* (1778) and by Jane Austen in *Pride and Prejudice* (1813), casts into comic form the precepts set out in conduct books for female behaviour. However, Haywood's novel is more than this, because it also looks back to her earlier fiction through its scenes of attempted rape, seduction, and unhappy marriage, and through its alertness to the workings of the double standard of sexual morality. *Betsy Thoughtless* is rightly described by Tobin as 'one of the first novels to depict a heroine struggling with the consequences of marrying the wrong man', and also as one of the very few novels of its period to deal with details of divorce proceedings and marital separation (xi, xii–xiii).

One of the obvious respects in which *Betsy Thoughtless* follows the new and more conservative morality is in its portrayal of women who yield to seduction. The conduct of its imprudent but virtuous heroine is contrasted with that of two of her friends, who both pay the price for sexual transgression, one descending to actual and the other to virtual prostitution. While these figures offer examples of how a young woman should not behave, the novel's two cases of female adultery and infidelity carry further implications. Lady Mellasin is twice guilty of double adultery. Remarried after the death of her first husband, she is blackmailed into continuing her affair with a married man who depends on her for money as well as sex. When the affair, and the blackmail, are discovered, her husband takes divorce proceedings against her; and, although these come to an end when he dies suddenly, she has to take refuge overseas. Still further down the scale of sexual immorality is a young Frenchwoman on whom Betsy takes pity, giving her refuge in her own home in ignorance of her proclivities. Mistress by choice first to a duke in her own country and then to Betsy's elder brother, she is ejected by both for infidelity, only to have an affair with Betsy's husband. Both these cases of female adultery illustrate changing social attitudes. Lady Mellasin's role signifies the growing association of sexual sin with members of the aristocracy, Mademoiselle de Roquelair's with the French. Indeed, an earlier episode foreshadows the novel's linking of France and sexual licence through the governess, crudely labelled Mademoiselle Grenouille, who helps lead Betsy's schoolfriend astray. The bourgeois attack on aristocratic behaviour had already begun to play a key ideological role in British fiction, with Richardson leading the way; and France was to remain a byword for sexual irregularity till well into the twentieth century. Both stereotypes mark a dramatic change in direction from Haywood's first novel, in which all the main characters are from the aristocracy, and in which much of the action takes place in a France identified not with libertinism but sophistication.

Betsy Thoughtless also evokes Richardson in its use of letters as devices both of narrative and plot, and, most explicitly, by ending with 'the virtues of our heroine [. . .] at length rewarded' (568). Yet Haywood by no means conforms entirely to the new codes of manners and behaviour. For instance, when the narrator refers to female sexual transgressors, in phrase after phrase she links a word of condemnation with one of sympathy, as when she describes Lady Mellasin's response to her exposure in court: 'After this dissolute *and unfortunate* creature was left by Mr Trueworth [. . .] she gave a loose to agonies, which only those who have felt the same can be capable of conceiving' (454; emphasis added). The same episode revealingly varies a sequence from *Memoirs of a Certain Island* in which it is a man who is cheated (I, 193–4). The difference consists not only in the victim's sex, but in the more complex response invited from the reader to a married woman who cannot buy her way out of trouble so easily. In this case and elsewhere, Haywood draws attention to the double standard. The most interesting example occurs when Betsy visits her friend who, without telling her, has become a kept woman as a result of seduction. Here, her unexpected meeting with her suitor Trueworth and his friend Sir Bazil exposes the double standard in two ways. While it is improper, even out of friendship and charity, for one unmarried woman to visit another whose reputation is doubtful, a man may not only visit such a woman but enjoy her sexually. Although it is made clear that Trueworth has no such intentions, he later yields to temptation when, in a further echo of her earlier fiction, Haywood has him fall into a liaison with a female admirer who writes to him anonymously.[32]

Betsy Thoughtless also looks back to Haywood's previous novels when, addressing his wife, an elderly male character offers a stock defence of wifely adultery: 'You forget, my dear, how many ladies of late have broke the conjugal hoop, and think themselves justified in doing so, by having been prevailed upon to enter into it without inclination' (426). Now, however, the emphasis is rather different. The point of the remark is to underline the importance of rooted affection between man and woman before they marry. Such an ideal, which gave more scope to male choice and, at the least, female power to refuse, had been gaining ground since the previous century.[33] Thanks to its increased acceptance, especially among the middle ranks, by mid-century the view was already dying out that adultery in an arranged marriage might be condoned. These changes of attitude are linked with a reversal in assumptions about female sexuality and in its representation. Beth Fowkes Tobin marks a radical difference between *Betsy Thoughtless* and Haywood's earlier fiction when she declares:

> *Miss Betsy Thoughtless* is quite unlike *Love in Excess* and the dozens of amatory novels that Haywood wrote in the 1720s and 1730s in that explicit delineation of female sexual desire is erased from the text. This erasure of female desire is of great significance as it signals a major cultural shift in ideas about gender, class, and authorship. (xxi)

Whereas in her first novel, *Love in Excess*, Haywood refers to women who, 'in secret, cursed that custom which forbids women to make a declaration of their thoughts' (41), in *Betsy Thoughtless* the heroine is not even allowed awareness of her love for Trueworth, and women who make approaches to men – Flora Mellasin and Mademoiselle de Roquelair – come off badly. Indeed, it could even be suggested that Haywood exploits the new prudery by drawing the twists and turns of her plot largely from her heroine's inability to recognize the nature of her feelings for the man she eventually marries. Two novels published within ten years of *Betsy Thoughtless* show how far the rule had become established that women should be pure in desire as well as in deed.

Sarah Fielding's *The History of the Countess of Dellwyn* might be described as a novel of wifely adultery before the fact. Unlike the two *romans à clef* discussed above, it did not trade on scandal. Instead, though first published in 1759, all but a century before *Madame Bovary*, it displays nearly all the features that Flaubert's novel was to confirm as central to nineteenth-century adultery fiction. The main character is a young woman who comes to grief through seduction by an unmarried man; the action pivots on her adultery and is the vehicle for wide-ranging criticism of contemporary social attitudes; the narrative form is impersonal, and the narrative voice ironic. Yet, if in these ways *The Countess of Dellwyn* seems to anticipate the novel of wifely adultery, it more strikingly suggests why the form was never to take root in Britain.

In her Preface – almost a critical manifesto – Fielding sets out her aims in writing the novel. She begins by distinguishing it from two kinds of fiction associated with female writers of the previous generation: the scandal chronicle and the romance. On the one hand she insists that her characters are 'universal, and not pointed at Individuals' (I, iv), a wise precaution, in the wake of trial reports and *romans à clef*; on the other, quoting Hamlet's advice to the players, she warns against deviations 'from the Paths of Nature, in either stopping short of her Mark, or wildly running beyond the Limits she prescribes' (I, viii).[34] *The Countess of Dellwyn* is to pivot not only on the sober, scrupulous imitation of 'Nature' identified with the novel rather than the romance, but on moral instruction, that, Fielding claims, 'is essentially necessary to render any Writing useful to the Reader' (I, xvii). These three principles – typical rather than individual characters, the close imitation of 'Nature', and the importance of the 'Moral' – combine in Fielding's central device of the humour. However, although she cites Ben Jonson, she uses humour theory not for satire or comedy but for moral psychology. Her object is to 'unravel the intricate Labyrinths of the human Mind' (I, xv), a metaphor of which she was fond; and by doing so to demonstrate 'That the Mind, under the Influence of any indulged vicious Passion, is of itself and essentially unhappy, even without the Consideration of any Consequences' (I, xxv).

These precepts, which the novel follows faithfully, take it in quite another direction from the novel of wifely adultery. The key difference is that the 'vicious Passion' on which it turns is not sexual desire but vanity. Although the heroine, when just 17, is manipulated by father and suitor into marrying an invalid of 63, the reader is invited less to sympathize than to note, critically, how easily she is deceived through her wish to shine in fashionable society. But Fielding's idea of vanity is complex, and it involves not only social success but self-esteem. For instance, Lady Dellwyn enjoys 'a new-acquired Liking to herself' by rebuffing the man who later becomes her lover; and the narrator claims that this action is the first 'which had given her any true Pleasure' since her marriage (I, 119, 121). Fielding is at pains to emphasize that Lady Dellwyn is never influenced by sexual attraction, so that she embarks on her affair not because she is in love but in a heedless bid for attention. Not only would she have been able to overcome 'the soft Allurements of Inclination', but she is vulnerable precisely because they do not affect her and so fail to put her on guard (II, 49–50). Her transgression is therefore rightly termed 'criminal Vanity' (II, 130) rather than 'criminal conversation', the period's standard legal formula for adultery. The novel is consistent, and often convincing, in explaining the heroine's behaviour through her ruling passion. Even when, after her divorce, the Countess becomes engaged for a second time, her motive is to recover social standing, so that the fiancé who would help her in this is 'the only Man she had ever even fancied she had loved' (II, 269). Vanity also accounts for the roles she plays both in the immediate aftermath of her divorce and after her hopes for remarriage are crushed.

The Countess of Dellwyn carries the potential for a thoroughgoing critique of patriarchy, for it is possible to infer that the story's real villains are Lady Dellwyn's father, husband and seducer. The first not only fails to give her a proper moral education, but destroys her calm and leads her into a wholly unsuitable marriage for his own self-interest; the second, a superannuated rake, treats her as a commodity to be discarded at will; while the third, experienced in seduction, abandons her and leaves the country rather than pay damages for divorce. Since Fielding nevertheless insists that her heroine is responsible for her actions, and should suffer their consequences, it is not surprising that two of the novel's recent critics have argued that its apparent attack on patriarchy is compromised.[35] However, though there are compelling grounds for such a view, it fails to take account of the traditional Christian values to which Fielding held. Those values are demonstrated in Mrs Bilson, the novel's leading example of female virtue. As Linda Bree has pointed out,[36] Fielding develops Mrs Bilson in part as a contrast to the eponymous heroine of her brother's last novel,

Amelia (1752). Unlike Mrs Booth, Mrs Bilson not only forgives her husband's adultery and bankruptcy but reforms both him and her daughter's suitor; and, having led the family from debt to affluence, becomes a model of enlightened charity. She does this without questioning either the social order in which men always take precedence, or her own responsibility for behaving both morally and modestly. Although Fielding shows a keen awareness of how often, and how grossly, men abuse their power, she stopped short of challenging masculine priority. Instead she maintained the view of women that had become dominant in Britain during her lifetime, and to which she refers in her Preface when she recommends 'that Gentleness which is the characteristic Beauty of the female Mind' (I, xxxiii). At least she did not bring her heroine to death or its equivalent, unlike most of the male novelists who wrote novels of wifely adultery in the following century.

Nevertheless, in light of the rise of the novel of female adultery, at least two questions remain: why Fielding should have devised for her purposes a plot centred on wifely adultery; and why, having chosen such a plot, she should so firmly have excluded any hint of the sexual passion that adultery is usually taken to involve. These questions are all the more interesting for reasons indicated by Linda Bree, that the novel is very unusual for its period in dealing with divorce, and that the sole ground for divorce was adultery.[37] Divorce was infrequent, not least because, except in Scotland, where the law was different, before the Matrimonial Causes Act of 1857 it could only be obtained by Act of Parliament.[38] Bree cites Lawrence Stone's statistics that 'there were 16 divorces in the period 1751–60, compared with 14 in the period 1701–1750'.[39] Written near the end of the decade, *The Countess of Dellwyn* may reflect the increase in the number of actions for divorce, still few but always prominent and often scandalous; yet Fielding is unlikely to have chosen her subject for this reason alone. Instead, she uses adultery and divorce as vehicles for a more general social criticism. Partly for this reason, she provides none of the details with which those who published accounts of divorce proceedings regaled their readers.

The extreme care that Fielding displays over any potentially titillating material also helps explain her strict exclusion of any hint of sexual feeling. Here, another statistic cited by Bree offers a telling juxtaposition. Summarizing research by Cheryl Turner, Bree points out that 'between 1725 and the early 1740s the number of novels published by women declined; one recent study has identified none at all between 1737 and 1743, and only one woman writing before 1737 who published anything later'.[40] The causes behind the gap pointed out by Turner are undoubtedly complex, but one crucial factor was the 'new ideology of femininity' identified by Jane Spencer, Janet Todd, Mary Poovey and others.[41] It is this ideology, clear from Fielding's affirmation of feminine 'Gentleness' quoted above, that helps account for the lack of direct successors to the previous generation of women novelists. Tarnished, often unfairly, by charges that their lives and their subject matter were improper, their reputation gave Fielding every reason to distinguish her novel from romance and scandal chronicle alike. Unlike them, she and other novelists of her period would eschew any suggestion of immodesty. Since the new code of moral decorum applied above all to women and to sex, it is a remarkable paradox that, pornography aside, it took a woman to write the only novel of this period to centre on wifely adultery. Hence the need for caution. Fielding was already established as a serious writer whose name was unblemished, and probably no woman without such a position could have published on such a theme. Even then, however, the novel was a failure. Unlike her next work, *The History of Ophelia*, it was never reprinted, and the critical response was mixed.[42]

In the 1760s, after Sarah Fielding's career as a novelist had ended, the culture of sensibility was at its height.[43] As Jane Spencer has demonstrated, one important result was a decisive shift in the fictional presentation of the theme of seduction. On the one hand, sentimental and humanitarian attitudes invited sympathy for the seduced woman; on the other, the still-growing obsession with feminine purity both restricted that sympathy and required models of triumphant virtue. As Spencer remarks, Fielding could centre *The Countess of Dellwyn* on a seduced woman 'because as a satirist she did not intend any sympathetic identification with her heroine'; but novelists of the next generation gave the virtuous role to the heroine, and consigned the seduction theme to the margins.[44] A characteristic example, published only two years after Fielding's novel, is Frances Sheridan's *Memoirs of Miss Sidney Bidulph* (1761).

What distinguishes Sheridan's heroine is her perfect fidelity to conduct-book canons of female behaviour. Sidney obeys her mother in withdrawing from her engagement to Orlando Faulkland, to whom she is strongly attracted, because it appears that he has seduced a young woman and got her pregnant; less than three months later, she yields to persuasion in marrying a suitor for whom she can only feel rational affection; and when her husband, Mr Arnold, has a flagrant and damaging affair with a young widow, she forgives him and takes him back, even though, wrongly suspecting that she is meeting Faulkland secretly, he had forced her to leave their home and children. As Jean Coates Cleary has shown, *Sidney Bidulph* acts out principles of female behaviour codified in three popular conduct books published by James Fordyce, Hester Chapone, and John Gregory respectively between 1765 and 1774 (Introduction, xviii–xxviii).[45] At the core of those principles is not only a woman's subordination to parents or husband, but the requirement that she quell all awareness – let alone expression – of sexual desire. Thus, advising Sidney to accept Arnold, her friend Mrs Vere tells her: 'if you find no disinclination, it is enough. I married for love, yet I was far from being happy. [. . .] if you marry him with nothing more than indifference, gratitude will soon produce love in such a breast as yours' (82). Two months after the marriage, Sidney shows she has done her best both to absorb this precept and to act upon it when she faithfully affirms: 'Mr Arnold's assiduity and tenderness towards me deserve the gratefulest return my heart can make him; and I am convinced it is not necessary to be passionately in love with the man we marry, to make us happy' (106). It is not for lack of effort on her part that the marriage for a time breaks down.

However, *Sidney Bidulph* is not only of interest for illustrating conduct book principles through its virtuous heroine. Sheridan also built into her novel several examples of female sexual transgression, heightening the contrast in such a way as to press home the dangers of yielding to desire. Indeed, the action turns on a series of seductions, some involving adultery. First, though represented as the chief offender, Faulkland is himself seduced by Miss Burchell at the prompting of her aunt Mrs Gerrarde. Second, Sidney's mother opposes her marriage to Faulkland because of a parallel in her own earlier life: a man whom she had been about to wed had left her in a desperate attempt at amends to a woman he had seduced and promised to marry. Third, Arnold is seduced by Mrs Gerrarde, who milks him of money and manipulates him into believing that Sidney is on the verge of an affair with Faulkland. Fourth, Arnold loses more money still as a result of an affair carried on by the estranged wife of his elder brother, who gives birth to an heir later established by fraud as legitimate. Finally, the plot reaches a dramatic climax when, having married Miss Burchell in response to persuasions from Sidney and her mother, Faulkland finds her in bed with another man. In this way the novel not only presents three figures of female vice, but paints them in lurid colours, not least by having two of them seduce its two leading men.

Miss Burchell and Mrs Gerrarde also contrast with each other as adulteresses. The former, demure enough to mislead Sidney's mother, exemplifies the dangers for a woman of expressing and acting on desire. Telling Sidney her story, though only in part, Miss Burchell confesses: 'I had nobody to accuse but myself. I had declared my frantic love to Mr Faulkland unasked; I had implored his in return: in one dreadful moment I fell a sacrifice to my own weakness' (305). Even before this Sidney has exclaimed: 'never was so extravagant a love as her's', calling it 'the warmest and most romantic love I ever saw or heard of' (298, 299); later she warns: 'let her beware of disgusting a man of his sense by too strong an expression of her fondness' (324). As Jean Coates Cleary has argued, 'What the novel tells us metaphorically and through the object-lesson of Miss Burchell is that the consummation of an ardently felt, passionate love, even if it is sanctioned by marriage, is to be feared and must be avoided lest it lead to a sensual debasement synonymous with prostitution' (xxviii). It turns out that Miss Burchell has already, before marrying Faulkland, had an affair with Sir George, his friend who is also Sidney's brother; and her adultery within two years of marriage confirms the latter's view of her as 'a female libertine' (383). If Miss Burchell represents the danger for a woman of yielding to desire, Mrs Gerrarde shows the damage a woman may cause when she exploits it for her own ends. Party to her niece's seduction of Faulkland, and seducer herself of Sidney's husband, she can only be fought with her own weapons. In what is perhaps the novel's most extraordinary episode, Faulkland saves Sidney's marriage by acting as a kind of anti-Lovelace. Feigning love to Mrs Gerrarde, he abducts her and takes her to France, where she is sufficiently taken in by his pretended gallantry to write to Arnold explaining why she has left him and disabusing him of his suspicions of Sidney. Having achieved his designs without infringing his chastity, Faulkland marries Mrs Gerrarde to his valet, whom she later leaves to become mistress to a French nobleman. Sheridan spares no effort to incite revulsion for this female sexual adventurer, branding Mrs Gerrarde with all the ruling stereotypes:

not only vain, avaricious, and low-born, but also a flashy young widow, brought up as a Catholic, who is utterly without principle. Faulkland calls her an 'Amazon' (211), and goes so far as to declare: 'I could hardly consider her as a female' (213). Indeed, Mrs Gerrarde has none of the features that define her sex, according to the eighteenth-century ideology of femininity.

Although the novel has Faulkland redeem his offence with Miss Burchell, it shows the double standard at work in Sidney's marriage. On the one hand, it gives full weight to a husband's adultery when Sidney exclaims in her journal-letter: 'O Faulkland! how light was thy transgression, if we consider the consequences, compared to that which has driven me from my home, and from my children! steeled my husband's heart against me, heaped infamy on *my* head, and loaded my mother's age with sorrow and remorse!' (158–9). On the other, Sidney is not only expelled by Arnold for mere suspicion of her relations with Faulkland, despite his continuing affair with Mrs Gerrarde, but she lavishes concern on him and also, when he repents, forgiveness. Her mother states the orthodox rule in distinguishing Arnold from Faulkland, whom she believes to have seduced Miss Burchell: 'a woman certainly ought not to marry a loose man, if she knows him to be such; but if it be her misfortune to be joined to such a one, she is not to reject him, but more especially if she sees him willing to reform' (257).

Sheridan clearly intended the difference in treatment of husbands and wives to be noticed, and in other ways too the novel not only displays conduct-book precepts but half undoes them from within. In *Sidney Bidulph*, as Margaret Anne Doody puts it, 'Virtue is not rewarded, even by personal development. Moral decisions based on high principles of honor and the nicest scruples turn out wrong.'[46] Following strictly all the codes of contemporary female virtue, Sidney marries the wrong man, only for him to betray her and die in an accident after she has forgiven him; similarly, Faulkland marries the wrong woman only for her to betray him and expose him to a charge of murder. The novel feints towards a happy ending when Sidney marries Faulkland, believing his wife to be dead; but the marriage is not only unconsummated but is almost immediately nullified when it transpires that his crime of passion succeeded only in killing the lover. Faulkland dies, apparently by his own hand, leaving Sidney to bear her lot with Christian patience and stoicism, even to the next generation, as Sheridan's sequel shows.[47]

Doody suggests that in some respects 'Sheridan has, in what looks like a feminist novel, taken us beyond feminism, opening out the complexities that arise in human life whenever human beings try to do right'.[48] But what determines the complexities in question are specific codes of conduct, and these Sheridan undermines even while giving them overt support. Cleary catches the novel's critical paradox when she points to its 'complex doubleness – an insistent promotion of conduct doctrine coupled with an aggressive exposure of its unfortunate effects' (xix). This view goes further than Doody's, especially when Cleary shows how the delicacy required by the conduct books ties Sidney's hands and tongue. Two problems, however, remain. First, neither Cleary nor Doody gives enough weight to the negative examples of Miss Burchell and Mrs Gerrarde. If the novel questions the code of female delicacy in Sidney's case, in theirs it appears to endorse it. Second, there is still a shocking discrepancy between Sidney's virtue and her fate. The way the novel resolves this is by appealing to Christian doctrine: as the fictitious editor writes in his Introduction, people are not necessarily rewarded or punished in their lifetime, but in 'an invisible world where the distributions are just and equal' (7). As Cleary indicates, this appeal contributed to 'the debate over "poetic justice" that raged with particular energy in England during the third quarter of the eighteenth century' (xi). Cleary also suggests that, though 'Sidney's resignation may be perfect, one feels that her author's was not' (xxix), but such a claim can only be speculative. Much more likely is that Christian doctrine gave Sheridan – and most of her readers – the only acceptable explanation for human disasters that happen arbitrarily and even to the virtuous. Writing at an historical moment when the cult of sensibility gave codes of female virtue a further twist, Sheridan put her readers through an emotional switchback. Though authorized by Christian belief, this had the effect of raising questions that could not be expressed directly. Perhaps because of the skill with which Sheridan touched sensitive nerves, *Sidney Bidulph* proved highly successful, entering a second edition within the year, a fifth by 1796, and enabling a sequel. The contrast with *The Countess of Dellwyn* is telling. Not till near the end of the century, and scarcely even then, could a novelist of any integrity attribute sexual transgression to a heroine.

This taboo stands out all the more in light of the impact of Lord Hardwicke's Marriage Act, passed in 1753. While on the one hand, as Lawrence Stone declares, the Act 'at last brought coherence and logic to the laws governing marriage', on the other, as he observes elsewhere, it 'significantly strengthened legal supports' for 'the rights of property and male primogeniture'. The result was 'direct conflict with the principle of affective individualism with regard to the free choice of a spouse'.[49] It might have been expected that novels of the period that involve female adultery would exploit that conflict to the full. The fact that they rarely do so shows how powerful were the codes of feminine purity.

Elizabeth Griffith's *The History of Lady Barton* (1771) is a classic example of how female novelists handled the theme of female adultery during the age of sensibility. As Jane Spencer points out, *Lady Barton* contrasts with *The Countess of Dellwyn* in three respects: the heroine of the main story keeps her virtue, but the heroine of one of the secondary stories succumbs; yet the narrative works to invite sympathy for both – in part through a blend of epistolary form and personal narrative in which the various women tell their own tales.[50] At the same time, Griffith's novel is more conventional than Sheridan's. While, like *Sidney Bidulph*, it relegates adultery to a subplot, it implies less questioning of the conduct books.

Though it contains several different stories, *Lady Barton* is tightly constructed. The heroine, married to a man she does not love who treats her with little respect, successfully resists her love for another man, who is also in love with her. She corresponds with her sister Fanny, who is first discarded by her fiancé and then reunited with him after he has had an affair with an Italian opera-singer who deceives and robs him. The letters in which the two advise each other provide a forum for examining how a wife should behave if she cannot help feeling for another man the love she owes her husband. They also supply a channel for the two main subplots. The first, relayed by Lady Barton, concerns a young Frenchwoman, Olivia, who marries in secret but whose libertine husband tries to disavow her, even imprisoning her and their child when she follows him to his home in Ireland. The second, relayed by Fanny, concerns an unhappy wife, Maria, who commits the sin Lady Barton eschews. Between them, the four stories offer a range of comparisons. For instance, Maria, who succumbs to adultery, contrasts both with Lady Barton, who refuses, and with Olivia, first disgraced but at last proved victim of a secret marriage. Indeed, Griffith even builds into Maria's story a further inner narrative, also involving a secret marriage between a virtuous wife and a tyrannical husband. However, not all the contrasts point the same way. In particular, Griffith tailored Maria's story in such a way as in part to extenuate her adultery.

Unlike Lady Barton, Maria falls for her lover before she marries, and she agrees to the marriage not only because she and her mother face penury, but because her lover rejects her after a rival deceives him into believing her inconstant. The same rival inflames her husband with jealousy that she does nothing to encourage, and her single act of adultery occurs after the lover has traced her to the remote estate where her husband has banished her. She then sends her lover away, only to recall him when, finding she is pregnant, she has no other way to escape even harsher marital retribution. They are about to elope when her husband surprises them and kills her lover. It later turns out that he is the same man who had tried to deny his previous marriage in the second inner narrative. The effect of these narrative complexities is to suggest that Maria succumbs as a result not so much of sexual desire as of overwhelmingly hostile circumstance. For this reason her story qualifies Jane Spencer's generalization that subplots involving seduction in novels of the period serve 'as repositories for all the problematic feminine weaknesses purged from the picture of the ideal heroine'.[51] Maria is no weaker than Lady Barton, just considerably unluckier; and this lends the subplot a subversive potential that the main plot lacks. What is significant is that Griffith insulated that potential by embedding the subplot in a story of adultery avoided. She also used her subplot to emphasize further the arbitrary male power and licence displayed by the husbands of Lady Barton and Olivia, and by the fiancé of Lady Barton's sister, Fanny.

Through her epistolary form, Griffith also sought to stage a real debate over marriage and illicit love. In a key passage, quoted by Spencer, she has the unhappy wife argue with herself:

> If passion is involuntary it cannot be criminal; 'tis consequences only that can make it so [. . .]. –
> Flattering sophistry! Alas! I would deceive myself, but cannot! Have I not vowed, even at the altar vowed, to love another? Yet can that vow be binding, which promises what is not in our power, even at the time we make it? But grant it were, the contract sure is mutual; and when one fails, the other should be free.

> Wretched Louisa! strive no more to varnish o'er thy faults –
> Thou wert a criminal, in the first act, who wedded without love;
> and all the miseries which proceed from thence, too justly are thy
> due. (II, 108–9)[52]

In the following letter Lady Barton's conclusion is accepted by her sister, who writes: 'the woman who stretches out an *empty hand*, at the altar, but mocks the institution; and, if I may hazard the boldness of the expression, becomes *guilty*, before her *crime*; receives an antepast of misery' (II, 116–17). The problem is that this leaves unsolved the problems not only of unhappy marriage but of adulterous desire. Lady Barton ends by dying of consumption.

It is the code of female purity that blocks more radical questions. In conformity with the code, Griffith has her heroine die rather than succumb, Maria die after succumbing; and the informed reader can easily tell that Olivia's secret marriage is valid from the insistence with which she is described as chaste. Conversely, the two female villains both act from guilty passion. One is a widow who fakes her daughter's death because she fancies her fiancé for herself; the other is an adulteress who betrays Maria out of jealousy, having previously had an affair with Maria's lover. As the latter example indicates, the novel also draws attention to the double standard. While a woman's lapse is fatal, not only can Maria's lover be forgiven for sexual indiscretion, but also Fanny's fiancé in his affair with the opera-singer. The ideal man is Lady Barton's lover, who gives sententious advice to Fanny's fiancé, and who keeps his own purity unsullied. It is he who advocates 'a strong, but chaste passion, for a woman of merit [. . .]; than which, nothing in nature more elevates the mind, improves the understanding, refines the manners, and purges the affections of man' (II, 200). The novel suggests, despite itself, that the laws and customs governing marriage often frustrate or obstruct such a prospect. But the code of feminine purity prevented Griffith, like other novelists of her period, from venturing further.[53]

Other forms of publication than the novel faced fewer restraints, and their proliferation after 1770 helps explain why for about the next fifteen years novelists avoided the theme of female adultery. Early in the century a market had developed for reports on the more notorious trials for adultery. Although, as Lawrence Stone has explained, adultery had been quietly decriminalized by 1746, a form of civil action had been introduced towards the end of the previous century by which adulterers could be called to account:

> the two superior courts of common law, the King's Bench and Common Pleas, extended the range of the action of trespass [. . .] to cover an action by a husband for damages against the seducer of his wife, the seduction being described as a 'criminal conversation', despite the fact that it was neither criminal nor a conversation in the usual sense of the word.[54]

An action for 'crim. con.', as it came to be known, was usually a precondition for divorce by Act of Parliament – the only possible method until after the Matrimonial Causes Act of 1857. Peter Wagner has shown that unscrupulous literary entrepreneurs such as Edmund Curll soon realized that there was money to be made from reports of trials for crim. con. and divorce, and collections began to appear from early in the century.[55] The genre faded in the 1730s as a result of competition from newspapers, though it rallied from time to time in such publications as the two *romans à clef* discussed above and in the 1761 collection *Adultery Anatomized*. Its progress is summarized by Lawrence Stone: 'Accounts of individual cases of trials for adultery began in about 1690, collections of the more sensational items in about 1750, and by the 1770s the genre had grown from a trickle to a flood' (249). The genre is epitomized by a seven-volume collection of especially colourful cases, first published in 1779–80, entitled *Trials for Adultery: or, the History of Divorces. Being Select Trials at Doctors Commons, For Adultery, Fornication, Cruelty, Impotence, &c.*[56] Stone suggests that the genre 'became a kind of didactic fiction drawn from real life, a substitute for the novel' (249). The difference was that trial reports could get away with material that respectable fiction had to avoid. Trading on quasi-factual status, and on spurious claims to morality, they constituted a form of pornographic narrative, to be heightened further from the following decade by pictorial frills.

A single highly publicized trial of 1770 did most to release the flood of crim. con. reports and associated items mentioned by Stone: Richard Grosvenor, Baron and later Earl of that title, prosecuted the King's brother, the Duke of Cumberland, successfully for adultery with his wife Henrietta.[57] Several factors ensured maximum public attention, ranging from the rank of the parties involved to the various salacious and at times ludicrous details brought to light by witnesses and by correspondence between the two lovers. Not only did the trial report go into more than five editions, as Wagner records, but a rash of other publications followed, including *Free Thoughts on Seduction, Adultery, and Divorce* by the translator of Rousseau's *Julie, or the New Heloise*, William Kenrick.[58] Two of these are of special interest. On the one hand, *A Full and Complete History of His R—l H— the D— of C—d and Lady G—r, the fair Adultress* (1770) takes the plaintiff's point of view, representing him as affectionate and generous and his wife as vain, wanton and ungrateful. On the other, a novel entitled *Harriet: or, The Innocent Adultress* (1771) denies that Lady Grosvenor ever committed adultery, paints the licentious Cumberland as a pattern of virtue, and, not without justice, accuses the noble lord of neglecting his wife both for the turf and for his own sexual adventures.[59] Both books develop a branch of the literature of crim. con. formed by 'articles which were written or paid for by the plaintiff or the defendant [. . .] and were intended to offer a highly partisan presentation of the affair in order to sway public opinion in their favour' (Stone, 250). Thus the *Full and Complete History* was probably written not only to cash in on the case but to curry favour with the Grosvenor family; whereas *Harriet: or, The Innocent Adultress* was clearly designed to counter the impact of publicity highly damaging not only to Lady Grosvenor's name but to the already tarnished reputation of the Duke. Indeed, a new edition of the novel appeared when the trial report was republished in *Trials for Adultery* at the end of the decade.[60] The *Full and Complete History* enjoyed a briefer but more profitable shelf life, on the evidence of the editions recorded – all dated 1770, three from London and one from Dublin.

Though it gestures occasionally to morality, the *Full and Complete History* outstrips the report of the trial in exploiting the Grosvenor / Cumberland case for comic, prurient and pornographic ends. Claiming that Cumberland 'never wrote to the dear object of his love, but was sure to commit some mistake, as to place or time of meeting' (I, 104–5), and representing Grosvenor as often coming home unexpectedly, it makes the most of the resulting altercations; and it gains full value from copies of correspondence which, it acknowledges, had been published already. At the same time, it also draws on traditions of libertine writing. Examples are a sensual description of Lady Grosvenor positioned invitingly in a room filled with erotic paintings (I, 177–80); an almost wholly irrelevant narrative of the sexual exploits of a man with whom she was hardly acquainted (II, 133–58); and a pretended 'defence of the fair sex' (I, 90) that ends with the deadpan protest that a woman should not be blamed for adultery 'who has been deceived by an impostor, who was in all respects as like her husband as one may appear to be in a dark room' (I, 99). Not only the *History* but, surprisingly, *Harriet: or, The Innocent Adultress* comes close to justifying wifely adultery. The latter even ends on a comically rueful note by giving the last word to the heroine's free-living confidante: 'Tho' we all agree in thinking the verdict provoking – not one of us has, I believe, the same reason for the opinion – [. . .] Your ladyship thinks it provoking to be found guilty when you are innocent – and I think it provoking, my dear, that you should be innocent when you are found guilty' (I, 176). It is significant that the more tightly controlled press in France could not go as far in exploiting similar material for erotic or bawdy purposes. Stone notes that

> in France before the Revolution there was an identical explosion of publications about sensational trials, including over seventy for adultery and bigamy. Thanks to the efforts of the censors, however, there are no records of eye-witness testimony, and no detailed descriptions of sexual activity. The general tone is one of moral satisfaction at the detection and punishment of wickedness. (251)

The contrast is all the more telling in light of the fact that during the eighteenth century France not only produced a tradition of libertine fiction but, as Peter Wagner has put it, 'dominated in almost every area of erotica'.[61] It indicates how strongly national institutions and culture influenced what could be offered to readers.

By the later eighteenth century, scandalous news and reports were published not only in books and newspapers but in 'elite scandal periodicals' such as the *Town and Country Magazine* and the *Bon Ton Magazine* (Stone, 252). According to Wagner, by the time the century ended 'crim. con. cases and similar trial reports had fully developed as a genre of erotica'.[62] If such a description suggests a limited, under-the-counter market, this was far from being the case. Stone quotes Leigh Hunt remarking in 1820, at the height of the sensational trial for adultery of Queen Caroline: 'You may look upon the British public as constantly occupied in reading trials for adultery' (253). But the very success of the genre, especially when embellished with pictures, had already drawn attention from the Vice Society. A series of successful prosecutions brought the books and magazines to an end, and crim. con. itself disappeared as a result of the Matrimonial Causes Act of 1857. Nevertheless, Stone observes that the new system

> failed entirely to keep the sordid details of divorce proceedings out of the newspapers. In 1859, two years after the act came into force, Queen Victoria wrote an anguished letter of protest to Lord Chancellor Campbell, asking for a curb to be placed on publication of items 'of so scandalous a character that it makes it almost impossible for a paper to be trusted in the hands of a young lady or boy. None of the worst French novels . . . can be as bad . . . and its effect must be pernicious to the public morals of the country.' (294–5)

Stone further relates how, in response, Lord Campbell proposed a bill requiring that court hearings for adultery be conducted in private, and how its failure left a notably juicy market open to the press until it was finally restricted by legislation over sixty years later. Barbara Leckie has discussed this divorce court journalism and its various effects, including the development by modernist novelists in Britain of oblique ways in which to handle a topic that was otherwise forbidden to them.[63]

However, while the tradition of a free press allowed newspapers to publish salacious material, fiction aimed at general readers had to follow a much narrower code. Writers were restricted not only by political reaction and Evangelical morality, as the next chapter will show, but at the same time they were striving to establish the novel as a respectable form. It is scarcely surprising that they did not venture into a subject that would threaten their reputations, and that was already firmly entrenched – at first in a demeaning corner of the book and magazine market, later in the press at large. Thus a further reason why the novel of wifely adultery never developed in Britain is that it was forestalled by publications that were already well established there in the later eighteenth century, and that continued to flourish in other forms.

6

Adultery, Revolution and Reaction: 1773–1814

Between the early 1770s and the mid-1780s, the topic of wifely adultery all but disappeared from respectable British fiction. One reason for this was the development of the literature of criminal conversation, another the still mounting constraints on the subjects that women novelists, in particular, could safely treat. It is all the more striking, then, that in the last fifteen or so years of the century several women novelists not only returned to the topic of wifely adultery but handled it in new and controversial ways. This chapter discusses several examples, and considers what was at issue in the partial and temporary freeing of restrictions and in their restoration.

Elizabeth Griffith's *History of Lady Barton*, discussed in Chapter 5, seems to be the only clear example of a novel addressed to respectable readers that dealt with wifely adultery in the years between 1771 and 1786. Its appearance in 1771 coincided with the first wave of success of the publications exploiting the Grosvenor case, also considered in the previous chapter, and with the bringing before Parliament of the first of a series of bills 'to forbid a wife divorced for adultery from marrying her lover'.[1] Griffith's career as a writer suggests that she changed tack in order not to lose reputation or sales by association with a dangerous subject. Her first novel, *The Delicate Distress* (1769), had addressed the problems of husbandly neglect and infidelity; as I have shown, her second, *Lady Barton*, had broached the more difficult question of a wife's adulterous desire and had dealt, in two of the three subplots, with wifely adultery. Her third and last novel, however, *The Story of Lady Juliana Harley* (1776), went back to the safer themes of forced marriage and unwanted courtship; and she had already begun to diversify into short stories and compilations. Apart from *Lady Juliana Harley*, her most substantial publications in the last decade of her career were *The Morality of Shakespeare's Drama Illustrated* (1775), a selection of extracts along with edifying commentary, and

A Collection of Novels (1777), a three-volume anthology that she took care to guard from impropriety by selection and bowdlerization.

The sole short story by Griffith to centre on wifely adultery offers further evidence of narrowing attitudes. 'The Unforced Repentance' was first published anonymously in the *Westminster Magazine* in September 1773 and collected seven years later in *Novellettes, Selected for the Use of Young Ladies and Gentlemen*, to which she was the main contributor. What is significant about the story is the care it displays to avoid indelicacy. Griffith distances it through its narration, in retrospect, by an elderly, unworldly narrator who is, moreover, a parson. She also adds the subtitle 'A Real Story', as if attempting not only to claim authenticity but to excuse the narrator or author from having invented a tale on such a subject. The tale itself, however, could scarcely do more to dispel any possible qualms. It begins with the narrator taking 'a very young and unhappy Lady' (2) into his home in response to a request from a young man who turns out to be her husband.[2] The cause of the woman's distress is unstated, and the narrator does not discover it until she is dying of grief for having betrayed her husband and then, she believes, caused his death through her inability to accept his forgiveness. Since almost all the action has already taken place by the time the narrator meets the heroine, and since he only meets her husband briefly, he has little to do but watch her die and listen to her story. Though it is a story of adultery, by the time she tells it her suffering already appeals for the reader's sympathy, and Griffith builds in a battery of mitigating circumstances. Having lost her mother in infancy and her father at the age of ten, Emilia has been brought up chiefly by her aunt, a society lady who pays little regard to virtue. Left without resources by the death of her uncle, she marries a man whom she finds admirable but does not love, only to succumb to a previous admirer, the Earl of S—, who would have married her himself had he been of age or allowed to do so by his family. She yields to the Earl out of pity when, seriously ill during a visit to her home, he confesses his love, at a time when her husband has already been away for several weeks looking after his dying sister. Griffith emphasizes that Emilia falls through the quintessentially feminine quality of sensibility: 'There are virtues which are dangerous even to virtue itself' (24). Her ingenuity in constructing a situation to explain how an otherwise blameless heroine could have transgressed would be absurd, if it were not for the ideological constraints on fictions of female adultery. It is also sensibility that accounts for Emilia's terminal penitence. This helps justify the appeal for her pardon with which the story ends.

Whoever compiled *Novellettes* must have thought well of 'The Unforced Repentance' because, though not the first of Griffith's stories to appear in the *Westminster Magazine*, it is placed first in the collection. The stories chosen to accompany it demonstrate a similar blend of sentiment and morality, appropriate to the 'Young Ladies and Gentlemen' of the subtitle. Three are about husbandly adultery and three about obstructed marriage; two about seduction and two about faulty education; while, of the remaining two, one is a tale of sensibility revolving on charity to a female orphan, and the other is best described by its title, 'Conjugal Fidelity: or, Female Fortitude'.[3] Though this last story has nothing to do with adultery, male or female, it is clearly aimed at providing a counter-example to what it represents as contemporary licence. At the same time, the narrator's dry reference to 'the Archives of Doctors Commons' (181) not only gives evidence of that licence, but draws attention to the kind of writing from which the author had to distance herself.

Nevertheless, despite the strengthening of the constraints on fiction to which Griffith's career attests, for some years towards the end of the century it again became possible not only to attribute sexual desire to a fictional heroine but also to suggest that wifely adultery might be condoned and even, in the most radical example, justified. It is not easy to explain why this change took place, but it was part of nothing less than a cultural revolution in which the professional middle classes played a leading role. The effect of this revolution, in Gary Kelly's summary, was

> to consolidate the middle classes under the leadership of the professionals, detach them from ideological and cultural dependence on the dominant classes of court, aristocracy, and gentry, and secure them from cultural and ideological contamination by the lower classes. [. . .] In this way the cultural revolutionaries would secure hegemony for themselves without using court government's resource of main force or the lower classes' resource of riot, and without the kind of revolutionary violence that haunted Britain from the seventeenth century and that took place across the Channel in the 1790s.[4]

As Kelly shows, political, legal and ideological restrictions on women rendered their part in the movement ambiguous, even contradictory. While educational opportunities for middle-class women had improved, and the number of women publishing works of fiction, non-fiction and poetry had greatly increased,[5] they operated in an ideological sphere in which the code of feminine purity still held sway. For this reason, fiction of the period by women shows many tensions in its handling of sexual themes. All the same, there is a clear development towards more enlightened ideas of female sexuality from Harriet Lee's *The Errors of Innocence* (1786) to Mary Wollstonecraft's *The Wrongs of Woman* (1798).

The Errors of Innocence is a novel less of adultery than of adultery avoided, and in this it looks back to *The History of Lady Barton*. In the main plot, Sophia Vernon is tricked into marrying George Obrien by an appeal to her sympathy; and, despite her husband's extravagance, ill-treatment and adultery, she successfully resists two attempts at seduction from the man she loves until the deaths of her husband and her lover's wife finally permit them to marry. The novel's project is to show that what one of the characters calls 'fatal sensibility' (I, 263),[6] in referring to Sophia's marriage, need not be fatal to female virtue. The heroine's task is therefore defined as 'Directing a fine understanding towards correcting the errors of a warm heart' (III, 61), while the adulteress is described as combining 'a wrong head, and a cold heart' (III, 87). Such an ideological move may be explained as an attempt to have the cake of sensibility and still eat it. Women who wished both to promote the claims of their sex and maintain its accepted qualities of compassion and feeling had to work hard to defuse the charges of weakness and susceptibility these entailed. Lee accordingly casts her adulteress as both unfeminine and unwomanly, seduced by fashion, not feeling.

Lee's novel offers a view of the aristocracy in keeping with Kelly's summary quoted above. Few members of the class emerge with any credit, and the four leading characters all distinguish themselves from it in various ways. The only estimable male, Edward Nugent, is the son of a painter; in response to the snobbery of the titled family into which he has married secretly, he all but boasts of his irremediably plebeian connections. His friend Henry Erskine begins and ends the novel illegitimate, inheriting a title in between only to lose it without regrets when his parents' marriage is proved invalid. Along with the main female characters, Lady Helen and Sophia Vernon, these two found a kind of alternative society at the end, based on moderate income and expenses, country retirement, and polite learning. However, what they reject in the novel's version of aristocracy is not only its snobbery but its licentiousness and excess. Lee furnishes almost a caricature image of seduction, liaisons and elopement among the upper classes of the day. Against this, the two model couples at the end hold out an ideal of bourgeois companionate marriage and domesticity.

While the fictional attack on aristocracy dates back at least as far as Richardson, Lee's emphasis on specifically sexual scandal had more recent origins. These become clear when, deploring the fall of her cousin Janetta, Lady Helen Nugent paints a picture of general fashionable licence:

> Frivolous, even in vice! yet these are the women, whose names disgrace our Courts of Justice: names, sacred in the annals of the past, and sanctified by the most illustrious actions, now adorning some scandalous anecdote in a newspaper, increasing the sale of a despicable pamphlet, or stuck up, amidst the vilest of their sex, at the windows of a licentious print-shop. (IV, 2).

So explicit an allusion to the literature of criminal conversation emphasizes not only the novel's moral attack on the aristocracy but also its care to avoid titillation and prurience. Despite its epistolary form, *The Errors of Innocence* leaves no doubt that its author follows an irreproachably conservative moral line. Among the several characters who refer to marital failure, it is the villain who claims that '*modern* matrimony [. . .] now privileges licentiousness', and all too often ends in 'the King's-Bench, or Doctors-Commons' (I, 168–9); while the betrayed husband asks: 'And what is a divorce? – A reward for licentiousness, that only confirms *my* infamy, and leaves her free to encrease her own' (IV, 46). This definition, perhaps at first surprising, refers not only to the exposure in court of the husband's cuckolding but to the absence of restrictions on the wife later marrying her lover. As Lee would have been well aware, bills had been debated in Parliament in 1771 and 1779 in an attempt to prevent such marriages.[7] The novel gives no hint of the counter-argument that in most cases such a ban would ruin the woman's life while leaving the man unscathed. This further underlines Lee's prudence in dealing with a topic rendered notorious by the trial reports and scandal sheets. As other women novelists took it up, however, they pressed it further both in substance and presentation.

The novels of Charlotte Smith illustrate the more progressive attitudes to marriage and sexuality that found increasing voice in British fiction of the period. Smith, described by her most recent biographer as 'the most popular English novelist of her time', published ten novels and a collection of novellas between 1788 and 1802;[8] she was also a fine poet. Though often grouped with those 'who were called by their detractors "Jacobins", writers who wanted radical reform or revolution', she is more accurately defined as 'a Girondin, not a Jacobin'.[9] Yet, while she does not go as far in raising social and political questions as some of her fellow novelists, the narratives in which she addresses adultery and seduction mark a clear change of direction from that of her immediate precursors. Her first novel, *Emmeline, the Orphan of the Castle*, published in 1788 only two years after *The Errors of Innocence*, is a clear example.

Emmeline follows a conventional plot that conducts its virtuous heroine both to her proper place in society and to an emotionally and materially desirable marriage. On the margins, however, are three subplots in which marriage fails; and two of them highlight the dangers of marrying too early. Emmeline's friend Mrs Stafford has been wedded at the age of 15 to a man who has proved grossly irresponsible, depleting their property and descending to 'low and degrading debauchery' (177).[10] At the same age, and largely because she dislikes the woman who is about to become her stepmother, Lady Adelina Trelawny has married a man who had just come into a fortune and who turns out to be a boor. She herself says: 'I had never thought of any thing so serious as matrimony; and indeed was but just out of the nursery, where I had never been told it was necessary to think at all' (211). Both marriages draw on Smith's personal experience,[11] but, while Mrs Stafford's married life follows the writer's more closely, Lady Adelina's leads her into adultery.

Four main features of Lady Adelina's story distinguish it both from adultery narratives earlier in the period and from the form that would develop on the Continent in the following century. Three of these features are emphasized by Jane Spencer, who calls attention not only to the subordination of the adultery plot to the main story, focused on a virtuous heroine, but to the circumstances that mitigate wifely adultery and support the prospect of it ending happily. As Spencer says, the unsuitable husband, married to Lady Adelina before she could judge better, 'is practically held responsible' for driving her into the arms of Fitz-Edward, who becomes her lover; and Lady Adelina proves properly repentant, leaving Fitz-Edward when she falls pregnant and, though she loves him, refusing to see or even name him until, after her husband's death, he meets her uninvited.[12] The fourth distinctive feature is that the subplot focuses not on seduction, or indeed adultery, but their aftermath. For this reason, and because Lady Adelina blames herself as much as her lover, it is not quite accurate to class the story, with Spencer, as one of seduction. Lady Adelina tells the first part herself, when Emmeline and Mrs Stafford find her awaiting childbirth in a miserable cottage where she has taken refuge, but it then becomes part of the novel's larger action. The effect is to move the emphasis from adultery to the trouble and misery it causes. Not only do both partners suffer painfully, but Emmeline has to struggle to prevent Lady Adelina's two brothers from fighting duels with her lover. Smith goes further still in her efforts to render acceptable what could easily have been represented as toleration of wifely adultery. She casts the lover as a libertine who recognizes the error of his ways and reforms; she has Lady Adelina, supported by Emmeline, refuse his proposal of marriage; and finally he is allowed only 'the hope, that at the end of her mourning she would relent, and accede to the entreaties of all her family' (526). Although Lady Adelina is widowed, not divorced, for a woman novelist to permit such a hope was an appreciable risk at this period, during which the series of bills, mentioned above, that aimed to bar divorced wives from marrying their lovers all gained majorities in the House of Lords.

Relegating the adultery story to a subplot, Smith was also able to offer improving alternatives in her presentation of Mrs Stafford and of the heroine herself. Mrs Stafford copes with several children, the management of her husband's debts, and his folly, infidelity and ill-temper, yet refuses to respond to the engaging libertine Fitz-Edward when he makes up to her. Emmeline's difficulties stem from her courtship by a series of suitors, especially her cousin Delamere, whose parents oppose their marriage because she is without money, rank or prospects. Smith builds a clever feint into her novel's action by which the conventional outcome of marriage between heroine and apparent hero is avoided. First, though for a long time she keeps that outcome open, it becomes clear that Delamere's volatility makes him wholly unsuitable as a husband. Second, she introduces a superior kind of hero in the shape of Lady Adelina's younger brother, Godolphin. The strategy behind this move emerges when, addressing the heroine, Lady Adelina calls attention to her luck:

Fortunate, too, were those circumstances which divided my Emmeline from Delamere, before indissoluble bonds enchained you for ever. Had it been otherwise; had *your* guardian angel slumbered as *mine did*; you too, all lovely and deserving as you are, would have been condemned to the bitterest of all lots, and might have discovered all the excellence and worth of Godolphin, when your duty and your honour allowed you no eyes but for Delamere. (469)

While this scarcely suggests that Emmeline, any more than Mrs Stafford, would have succumbed to adultery, it identifies the kind of marital misery in which she might, but for the providential plot, have found herself. At the same time, it reinforces the dangers for women both of early marriage and of giving way to male will.

If Emmeline's lucky escape shows the perils women face in courtship, she also exemplifies moral and affective qualities required at the period of a woman of her class. The most she feels for Delamere is 'a sentiment warmer perhaps than friendship' (149), but this is chastened when, in a rewriting of a famous episode in *Clarissa*, Delamere abducts her and tries to get her to agree to a marriage in Scotland. After she meets Godolphin, she monitors her feelings closely so as not to 'allow any partiality to rob Delamere of that pure and sincere attachment with which he would expect her to meet him at the altar' (289). However, unlike Betsy Thoughtless or the Countess of Dellwyn, Emmeline is allowed not only to feel such partiality but to become aware of it and to act upon it. The fact that she refuses to marry Delamere once she has fallen in love with Godolphin marks the progress made by the ideal of affective marriage since the 1750s. As Loraine Fletcher notes, Smith 'breaks the novelistic etiquette that a virtuous heroine must marry the first person she seriously considers as a husband, an innovation felt to be dangerous by some readers'.[13] Yet the novel still confirms the code of feminine purity by defining Emmeline's and Lady Adelina's love not in terms of passion but of softness of heart. It also goes further by taming and domesticating the men they love. Though one is a colonel and the other a sea-captain, Emmeline persuades each of them not to fight the duel required by military honour; and Godolphin is not only credited with feeling for Emmeline 'the most pure and ardent passion that was ever inspired by a lovely and deserving object' (304), but is portrayed in a thoroughly domestic light when he sets up house for his sister and her child.

The third subplot in *Emmeline* in which marriage fails offers a quite different set of contrasts. Although it is a story of wifely adultery, sexual passion still plays no part; what it shows instead, through its three participants, is a set of revealing antipathies. The adulterous wife is an example of aristocratic hauteur, the betrayed husband one of petit-bourgeois self-seeking, and the lover one of French libertinism, religious as well as sexual. In this way the subplot performs several obvious kinds of ideological work: it promotes an ideal of conduct that is genteel but affected neither by the faults of upper-class vanity, nor by those of expedience and cupidity, attributed to its three bourgeois figures, all lawyers; and it distinguishes very explicitly between what it presents as proper English morality and French and aristocratic licence. Its outcome is suitably sensational, for the affair leads to a duel in which Delamere, the adulteress's brother, is killed, and then to her abandonment by her lover, a period in Paris 'most disgraceful to her family and herself' (525), and her confinement in a convent.

Neither the lurid ending of this subplot, nor the conventional outcome of the main plot, in which Emmeline is discovered to be legitimate and wealthy, materially compromises what was for the period a liberal approach to the problems faced by women in courtship and unhappy marriages. In her ten novels, Charlotte Smith displays what Loraine Fletcher rightly calls 'a more tolerant attitude to extramarital sex and divorce than is usually found in English novels of the eighteenth or nineteenth centuries'.[14]

The presentation of adultery in Elizabeth Inchbald's *A Simple Story* (1791) betrays a more complex range of attitudes than those either in *The Errors of Innocence* or *Emmeline*. As Jane Spencer has shown, 'the heroine's desire [. . .] and its prohibition are Inchbald's main concerns'.[15] The desire is certainly explicit, as when Miss Milner confesses of her guardian: 'I love him with all the passion of a mistress, and with all the tenderness of a wife' (72). It is also dangerous, for, as a Roman Catholic priest, its object is pledged to celibacy, and, as her guardian, his relation to her is paternal. The first obstacle is removed when, having unexpectedly succeeded to a title, Lord Elmwood obtains dispensation from his vows so that he may perpetuate the family line. The second appears surmounted when he marries the heroine, just as the father figure Lord Orville marries Frances Burney's at the end of *Evelina* (1778). At this point, however, Inchbald's story is only half told. The second two volumes begin with a chapter summarizing the failure of the marriage as a result of Lady Elmwood's adultery and her husband's intransigence. They then trace the difficult stages through which, after her death, Lord Elmwood takes their only child, a daughter, back into his family. It is therefore possible to argue that the novel enacts a female version of the family romance in which the daughter's desire for the father is both punished and, through displacement, finally gratified. There is ample evidence for such a reading, especially in the fraught interaction of ward and guardian, and later of daughter and father, where the mother's erotic desire is transposed into the filial devotion of the child. Yet, despite the novel's title, the story is not so simple.

First, though Elmwood gains absolution from his vows, the taboo against desiring a priest is formidable. The narrator not only compares it to 'that barrier which divides a sister from a brother' (74), but shows what it means to Miss Milner's Catholic confidante:

> there was no guilt, except that of murder, which she thought equal to the crime in question, provided it was ever perpetrated.— Adultery, her reason would perhaps have informed her, was a more pernicious evil to society; but to a religious mind, what sounds so horrible as sacrilege? Of vows made to God or to man, the former must weigh the heavier.— Moreover, the dreadful sin of infidelity in the marriage state, is much softened to a common understanding, by the frequency of the crime; whereas, of vows broken by a devotee she had scarce heard of any; or if any, they were generally followed by such examples of divine vengeance [. . .] that served to exaggerate their wickedness. (78)

Second, although the passage hedges to some extent over which form of infidelity is more heinous, it not only introduces the sin of adultery that the heroine is to commit later, but also suggests that it is a more serious evil 'to society'. The problem with Miss Milner may therefore be defined as ungovernable female desire.

Jane Spencer, to whom this discussion is indebted, declares: 'Only Inchbald's extreme delicacy of handling could have made her theme acceptable to her readership' (xv). This delicacy ensures that the mother's indiscretions in the first two volumes are repaired by the daughter's rectitude in the second two, and insists, in the closing words, on a moral: the need for 'A PROPER EDUCATION' (338).

Where it is most manifest, however, is in the novel's remarkable tact about the heroine's adultery. Although the story turns on the affair that leads to Lady Elmwood's separation from her husband, and ultimately her death, the narrative all but elides it. The narrator cautiously remarks: 'To state the progression by which vice gains a predominance in the heart, may be a useful lesson; but it is one so little to the satisfaction of most readers, that it is not meant to be related here, all the degrees of frailty by which Lady Elmwood fell' (195). This drastic narrative condensation may suggest that *A Simple Story* should not be called a novel of adultery. From another point of view, it points again to the difficulty of handling the theme at all. When Lord Elmwood's chaplain precipitates the marriage, he presents a stark alternative: 'this moment give her up for ever; or this moment constrain her by such ties from offending you, she shall not *dare* to violate' (191). As Patricia Spacks has observed, these words emphasize that marriage 'provides the definitive means to quell female insubordination'.[16] If marriage is given such importance, the heroine's adultery might well demand narrative circumspection, even though it provides the novel's turning point.

What is beyond doubt is that the second two volumes of *A Simple Story* work hard to reverse the desires that disrupt the first. Lady Elmwood's daughter, Matilda, is distinguished not only by utter devotion and obedience to her father, despite his refusal to see her even when they share the same house. She is also portrayed as innocent of sexual passion, indeed unaware of what is meant by the attentions of the young man whom Elmwood has made his heir: 'The idea of love never once came to her thoughts; and she would sport with Rushbrook like the most harmless child' (334). Whereas the mother has flirted with a man she did not love to gain attention from her guardian, and later had an affair with the same man during her husband's protracted absence, the daughter is abducted by a parallel figure who threatens to rape her. As Spacks wittily puts it, 'Lord Elmwood's rescue of his daughter from a would-be ravisher reestablishes the appropriate sublimations.'[17] At a time of radical questioning about the whole social order, the novel holds out the disruptive potential of female desire, and suggests that only feminine purity, marital or virginal, can bring it within bounds.

Written in the wake of Wollstonecraft's *A Vindication of the Rights of Woman* (1792) and of William Godwin's *Enquiry Concerning Political*

Justice (1793), Mary Hays's *Memoirs of Miss Emma Courtney* (1796)
goes further than *A Simple Story* in three main respects. It is more a
novel of ideas, citing freely not only Wollstonecraft and Godwin –
including also the latter's *Caleb Williams* (1794) – but other
philosophers such as Rousseau and Helvétius; it is more explicit,
and more approving, about female sexual desire; and yet it shows
even greater contradictions between the open avowal of that desire
and the need to repress it. The novel is framed as a cautionary tale.
Writing to her adopted son, desperately in love with a woman who
does not love him and who has just married another man, the
heroine tries to persuade him to give up his hopeless passion by
telling the story of her own unrequited love for his father. Yet,
despite herself, and in a way that recalls *A Simple Story*, the force of
her desire speaks more powerfully than the intended lesson.

This paradox may be explained in part by tensions between
Hays's version of philosophical radicalism and eighteenth-century
codes of feminine purity. Disclaiming double standards of sexual
morality, Emma Courtney advises her adopted son from her own
experience: 'be not the slave of your passions, neither dream of
eradicating them' (8).[18] On the one hand, she believes it natural and
right both to feel desire and to express it. She tells how, therefore,
she had pursued Augustus Harley, the man she loved, relentlessly,
refusing to accept his evasions and bombarding him with letters in
which she not only declared her love for him directly but offered to
live with him outside marriage. Such outrages of female delicacy
shocked many contemporaries, but Hays grounded them in moral
principle. The reason for Emma's proposal is that most of Harley's
income depends on his staying unmarried; she gives it further
sanction by encouraging him to free himself from dependence, by
imposing her own condition that the attachment be permanent and
binding, and by insisting repeatedly on the purity of her love. On
the other hand, when Emma discovers that Harley, though in love
with her, is already secretly married, she gives up her passion and
becomes a conduct-book wife to a man she does not love. This
marriage is precipitated by the loss of all her money thanks to the
failure of her banker, but it does not contradict the principle she has
declared earlier: 'I would not marry any man, merely for an
establishment, for whom I did not feel an affection' (56). Her
marriage is not for social or material advantage; more important,
she is able to say to her husband: 'I feel for you all the affection that
a reasonable and a virtuous mind ought to feel – that affection

which is compatible with the fulfilling of other duties' (170). Since the duties in question are domestic, this is to fill the normative role for a bourgeois wife of the period. But the novel shows that contradictions between sexual desire, material need, and the codes of feminine purity cannot be resolved so easily.

Hays's plot brings the contradictions to a head in a melodramatic ending a few years after the heroine's marriage. Harley, seriously injured by a fall from his horse, is brought to Emma's home where her husband practises medicine. Dying, and tended by Emma because her husband is absent, he tells her he has always loved her, but that he has had to keep distant because of his marriage; also, since his own wife has just died, according to him as a result of his unkindness, he entrusts her with his son. Emma behaves with perfect propriety, claiming 'I forgot not that I was a wife and a mother' (177), but when she herself falls ill she cannot help giving vent in delirium to her grief-stricken love. The reaction of her husband, already jealous because she has been unable to feel for him the passion she felt for Harley, is moral collapse. After an affair with a maidservant, ending with the latter's pregnancy and the death of their baby, apparently at his hands, he shoots himself in despair. Such, the novel appears to suggest, are the fruits of sexual repression and frustration. Eleanor Ty goes so far as to argue that, despite Hays's purported moral, 'the unstated but undoubtedly calculated thesis of the work seems to be the fatal repercussions of repression on the eighteenth-century middle-class woman.'[19] In light of the fate of both lover and husband, the same remark might also be applied to men.

Whether or not Ty's inference is valid, the strongest taboo in *Emma Courtney* is that against adultery. First, while the heroine is willing to live with Harley outside marriage, she is shocked to the core by the discovery that he is already married: 'Ignorant of his situation, I had been unconsciously, and perseveringly, exerting myself to seduce the affections of a *husband* from his *wife*. He had made me almost criminal in my own eyes – he had risqued, at once, by a disingenuous and cruel reserve, the virtue and the happiness of three beings' (135). Second, the outburst just quoted suggests not only that Harley was right to suppress his own desire in refusing to respond to Emma, but that he was entirely wrong to leave her any hope by not telling her about his marriage. Third, the consequences of adultery on the part of Emma's husband are devastating, leading as they do both to his own death and that of his adulterine child, and to misery for his wife and his mistress. The story's frame is therefore more than a convenience. Not for nothing does Emma try to dissuade her adopted son from pursuing a woman divided from him by what she terms 'the insuperable barrier' of marriage (8).

It is not easy to explain why the novel gives such weight to an institution that, on its own evidence, is all too often abused. Since much of the text has an autobiographical basis,[20] it is possible that Hays had personal as well as moral reasons for presenting even a bad marriage like Harley's as inviolable. But the most telling evidence offered by the novel itself is the value it gives to the heroine's purity. For all the passion and importunity with which Emma expresses her desire, she insists that it is pure and right, even when arguing that circumstances might justify her unchastity. It seems likely that Hays felt obliged to maintain feminine purity in order to urge the legitimacy of female desire. If so, she could best demonstrate her heroine's virtue by having her uphold the sanctity of marriage. Even when Emma offers herself to Harley, what she proposes is a quasi-marital arrangement based on mutual sexual exclusivity. This is clear from her statement that '*the individuality of an affection constitutes its chastity*' (123; original emphasis). A further important factor is the value the novel accords to actual and surrogate motherhood. Emma's relation both to Harley's mother, and to her own child and Harley's, endorses a code of domestic care and affection that is grounded on marriage and that outlives the husband's death or failure. The novel's construction of adultery shows not only how firm a grip the ideology of feminine purity continued to hold, but how solidly established were the canons of bourgeois marriage. It also indicates the limits beyond which Hays, for all her radical views, would not pass.

All the same, there are clear signs that Hays had taken a bold step with *Emma Courtney*. One, as Anjana Sharma argues, is her choice of narrative form.[21] Instead of the decorous epistolary style of Lee's *Errors of Innocence*, or the impersonal voice of Smith's *Emmeline* and Inchbald's *Simple Story*, Hays opted for a compound of memoir and letter. The use of the personal voice is significant because of the more direct expression it enables of feeling and desire. In contrast, Griffith had framed the heroine's confession in 'The Unforced Repentance' very carefully as a story told by an elderly clergyman, and in *Emmeline* Smith had placed Lady Adelina's story in a subplot and only allowed her to tell part of it in her own voice. Another sign of Hays's audacity is the offence her novel caused – an offence based partly on the assumption that its personal narrative was also autobiographical.[22] Two years later, within an impersonal narrative framework, Mary Wollstonecraft's *The Wrongs of Woman* was to deploy personal narratives to more potent effect, and, not surprisingly, attracted even greater opprobrium.

While adultery is punished in *A Simple Story*, and evaded in *Emma Courtney*, in *The Wrongs of Woman* it is justified. Wollstonecraft had written only about a third of the novel when she died from puerperal fever, but even in its unfinished state *The Wrongs of Woman* presents a far-reaching critique both of marriage at the period and of received wisdom about seduction and adultery. Wollstonecraft had begun her fictional appraisal of matrimony in *Mary, a Fiction*, published ten years earlier. Here she demonstrates the emptiness to which marriage can be reduced through a plot in which the heroine is married at the age of 17 to a boy of 15 in order to extricate two estates from litigation in Chancery. Mary's husband leaves on the same day as the wedding to complete his education on the Continent, and, repelled by his weakness and superficiality, she avoids him for as long as she can. She meets a much more congenial companion when she accompanies an invalid friend to Portugal, but both feel inhibited by her marriage and he dies. The novel leaves her compelled at last to live with her husband, and able only to look forward to a world evoked in the closing words *'where there is neither marrying,* nor giving in marriage' (68).[23]

The deadlock that brings *Mary, a Fiction* to an end is the same that Hays had tried to bypass in *Emma Courtney*: the conflict between female desire and the requirement of female purity. Because the man she loves is ill, Mary is able to give him 'little artless proofs of affection, which the purity of her heart made her never wish to restrain' (31); he sounds a similar note on his deathbed when he exclaims: 'The passion I have nursed is so pure, that death cannot extinguish it' (61). The relationship is therefore never consummated; indeed, Henry's death seems almost designed to preclude adultery. A few years later, in *A Vindication of the Rights of Woman*, Wollstonecraft would deplore the same melancholy and quietism that her own heroine displays in *Mary*. However, in shying away from sexual passion and its likely consequences, the novel seems to anticipate the treatise, in which, Cora Kaplan has claimed, 'a sexually purified femininity was equally a precondition for any optimistic, liberal re-ordering of intra-class gender relations, or female aspiration', and in which the price of 'equal rights' is 'self-abnegating sexuality'.[24] Kaplan's interpretation has been questioned by Elaine Jordan and Jane Moore, who argue in different ways that 'Wollstonecraft does not prohibit women's sexual passion *per se*'.[25] Nevertheless, the *Vindication* shows an anxiety on the subject that casts in relief the more radical stance Wollstonecraft was to take in *The Wrongs of Woman* both on marriage and on female sexuality.

The later novel is much more explicit than the earlier about the abuses to which marriage exposes women. Its heroine, Maria, marries in an attempt to escape an oppressive household run by her father's mistress after her mother's death. She has little chance till it is too late to get to know her husband, George Venables, whose chief motive in marrying her is financial and who already has an illegitimate child by a servant whom he has seduced. Disgusted by Venables's vice and extravagance, Maria leaves him while she is pregnant, and gives birth; but she is parted from her baby and confined in a madhouse while he tries to appropriate her fortune. There she meets Jemima, a servant who had previously been raped by her master and forced into prostitution, and Henry Darnford, who has been imprisoned in an attempt to deprive him of his inheritance. The three get away to live together, only for Venables to sue Darnford for criminal conversation (though the novel does not actually use the term).[26] This is despite his own repeated infidelity before Maria's departure, and also his attempt to prostitute her in return for a loan – an offence he tries to disguise as a tacit agreement 'to let each other follow their own inclination' (168). The novel also contains various other examples of empty or abusive marriages, including not only that of Maria's parents but Darnford's. In two cases, those of Jemima's first employers and of a landlady with whom Maria stays during her pregnancy, the husbands are furthermore adulterers.

Wollstonecraft also provides a detailed analysis of how the laws of marriage and property enable such abuses. In her personal testimony, written for her daughter, Maria challenges the double standards that permit a wife no redress for the intemperance or adultery of her husband, while entitling him to gain compensation and have her punished for the same offences. She presses this case when she defends Darnford, away in Paris, against the charges alleged by her husband. Having instructed Darnford's counsel to plead guilty to the charge of adultery but to deny that of seduction, she writes a paper to be read out in court because, as a woman, she is not entitled to a voice there in person. Here, as a woman who is of an age to choose and act independently, and whose spouse has ruined their marriage through misconduct, she claims the right to take another man as her husband: 'To this person, thus encountered, I voluntarily gave myself, never considering myself as any more bound to transgress the laws of moral purity, because the will of my husband might be pleaded in my excuse, than to transgress those laws to which [the policy of artificial society has] annexed [positive] punishments' (197).[27] In this way she rebuts the charge of seduction against Darnford, bearing out her previous statement that 'a man of feeling' who seeks to console an abused wife 'thinks not of seducing, he is himself seduced by all the noblest emotions of his soul' (155). She therefore challenges not just the laws of marriage but received ideas about both adultery and seduction. Jane Spencer makes this point very clearly: 'In *Emmeline* Charlotte Smith had allowed her adulteress, Adelina, to be forgiven, but Wollstonecraft denied that her adulteress, Maria, had committed any crime. She also went much further than earlier novelists in the tradition of protest, by criticizing not only the seducer and the social ostracism of his victim, but the very definition of seduction'.[28] Indeed, to contemporaries Wollstonecraft must have seemed to turn law and morality upside down in the conclusion reached by her heroine: 'Marriage, as at present constituted, she considered as leading to immorality' (193).

The morality for which Maria appeals is one of '*active* sensibility and *positive* virtue' (153). She deplores the sexual submission recommended by the conduct books, arguing: 'Truth is the only basis of virtue; and we cannot, without depraving our minds, endeavour to please a lover or husband, but in proportion as he pleases us.' For this reason she confesses: 'The greatest sacrifice of my principles in my whole life, was the allowing my husband again to be familiar with my person', even though her concession led to the birth of the daughter she loves. On the same principles she refuses to keep her relationship with Darnford secret, though the deceit she repudiates protects from ostracism some of the same ladies who boycott her: 'If, instead of openly living with her lover, she could have condescended to call into play a thousand arts, which, degrading her own mind, might have allowed the people who were not deceived, to pretend to be so, she would have been caressed and treated like an honourable woman' (192).

In presenting the summing-up of Darnford's trial, Wollstonecraft showed how well she knew the opposition that views such as these would provoke. According to the judge,

> We did not want French principles in public or private life – and, if women were allowed to plead their feelings, as an excuse or palliation of infidelity, it was opening a flood-gate for immorality. What virtuous woman thought of her feelings? – It was her duty to love and obey the man chosen by her parents and relations, who were qualified by their experience to judge better for her, than she could for herself. [. . .] he hoped that no Englishman would legalize adultery, by enabling the adulteress to enrich her seducer. Too many restrictions could not be thrown in the way of divorces, if we wished to maintain the sanctity of marriage. (199)

The context for these remarks is reaction not only to the Revolution in France, including the liberal divorce laws introduced there in 1792, but to the libertinism associated both with the aristocracy of the Old Regime and with their revolutionary successors. At the same time, the judge clearly also refers to the campaign in Britain cited above to bar divorced women from marrying their lovers. Wollstonecraft's sense of the backlash proved only too accurate when, shortly after her death, Godwin published his biography, revealing to a public all too ready to be outraged such episodes in her life as her liaison with Gilbert Imlay and her bearing of an illegitimate child. As Jane Spencer points out, Wollstonecraft met the same treatment as Manley and Haywood before her, in that 'once again the connection between her life and her writing was used against a woman writer'.[29] *The Wrongs of Woman* had a hostile reception, highly discouraging to others with radical ideas.

In Gary Kelly's words, 'British "anti-Jacobins" welcomed revelation of Mary Wollstonecraft's sexual transgressions as proof that Revolutionary feminism was inimical to bourgeois domesticity and femininity'.[30] But the reaction also went much further. As Barbara Taylor argues, 'the major shift in ideological stance that occurred in these years' cannot be explained by opposition to the French Revolution alone, for it drew part of its strength from 'religious enthusiasm': 'Irresponsible high life and insubordinate low would both be swept away, and in their stead would emerge the model Christian – industrious, sober, pious, narrow.'[31] Paradoxically, this reaction, based as it was in the middle class and to a large extent also in traditions of Protestant Dissent, had common roots with those of most of the radical writers themselves. For example, Mitzi Myers has demonstrated a number of close parallels that might otherwise seem surprising between the thinking of Wollstonecraft and Hannah More.[32]

Although Wollstonecraft mounted the most forceful challenge of her time to the subjection of women, massive political, social and economic changes were already overtaking her as she wrote. According to Gary Kelly's overview,

> Such developments as the professionalization of *belles-lettres*, the founding of literature as a national institution, the dissemination of professional method, the imposition of the utilitarian agenda, the *embourgeoisement* of the sublime – in short, the re-masculinization of writing against the subversive feminizations of the 1780s and early 1790s – left Wollstonecraft's writing, and women's writing of all kinds, outside or subject to the dominant (men's) discursive order of the professional middle-class cultural revolution.[33]

What put beyond the pale a progressive understanding of marriage and adultery such as Wollstonecraft's was a reassertion of the code of female purity that paved the way for Victorianism. Within a few years, the reaction against the French Revolution, bolstered by the Evangelical revival, made it virtually impossible for any respectable British novelist to address sexuality with any directness at all. One result was that no tradition of novels of wifely adultery could develop in Britain in the following century. Another was that no radical alternative was possible either. *The Wrongs of Woman* in several ways prefigures work by George Sand and Flora Tristan in France, and Nikolai Chernyshevsky in Russia,[34] but in Britain it marked the end for more than a century of writing about female sexual desire that was neither censorious nor prurient.

Ros Ballaster has described how the work of Behn and Haywood was first edited to bring it in line with the more delicate tastes of the later eighteenth century, and then, in the earlier nineteenth century, removed from the canon of English fiction altogether. Ballaster shows how Elizabeth Griffith, in her *Collection of Novels*, deprecated what she termed 'the gross effusions of amorous nonsense' that had enjoyed such popularity earlier in the period, and 'edited Behn's and Haywood's texts so as to make them conform to the sentimental and domestic moralism that dominated the novelistic discourse of her time'.[35] In particular, Ballaster cites Griffith's version of Haywood's *The Fruitless Enquiry*, from which she removed 'those stories most concerned with marital infidelity, male sexual violence, active female desire and female duplicity or personal ambition'.[36] Both Ballaster and Catherine Gallagher also quote Sir Walter Scott telling how his elderly great aunt responded to Behn's fiction in 1821, many years after first enjoying it, when he brought her a copy at her request:

> So I sent Mrs. Aphra Behn, curiously sealed up, with 'private and confidential' on the packet, to my gay old grand-aunt. The next time I saw her afterwards, she gave me back Aphra, properly wrapped up, with nearly these words: 'Take back your bonny Mrs. Behn; and, if you will take my advice, put her in the fire, for I found it impossible to get through the very first novel. But is it not,' she said, 'a very odd thing that I, an old woman of eighty and upwards, sitting alone, feel myself ashamed to read a book which, sixty years ago, I have heard read aloud for the amusement of large circles, consisting of the first and most creditable society in London?' This, of course, was owing to the gradual improvement of the national taste and delicacy.[37]

It is not surprising, then, that Behn, along with Manley and Haywood, disappeared from the canon. The three were excluded both from Anna Laetitia Barbauld's fifty-volume *The British Novelists* (1810), and from Ballantyne's ten-volume *The Novelist's Library* (1821–4), for which Scott wrote the introductions – though, unlike Scott, Barbauld at least mentioned them in her preface.[38]

Perhaps equally significant, not least for readers and writers of the period, was Scott's own practice as a novelist. Throughout his career he took care, sometimes on the advice of his friends, to avoid giving any offence in dealing with sexual passion. Contemporary French culture imposed fewer such inhibitions, and Balzac's response is instructive. Balzac saw Scott's forbearance as a crucial limitation, criticizing him through his character Daniel d'Arthez:

> Walter Scott lacks passion; it is a closed book to him; or perhaps he found it was ruled out by the hypocritical morals of his native

land. Woman for him is duty incarnate. With rare exceptions, his heroines are absolutely identical; as painters say, he has only one template. His women all proceed from Clarissa Harlowe; reducing them all to one simple idea, he was only able to strike off copies of one and the same type and vary them with a more or less vivid colouring.[39]

D'Arthez therefore advises the aspiring novelist Lucien de Rubrempré: 'depict the passions and you will have at your command the immense resources which this great genius denied himself in order to provide reading matter for every family in prudish England'. A few years later, in the Preface to *The Human Comedy* (1842), Balzac wrote in similar terms, qualifying his praise for the inventor of the historical novel with the charge of prudery: 'Walter Scott was obliged to conform to the ideas of an essentially hypocritical country, and consequently, in terms of humanity, he was false in his portrayal of woman, because his models were Protestant ones.'[40] Balzac reproached Scott for regretting in old age his creation of Alice Brand, who lives with her lover after he has killed her brother in *The Lady of the Lake* (1810), and of Effie Deans in *The Heart of Mid-Lothian* (1818), who bears an illegitimate child and is accused of having murdered him. But the problem was much more complex than Balzac alleged when he claimed that confession gave Catholicism more scope than Protestantism for acknowledging and dealing with sin. It was rooted in the different development of French and British culture, especially during the eighteenth century, and including British reaction to the French Revolution.

What Scott styled as 'the gradual improvement of the national taste and delicacy' was already well established by the time the first of the Waverley novels appeared in 1814. In his history of literary censorship in England, Donald Thomas traces the main steps by which prudery gained ground.[41] These include the founding of the Proclamation Society by William Wilberforce in 1787, and its successor, the Society for the Suppression of Vice and the Encouragement of Religion and Virtue, in 1802. The Vice Society, as it was known, 'rather to its own chagrin' (189), successfully prosecuted Alexander Hogg for publishing *A New and Compleat Collection of the most Remarkable Trials for Adultery*; and it was claimed that by 1857 it 'had brought 159 cases against pornographers and had been successful in no less than 154 of them' (190, 213). But, as Thomas indicates, the Society was not only concerned with writing that might tend to deprave and corrupt its readers. It was also preoccupied 'with a type of literature that might "bring a blush to the cheek of modesty,"' even though 'except in cases of extreme coarseness of language this was not generally regarded as a matter for legal censorship'. One effect was that, as in the case of Scott, 'authors, editors, and the circulating libraries were encouraged by the moral climate of the age to be their own censors' (193). Another was a more drastic form of editing than that already applied by Elizabeth Griffith to the works of Behn and Haywood. Although Thomas Bowdler's *Family Shakespeare* of 1818 is the most famous example, by the beginning of the nineteenth century, as Thomas declares, 'The great age of expurgation had begun' (186). It is a symptomatic irony that Addison and Steele, who had promoted polite literary and moral standards with the *Tatler* and the *Spectator*, were themselves found wanting a century later by no less a figure than Coleridge, who wrote in the second issue of *The Friend*: 'a man – I will not say of delicate mind and pure morals, but – of common good manners, who means to read an essay, which he has opened upon at hazard in these volumes, to a mixed company, will find it necessary to take a previous survey of its contents' (75).[42]

While Scott helped define standards for the social and historical novel, Austen pointed the way for British domestic fiction. In each of her novels, as Gary Kelly puts it, 'A central female consciousness has to negotiate her way through the social temptations of courtly emulation on the one hand and contamination by bourgeois vulgarity on the other, but she also has to avoid the subjective pitfalls of pride or humility.'[43] This is a far cry from dealing with the problems of marriage, whether or not they involve male or female adultery. A case in point is *Sense and Sensibility* (1811), which contains a narrative of wifely adultery but leaves it discreetly in the background. In Chapter 31, Colonel Brandon tells Elinor Dashwood the story of Eliza Williams, with whom he had been in love. Ward to his father, and an heiress, Eliza had been 'married against her inclination' to his elder brother because the Brandon estate was 'much encumbered' (205).[44] Colonel Brandon had tried to forestall the marriage by eloping with her, but the plan was discovered and he went to India in an attempt to ease the consequences for them both. The marriage failed, chiefly because of his brother's misconduct and ill-treatment, and, with no friend 'to advise or restrain her' (206), she had an affair that led to her divorce two years later. On his return to England after a further three years,

Brandon found her by accident in a spunging-house where he had gone to visit a friend in debt. She was suffering from consumption, and he provided for her until she died, leaving a child of about three, 'the offspring of her first guilty connection' (208). Because he had no family, he placed the child in a boarding school, and brazened out innuendoes that he was the father. It is this child, also called Eliza, whom John Willoughby turns out to have seduced, so making him unworthy as a suitor for Marianne Dashwood.

The themes in Brandon's story of guardianship, forced marriage, the dissolute husband, seduction, adultery, and descent into misery are entirely familiar from the early eighteenth century onwards; though it would soon cease to be possible for authors to refer as explicitly as Austen to a 'guilty connection'. More revealing, however, is the small part this story of wifely adultery is allowed in the novel's narrative economy: it is not merely marginalized, as in most previous novels after *Betsy Thoughtless*, but distanced through retrospect. Even more important, it is related neither by the impersonal narrator nor by the character herself. Austen's choice of Colonel Brandon as narrator is adroit, for it allows – indeed motivates – a plea in mitigation for female transgression while dissociating both the plea and the story itself from the central narrative voice. First drafted near the end of the previous century, *Sense and Sensibility* looks back as well as forwards. The single case of wifely adultery of any importance in Austen's fiction better illustrates the taboo on the theme that was already taking hold. When, in *Mansfield Park* (1814), Henry Crawford elopes with Maria Rushworth, all the reader is allowed to know is the limited and indirect information that reaches the heroine Fanny Price; and the novelist famously washes her hands of the business with the words: 'Let other pens dwell on guilt and misery' (461).[45]

As Nicola J. Watson has shown, Austen's shift towards novels of female improvement and courtship was itself part of a project to rewrite an earlier tradition. Commenting on *Emma* (1816), for example, Watson points out: 'It is regularly remarked that the narrative of Emma's "education" depends upon disciplining Emma into right reading; what is not recognized is that this education in close reading is designed [. . .] to exorcize the epistolary novel of passion, and is therefore closely tied to a broadly conservative political agenda.'[46] Once exorcized, few serious writers in Britain would dare attempting a novel of passion, epistolary or otherwise, until near the end of the century.

7
After *Madame Bovary*: Female Adultery in Zola

As late nineteenth-century British readers were all too well aware, it was a far cry from the novels of Scott and Austen to those of Flaubert and Zola. *Madame Bovary* was not translated into English until 1886, and, though English translations of Zola and Maupassant appeared much sooner, it was for publishing these among others that were considered obscene that in 1888 and 1889 Henry Vizetelly was first fined and then imprisoned.[1] It was, however, not on behalf of progressive or proto-feminist thinking that canonical French fiction of the late nineteenth century addressed questions of female sexuality. This and the next chapter seek to show instead that intrinsic to much of that fiction was a deep-rooted misogynism.

In the wake of *Madame Bovary*, novelists in France who wished to treat the theme of adultery had two main choices. First, they could follow what had become the popular conventions for basing a story on that topic. These conventions had developed from about 1830 in the work not only of Balzac, but, as Nicholas White points out, in that of 'figures such as Kock, Feuillet, Champfleury, Cherbuliez, and Ponson du Terrail'.[2] They were still going strong in the 1870s and 1880s – Joris-Karl Huysmans (1848–1907), looking back early in the following century at his novel *Against the Grain* (*A rebours*, 1884), sketched them drily when he described how the reader 'still continues to savour the scruples and hesitations of the Marquise on her way to meet her seducer at a dainty little flat, whose aspect changes according to the varying fashion in furniture'.[3] The second alternative was to challenge the conventions, but Flaubert had made this more difficult. As Baudelaire recognized in his review of *Madame Bovary*, he had chosen the most hackneyed of themes for his subject but had renewed it through his treatment and style.[4] To write about adultery without rehearsing the stock conventions therefore demanded enterprise, not least after 1869 when Flaubert capped his novel of adultery with a novel of adultery *manqué*,

Sentimental Education. It was the Naturalists who mounted the most radical challenge, and, not surprisingly, Émile Zola (1840–1902) who led the way. In order to highlight the extent to which Zola rewrote the conventions of adultery fiction, this chapter begins by commenting on three novels that offered alternative forms of the novel of wifely adultery in France between 1857 and 1870.

The writers of these novels were Ernest Feydeau (1821–73), Alexandre Dumas the younger (1824–95), and Octave Feuillet (1821–90). In *Fanny: A Study* (1858), Feydeau's innovation was to focus on the lover's jealousy of the husband. This, however, was less a variant of the adultery plot developed by Balzac and others, as Hans Robert Jauss has argued, than of an older form, the French Romantic confession, in which the role Feydeau gave the husband was quite new.[5] Dumas showed the continuing vitality of this form by adopting it for his polemical novel *Affaire Clémenceau: Mémoire de l'accusé* (*The Clémenceau Affair: Memoirs of the Accused*, 1866).[6] As its subtitle suggests, Dumas's novel is a personal narrative, though its aim is less confessional than defensive: the narrator tells the story of his life, and especially his marriage, to a lawyer in an attempt to justify murdering his adulterous spouse. *Affaire Clémenceau* obeys the formal conventions of the Romantic confession in that it is a retrospective account with a male author, narrator and addressee. It follows the orthodox confessional plot by having its hero kill the woman he loves, but diverges in the motive it gives him. In the Romantic confession, as Naomi Segal has shown, the plot stems from the 'anger and guilt' felt by the hero who 'has generally lost his mother in childbirth'.[7] Dumas varies this not only by making the victim the hero's adulterous wife, but by giving him the further motive not of his mother dying at birth – she dies as a result of his wife's adultery – but illegitimacy. As Dumas's biography suggests, much of the animus behind his novel came out of his suffering as the illegitimate son of a father who was as successful in his philandering as with his pen.[8] He was to follow *Affaire Clémenceau* in 1872 with his pamphlets *La Question de la femme* and *L'Homme-Femme*, in the latter of which he again, this time in a work of non-fiction, advocated wife-killing for adultery; and, in 1873, with *La Femme de Claude*, a play based on the career of an adulteress. But his obsession with wifely adultery was not just private or pathological. *Affaire Clémenceau* is of interest not only as a Romantic confession inflected by the novel of wifely adultery, but as an especially blatant example of the misogynism inherent in both.

It is in light of that misogynism that Feuillet's *Monsieur de Camors* requires special attention – for, unlike almost all nineteenth-century European fiction of marital infidelity, it deals more with male than with female adultery. Published in 1867, after serial issue in the *Revue des deux mondes*, it attracted an admiring review from Émile Montégut in the same journal, and five years later was hailed by Larousse's encyclopedia as having gained 'one of the foremost places in contemporary literature'.[9] Though the novel failed to hold such a position in the twentieth century, it casts interesting light on adultery fiction in its period.

Despite the fact that the hero's adultery is pivotal to the plot of Feuillet's novel, it can scarcely be characterized as a novel of male adultery. The writer had grander aims in view, as Montégut recognized when he described *Monsieur de Camors* as the tragedy 'of a man born for great things in the intellectual or political order, destroyed by a natural vice imprudently indulged, by a flawed will or by an inordinate disproportion between ideas in the abstract and the means of realizing them'.[10] Inconceivably for a woman at the centre of a stock adultery plot at the period, Camors is a politician and a financial magnate as well as an unfaithful spouse; and his sexual infidelity is of a piece with, indeed part of, the corruption of his role in the public sphere. In this way the novel gestures towards a critique of life under the Second Empire, an aspect emphasized in the subtitle and Preface of the American translation.[11] But Feuillet's ambitions went further still. As he hinted through a parallel drawn by one of his characters between his hero and that of Goethe's great philosophical drama, he aimed at nothing less than a contemporary version of *Faust* (II.viii.280–2).[12] If, as in some conceptions of female adultery, the wife's betrayal of her husband is seen as threatening the whole social fabric, in *Monsieur de Camors* the husband's betrayal of his wife is one example among others of his repudiation of all traditional religious, moral and social codes.

Feuillet stages three adultery scenarios to show how Camors tries to deny the moral order. First, already celebrated for his liaisons as a fashionable unmarried man, Camors seduces the wife of a friend. This highlights in the most lurid colours the difference between adultery for a woman who is married and a man who is not, since a single act of intercourse that leaves him unscathed leads to her death soon after. The point, however, is not to give an only too dramatic example of the double standard, but to present one of the critical steps taken by Camors on his path of moral negation.

Second, still unmarried, Camors embarks on an affair with the wife of his relative, friend and benefactor, General de Campvallon. In doing so he transgresses the only code of conduct to which he still subscribes, that of honour. Third, the liaison becomes doubly adulterous when Camors, who has long resolved to stay a bachelor, is forced to marry. The sole purpose of his marriage is to prevent the General from detecting, even suspecting, the liaison, which it in no way disrupts, even after his young wife discovers it. The novel therefore constructs adultery on the part of Camors not as a challenge to moral order, but as the betrayal of two male friends, and, by extension, as an example of the inadequacy of a moral code based only on honour. Indeed, the evil Camors does to his wife consists less in his sexual infidelity than in his perversion of marriage, since it has no other motive than to screen his affair. This perversion receives a due return when, having discovered the affair, Marie de Camors withdraws from her husband and the marriage becomes merely nominal. For a few more years the liaison is able to continue, until the General, acting on a tip-off, surprises the lovers together and dies of a heart attack.

The writer of the entry on *Monsieur de Camors* in Larousse's encyclopedia was partly right in observing that 'the thesis of M. O. Feuillet's novel, which is arguable, consists precisely in maintaining that honour is insufficient against passion if it is not supported by a sense of religion'.[13] This is not, however, the whole story, because Camors is finally destroyed not by the death of the friend he has betrayed but by what Feuillet defines as his humanity. His defiance of the moral order reaches its limit when his lover, now widowed, tempts him to murder his wife. Though he refuses, and decides to break with her as a result, before he can do so his wife, convinced that he aims to kill her, rejects him for good. Camors and his lover can do little with their new-found freedom, because he can bear neither his wife's accusation nor his separation from the young son she has borne him. He sickens and dies soon after.

Monsieur de Camors is therefore not a novel of male adultery in the sense that *Madame Bovary* is a novel of female adultery. Even though Feuillet endorses most of the moral and other codes that Flaubert had undermined, adultery itself is not at the centre of his text. Camors is presented as offending against a male code of honour, and ultimately against what Feuillet terms 'the most simple laws of nature', indeed, 'nature and truth' (II.ix.311, 314). Marriage is simply one of the institutions he defies in his campaign to become an 'almost superhuman type' (II.i.195), superior to all moral laws whatever. This idea suggests that Feuillet may have been responding in part to the cult of the superman represented, for example, by Napoleon III's *Life of Julius Caesar* (1865–6). Indeed, the Larousse entry on the novel suggests that in name and nature Camors combines characteristics of Caderousse and the Duc de Morny, 'the one marked by all the eccentricities of pleasure pushed to the limit, the other known as one of the main architects of [the coup of] 2 December'.[14] Morny was as notorious for his lack of moral and financial principles as for his role in politics, though the novel also refers to his bravery in saving the life of his commanding officer in Algeria when it attributes a similar act to Camors's father (I.iii.73–4).[15] But Feuillet keeps his hero's financial and political dealings offstage, and *Monsieur de Camors* is as far short of serious political critique as it is of another work that responded to the cult of Napoleon, Dostoyevsky's *Crime and Punishment* (1866).

Although the political and philosophical interest of Feuillet's novel is slight, and although it is even less about female adultery than male, its construction of female characters and its narratorial perspective illustrate contemporary masculine attitudes to women. This is especially significant in view of its early popular and critical success. First, the only female characters to whom the novel gives any space are those who are sexually available. These fall into three classes: that of 'respectable women' (I.i.26), represented by the wife of Camors's friend whom he seduces at the start; virtuous women, represented by Elise de Tècle, who refuses him, and by her daughter Marie, who marries him; and dangerous women, represented by the Marquise de Campvallon, who offers herself to him as his wife or mistress, marries the rich General when he declines, but later becomes his lover anyway. As Camors tells his friend's wife before leaving her, the charm of the first type is respectability, 'and, in losing that, they lose everything' (I.i.29). Though 'a young woman who does not believe much in anything', she is destroyed by a kind of return of the moral repressed – the 'thousand old prejudices', as the narrator ironically calls them, that she had thought buried (I.i.30). The second type is offered as a model of female goodness, especially in the roles of wife and mother. Thus the narrative invites its reader to assume that Camors will seduce Elise, only for her to refuse both this and his offer of marriage, and then go on to sublimate her love for him by raising her daughter as his wife instead. Marie in turn stays loyal to her husband by not exposing his treachery, and by leaving it open for him to repair the marriage by reforming; needless to add, she is a devoted mother to their son.

While *Monsieur de Camors* focuses only occasionally on its principal adulteress, it nevertheless displays most of the other patterns common to French fiction of female adultery. According to type, a passionate woman will go further than a passionate man, so the Marquise de Campvallon not only instigates Camors's marriage to protect her own as well as their affair, but shrugs off the death of her husband and hints at poisoning Camors's young wife. More revealing, however, is a series of narratorial generalizations not so much about her as about women in general. Like *Madame Bovary*, but uncritically and without finesse, *Monsieur de Camors* rehearses the received ideas of its time about femininity, while still offering its various female characters to masculine connoisseurship through passages of description.[16] Indeed, the novel even shows traces of the libertine tradition of the previous century. This is less through the parallels between Camors's pursuit of Elise and Valmont's of Mme de Tourvel – coyly signalled by the name of Laclos's hero in the title of an engraving (I.iv.106) – than through the implication that Camors is to be admired as well as condemned. Though in some places the narrator criticizes Camors, in others he presents him as the superior figure he aims to be; his tone of a man of the world tends to merge with the cynical materialism he professes to question; and he can manage no more than a conditional assertion of religious belief.[17] In these ways the novel not only compromises its support of the traditional pieties, but, despite pivoting on male adultery, endorses the prejudices of its time about women.

Adultery – male and female, single and double – occurs in many of Zola's novels, and plays a central role in five: *Thérèse Raquin* (1867), written and published before he began the *Rougon-Macquart* series; *A Love Affair* (*Une Page d'amour*, 1878); *Nana* (1880); *Pot Luck* (*Pot-Bouille*, 1882); and *La Bête humaine* (1890). While each of these novels treats adultery differently, and while they show increasing technical and imaginative sophistication, they depend on similar attitudes to women and sexuality. For example, F. W. J. Hemmings points out 'the recurrence in *La Bête humaine* of the obsessive associational complex between sexual love and death, never far below the surface in Zola's writing, but never so strongly marked since *Thérèse Raquin*, written over twenty years earlier'.[18] Zola himself recalled *Thérèse*

Raquin in the first of his notes towards the later work.[19] What ties the two novels together even more closely, however, is that each links wifely adultery and murder.

If, as Henri Mitterand has suggested, *Thérèse Raquin* marks Zola's birth as a novelist,[20] it is equally significant that he made his name with a novel of female adultery. Not only was the subject well established – and *Monsieur de Camors* was first published in the same year, 1867 – but Mitterand has shown how commonplace were the materials on which Zola drew. Although the initial inspiration came from *La Vénus de Gordes*, a melodramatic tale by Adolphe Belot and Ernest Daudet serialized the year before in *Le Figaro*, Zola's other chief literary sources were Charles Barbara's *L'Assassinat du Pont-Rouge* (1859) and Eugène Sue's *Atar-Gull* (1831).[21] As David Baguley has observed, 'It is not unusual for emergent literary genres to draw in this way upon such popular generic forms for their sustenance.'[22] But, just as with *Madame Bovary* eleven years earlier, what is most striking about *Thérèse Raquin* as a novel of wifely adultery is Zola's highly original treatment of material that was in itself conventional.

The originality of *Thérèse Raquin* stems from Zola's annexation of contemporary materialist science to inform and justify what is in other respects a work of lurid melodrama. At every stage of the narrative – and, it sometimes seems, the more so as it approaches the condition of Gothic – Zola cites what he styles as scientific fact in an attempt to validate its improbability. A case in point is Laurent's unlikely transformation from oaf to artist, which, via a nineteenth-century version of ancient humoral theory, the narrator explains as 'a result of the drastic upheaval that had thrown his body and his mind off balance' (XXV.151; 629).[23] What has attracted most critical attention, in Zola's redaction of Gothic, is therefore not only his choice of mundane characters and setting, but above all his insistence that the behaviour of his characters is to be explained by physical and psychological rather than moral causes. At least equally striking is the symmetrical form of the action, in which the most extraordinary changes and reversals proceed with the elegance of a theorem – as when, 'At exactly the same time', Thérèse and Laurent experience 'a sort of nervous crisis' that throws them back together (XVIII.99; 592), or when, at the end, the two simultaneously decide to kill one another.

Nevertheless, for all Zola's formal and thematic innovations, *Thérèse Raquin* subscribes with perhaps unexpected fidelity to the dominant assumptions of its cultural and historical moment about women and adultery. Central to those assumptions is the idea of hysteria that Janet Beizer has demonstrated not only in medical but also in literary texts of the period – including, not least, *Madame Bovary*.[24] According to that idea, the sexually wayward woman is an hysteric. Following positivist thinking on heredity, bound in with prejudices about sexuality and race, Zola predetermines his heroine's fall by giving her an hysterical personality as well as an African mother: 'All the instincts of a highly strung woman now burst to the fore with incomparable violence, as her mother's blood, that African blood which burned in her veins, began to pulse furiously through her slight, still almost virginal body' (VII.36; 548). Thérèse has 'a fit of hysterics' (*une crise de nerfs*, XI.66; 570) after Laurent murders her husband, and the narrator refers several times to her 'nervous anxiety' (V.30; 543) and her 'over-wrought nerves' (XXII.129; 613). According to Beizer, medical writers of the period 'repeatedly paint woman as incontinent slave to her secretions, unable to control her dripping, flowing, spurting, oozing bodily fluids'.[25] Picking up the notion of fluidity, Zola follows suit:

> Since the age of ten she had been troubled by nervous disorders, due in part to the way she had been brought up in the fetid, nauseating air of little Camille's sick-room. Thus there had built up within her an accumulation of stormy impulses and powerful fluids, which would give rise in later life to truly tempestuous outbursts. (XXII.131; 614)

Beizer has also shown how, within the ideology of the period, hysteria was often associated with, and traced to, the reading of novels.[26] Thus, when Zola makes his heroine a novel-reader too, he owes the motif not necessarily to Flaubert, as is often and plausibly suggested,[27] but rather to the network of assumptions that linked the erring woman with hysteria: 'She joined a subscription library and became passionately involved with the heroes of all the novels which came into her hands. This sudden love of reading had a great influence on her temperament; she developed a nervy sensitivity which made her laugh or cry for no reason' (XV1.87; 584).

The presentation of Thérèse also displays other forms of the implicit or explicit misogynism that runs through the novel of adultery. Although her affair with Laurent begins when he rapes her, the narrator suggests that she quickly turns the tables: 'He was no longer in control of his actions; his mistress, with her cat-like suppleness and nervous sensitivity, had slowly insinuated herself into every fibre of his body' (IX.48; 555–6). Indeed, in the scene that follows it is Thérèse who first seems to hint at murdering Camille – as the narrator confirms a dozen chapters later (XXI.119; 606). Most remarkable of all, Zola attributes Camille's transformation to a kind of hysterical infection from Thérèse: 'under the passionate influence of his wife, his temperament had gradually become that of a young girl suffering from an acute neurotic condition' (XXII.129; 613). Although Zola does his best to explain his characters' behaviour as produced by their crimes, it is in keeping with this kind of misogynistic fantasy that Thérèse is presented as sleeping better for Camille's beatings (XXIX.182; 650), and as using his kicks to provoke a miscarriage (XXX.187–8; 654). The novelist even brings his heroine to prostitution and suicide, set out as almost inevitable consequences of wifely adultery by Hippolyte Lucas a generation before[28] – although, maintaining the symmetry of his design, he has Laurent succumb to debauchery and suicide too.

Yet Zola's presentation of Thérèse is not wholly one-sided. In the novel's opening phase, before the affair begins, he emphasizes her repression and frustration, for instance through vignettes at the ends of the first three chapters and through images of live burial (III.19; 534, IV.24; 538). He invites almost no sympathy for Camille, even endorsing, just before the murder, what is clearly a view coloured by Thérèse's animosity with the remark that the husband 'was an exasperating and unprepossessing sight' (XI.60; 565). Most strikingly, since it is the only monologue of any length in the novel, he allows Thérèse to tell her own unhappy story; and the scene in which she does this, to Laurent, carries more weight for occurring after, not before, their affair has begun (VII.37–9; 548–50). Although this evidence of sympathy with Thérèse is concentrated in the period before the murder, one of the reasons why it is significant is that it is linked with hostility to the bourgeoisie. In her monologue to Laurent, Thérèse attacks Mme Raquin and Camille by exclaiming: 'They've made me into a hypocrite and a liar . . . They so smothered me in their bourgeois comforts that I can't understand how there can still be blood in my veins' (VII.38; 549); and when, a few pages later, the narrator refers to her 'savage laughter' at 'their complacent relaxation, their bourgeois pleasures' (VIII.45; 554), her view is difficult to distinguish from his own relentless depiction of the stupid, narrow routine they share with the Michauds and Grivet.

In attributing to an adulteress some of his own contempt for the bourgeoisie, Zola echoes Flaubert; and the contradiction may be explained in part by the relation in Second Empire France between the serious professional writer and the public. Ten years before *Thérèse Raquin* was published, in his review of *Madame Bovary*, Baudelaire had defined part of that relation when he declared that the novelist of the time 'is confronted with a completely worn-out public or, worse even, a stupefied and greedy audience, whose only hatred is for fiction, and only love for material possession'.[29] Yet, like his senior colleague, Zola was well aware that he belonged to the class he hated; and his awareness was all the keener because, unlike Flaubert, he had to make his way from a subordinate position through what his writing could bring him. Just as, in Janet Beizer's formulation, 'Flaubert's use of hysteria consistently exposes his discursive collusion with ideological constructs that he ostensibly rejects',[30] so Zola satirizes the same class whose basic values he accepts.[31] This helps explain why, for all Zola's attempts at denying any moral grounds for his novel's action, it could hardly paint in starker colours the message that adultery and murder bring their own retribution. Zola has his lovers realize that killing Camille solves nothing, because 'Thérèse was not a widow, and Laurent found himself married to a woman who already had a drowned man for a husband' (XXII.135; 617); and he goes so far as to present their marriage as 'the inevitable punishment for the murder' (XXVIII.169; 641).

There is one important way in which, in its presentation of the adulteress, *Thérèse Raquin* differs from *Madame Bovary* and most of its other predecessors. Since the heyday of libertine writing in the eighteenth century, the conventional viewpoint from which French fiction presented the erring woman was erotic and masculine.[32] Zola breaks with this practice, though he offers a glimpse of it in the phrase 'between her half-open lips could be seen the pink highlights of her mouth' (V.29; 543), and though his description of female bodies in the Morgue is prurient. Although he protested that his concerns and methods were strictly scientific, his moralistic aims are clear from the text's earliest printed embodiment, a story entitled 'Un mariage d'amour' first published in *Le Figaro* in 1866. Here, in the opening paragraph, he explains that the importance of the story is 'that it reinforces a weighty lesson, and that it shows the guilty finding a terrible punishment, even in a crime committed with impunity'.[33] He retained the story's title when he developed it into the novel first published in serial form in *L'Artiste*, renaming it as *Thérèse Raquin* only when it was issued in book form later the same year. The irony of the original title is significant, for to apply the phrase 'marriage for love' to a couple joined by adultery and murder is to imply a deep cynicism about love and marriage alike.

This jaundiced, even pathological, view of sexuality and marriage also informs several other novels in which Zola addressed the theme of adultery, including the last of the group, *La Bête humaine*. As Henri Mitterand has shown, Zola's thinking about the novel goes back to his original plans for the *Rougon-Macquart* series, in which he intended it as the story of a man who commits murder 'through animal instinct', framed by a presentation of the world of the law. As the ten novels that Zola first planned grew to twenty, he added a novel about the railways, which was to climax in a catastrophic accident; then, as he neared the end of the series, he was obliged to combine the two projects into a single work so as not to exceed the already much expanded bounds of his design.[34] The result, as he put it in his preliminary outline, would be to show, beneath the progress represented by the railway, 'the unchanged state of feeling, the savagery which is at the root of man', or, in another phrase, 'the beast in civilized man'.[35]

From such remarks as these it would seem that *La Bête humaine* was not intended as a novel of adultery. However, in comparing *La Bête humaine* to *Thérèse Raquin*, F. W. J. Hemmings draws attention not only to the link in both novels between 'sexual love and death', as he puts it in the remark already quoted, but to two further parallels: the conversations between the lovers in which the idea of murdering the husband is first mooted, and the confessions of murder by Thérèse to Mme Raquin and by Séverine to Jacques.[36] Indeed, the first of these parallels is still closer. Although Hemmings is correct to state that the initial thought of murdering Roubaud occurs to Jacques and Séverine at the same time, straight after they have become lovers, in both novels it is the adulterous wife who in effect proposes the murder.[37] Crucially, both the confession and the proposal of murder draw on stereotypes of femininity: the first, that a woman cannot hold her tongue; the second, that she is passive and requires a man to act for her. Like his memory of the earlier novel, the fact that the woman should propose the murder was in Zola's mind from the start;[38] but it is only in the later novel that he brings the female stereotypes he exploits into ironic and fatal relation. Whereas, thanks to Mme Raquin's paralysis, and the stupidity of her friends, she is unable to communicate what Thérèse has told her, Séverine's confession of Grandmorin's murder rekindles what can only be called femicidal mania on the part of Jacques, with the result that he kills her.

In *Thérèse Raquin*, adultery leads to the cuckolded husband's murder, and, after unbearable physical and psychological suffering, to the lovers' suicide. In *La Bête humaine* Zola greatly complicates this simple, even moralistic, design. First, he introduces other adulteries, other murders, pushing the link between sexual betrayal and killing much further. In this way, generalizing his central theme, *La Bête humaine* is the story not of a single murder, but of several. Second, he has a situation parallel to the one in the earlier work lead not to the death of husband or lover but to the murder of the adulterous wife. This is the most significant difference between the two novels. In his notes Zola defined the theme of *La Bête humaine* as 'the maniacal need to kill', then as 'The need to kill and to kill a woman.'[39] In an early and enthusiastic review that he welcomed warmly, Jules Lemaître further refined this formula by stating that in his novel Zola studies 'the most frightening and the most mysterious of the primordial instincts: the instinct of destruction and murder and its obscure correlation with the love instinct'.[40] As Roger Pearson has argued, all but one of the murders in the novel 'appear to have their origins in sex' (Introduction, xix): not only the initial crime of passion, in which Roubaud forces Séverine to help him kill her abuser Grandmorin, or the final one, in which Pecqueux attacks Jacques from sexual jealousy and both die under the wheels of the train, but also Louisette's death after Grandmorin's attempted rape, Misard's poisoning of Phasie (as Pearson suggests, not for her money but for the sexual power and vitality it represents), the killing of passengers in the derailment caused by Flore out of jealousy for Séverine's affair with Jacques, and, at the novel's climax, Jacques's murder of Séverine.

More significantly still, three of the novel's murders are carried out by men in response to the actual or virtual adultery of their partners. Roubaud kills with his wife's help because Grandmorin has not only abused Séverine as a young girl but continued to abuse her after her marriage. Pecqueux, on the other hand, is in a quasi-marital liaison with Philomène, spending as much time with her in Rouen as with his legal wife in Paris. Philomène enjoys 'the subtle flavour of forbidden fruit' with Jacques, for 'With Pecqueux it was like being married' (IX.252; 1226), and it is in drunken fury over the affair that Pecqueux sets upon Jacques in the final chapter. Jacques's murder of Séverine stems from a much more shadowy sense of adulterous infidelity. As Pearson suggests, 'his fear of women is the fear that he may carry out an act of vengeance for some primordial female betrayal' (xix), for the narrator attributes to Jacques 'some unquenchable thirst to avenge wrongs suffered in the distant past and yet which he could not precisely remember', and goes on to ask: 'Did it all go back so far, to the evil which women had perpetrated upon his sex, to the sense of grievance accumulated from male to male ever since that first betrayal in the depths of some cave?' (II.54; 1044). Pearson also points out that the narrator uses the same language just before Séverine's murder: 'Had that thirst of his returned, that thirst to avenge ancient wrongs which he could no longer quite remember, that sense of grievance accumulated from male to male ever since that first betrayal in the depths of some cave?' (XI.329; 1297). In his notes to the Pléiade edition, Henri Mitterand traces this idea to Cesare Lombroso's *L'Uomo delinquente* (*The Criminal Man*), which Zola had read before starting to write the novel and which clearly influenced him.[41] However, since Lombroso makes no mention of an atavistic sense of sexual betrayal as a motive for violent crime, either in the passage quoted by Mitterand or elsewhere,[42] this must be Zola's addition. Although the narrator also speaks of 'the terrible shadows of male egoism, the desire to possess her, and to possess her to the point of destroying her' (XI.319; 1287), after the murder he refines this desire as a need not to share the woman with others: 'he possessed her now as he had for so long desired to possess her, completely, even unto destruction. She was no more, she would never belong to anyone now' (XI.331; 1298).

The motive of a male's sexual betrayal by his partner, or his inherited sense of this, is revealing not only because it is Zola's addition to Lombroso. It goes along with a number of explicit or implicit generalizations about what is presented as male and female human nature. Though Pearson claims that, with a few exceptions, 'The narrator withholds all commentary' (xxxi), the narrative voice is not quite so impartial. For instance, the remark just quoted concerning 'the terrible shadows of male egoism' depends on a narratorial sleight-of-hand in which a generalization about maleness is finessed past an unsuspecting reader; and Zola uses the same ploy elsewhere. The passages in which he does so are about women rather than men; and they betray assumptions matching those I have already shown from *Thérèse Raquin*. Examples referring to Séverine are 'the inborn art of feminine hypocrisy' (V.127; 1110); 'the insatiable passion of a woman finally awakened' (IX.254; 1228); 'the unconcern of a woman whose nature is to love, to be the willing helpmeet' (XI.327; 1294); and, perhaps most interesting of all, 'the invincible and despotic smile of a woman who knows herself all-powerful through another's desire' (XI.328, TM; 1295).

The idea of 'woman' that phrases such as these inscribe is that of a comparatively weak and passive figure who gets what she wants through arts of pretence and seduction. Thus Séverine is presented in the same chapter as effectively seducing both Jacques, who has fleetingly witnessed the murder in which she has taken part, and Camy-Lamotte, who has the power to call off the investigation. With Jacques, the narrator observes, 'What she had just done, doubtless, was to give herself; for she was yielding to him, and if later he should ever come to claim her, she would not be able to refuse him' (V.141; 1122). To Camy-Lamotte she simply says 'I am yours', though he is no longer young enough to take advantage (V.145; 1126), and the narrator compares her behaviour to that of 'some sweet domestic pet rubbing itself against its benefactor by way of thanking him' (V.144; 1126). Once her affair with Jacques is in full progress, Séverine not only proposes murdering Roubaud, through hints that Jacques cannot fail to understand, but thanks him with a kiss for agreeing, 'promising him full possession, full communion with her body' (IX.267; 1239); and, when the first attempt fails, she plans the next in every detail. Two features of the role Zola gives Séverine are even more disturbing. First, it is her attempt to stiffen his resolve, by giving herself to him sexually, that finally renders Jacques's bloodlust uncontrollable and so brings him to kill her instead of her husband. Second, although Zola might have explained her all-too compliant sexuality as the result of her abuse when 16, his narratorial generalizations present it as an element of femininity itself.

Through his characterization partly of Séverine, partly of other female figures in the novel, Zola also conveys his sense of what a normative female role would be. Although he presents Séverine as typically female in her submission to male power, he describes her as 'a creature intended solely to caress and be caressed, a lover first and last, a woman who was not a mother' (IX.254; 1228). This both casts her in exclusively sexual terms and implies that motherhood is women's proper role. Philomène, who is childless despite a series of lovers and who is described in relation to Jacques as 'rubbing against him for ages like some scrawny cat on heat' (XII.334; 1301), is a counterpart to Séverine; and Flore, Jacques's cousin who is also in love with him, is another kind of non-maternal woman, a virago. The role the narrator gives her is that of 'a virgin and a warrior' (II.48; 1039, X.303; 1273), and he states that the sexual jealousy that drives her to derail the train on which Jacques and Séverine are travelling is of 'manly potency' (IX.256; 1230). Zola's assumptions about female human nature lead him to construct Séverine and Philomène as typical except in their avoidance of motherhood, but Flore, in her activity and violence, as a masculine aberration.

Through his portrayal of Jacques, Zola was to some extent able to externalize misogynistic assumptions. It is Jacques who is presented as feeling 'these woman's arms that were tightening round his neck and waist like coiling knots of snakes' (VIII.220; 1196), and to whom Séverine seems 'a bottomless pit filled with the darkness of which she spoke' (VIII.223; 1199); and it is the narrator who speaks, in a phrase already quoted, of 'the terrible shadows of male egoism' (XI.319; 1287), and who reports, after Séverine's murder, Jacques's 'sudden surge of pride, as though his supremacy as a male had somehow been enhanced' (XI.331; 1298). Nevertheless, *La Bête humaine* still has much in common with Zola's first novel of female adultery, *Thérèse Raquin*, including misogynism. It is not just, as I have emphasized, that in both novels a wife and her lover plan, at the wife's instigation, to murder an unsuspecting husband, or that Zola goes even further in *La Bête humaine* – both by having the husband kill not the lover but the wife, and by presenting her as virtually asking for it. Geoff Woollen provides an additional insight into the novel's discourse of sexuality, femininity and violence when he discusses Zola's repeated use of the word *éventrer*. Referring to the contemporary panic over Jack the Ripper, an often-noted influence on *La Bête humaine*, he points out that the word *éventrer* 'has semantic resonances beyond "to rip", "to disembowel" or "to eviscerate" in English, opening up a wider conceptual field because of the fact that in French, "ventre" can be taken to mean uterus'.[43] Zola's compulsive recourse to the verb goes hand in hand with the fact that the really unusual twist he imparts in *La Bête humaine* to the novel of female adultery is that the main plot issue is not when the lover will seduce the wife but when he will kill her.

At the start of his preliminary outline, Zola had set out his aim 'to give all Paris a nightmare'.[44] To derive suspense from the threat of violent death rather than of adultery was an apt refinement for a culture in which a woman's murder could be judged to offer an ultimate frisson.

In an essay on *La Bête humaine* as a parody of the conventional detective story, Nelly Wilson points out that Zola conceptualized crime in terms of class. According to him, she says,

> crimes, in bourgeois thinking, are committed for money; inheritance and theft in our context. The various *brutes,* on the other hand, all of whom belong to the lower classes, commit crimes of passion. [. . . W]hatever the precise source or nature of the driving passion, *la bête humaine* does not kill to inherit property or fortunes but is the victim of inherited ancestral instincts which are both vital and destructive, pertaining to the forces of Eros and Thanatos.[45]

The two novels discussed so far, both of which focus on characters from the lower and lower-middle classes, clearly bear out this distinction, and in doing so combine stereotypes of class with those of femininity. In this way it is not only Jacques, Roubaud and Pecqueux, for example, who are proto-criminal types, conforming in their physical appearance to Lombroso's theories.[46] Séverine also comes into the same category, as Thea van Til Rusthoven shows in a discussion of two articles on criminality in *La Bête humaine* published by Jules Héricourt and by Lombroso himself within two years of the novel's appearance. Van Til Rusthoven remarks that, in their book on female criminality and prostitution, Lombroso and his associate Ferrero 'define "hystericism" as "the exaggeration of femininity"; the female criminal displays in an exaggerated way the tendencies of normal women, such as impressionability and inclination to lying'.[47] She also demonstrates how far Séverine corresponds to such a type. Zola did not draw directly on Lombroso and Ferrero for his characterization of Séverine, since their book was not translated into French until six years after the novel was published. Instead, the fact that his notions about the female transgressor so closely resemble theirs is attributable largely to the widespread distribution of misogynistic stereotypes in European culture at the period. The impact of those stereotypes, compounded by assumptions about the lower classes, is also clear in *Nana* (1880).

The central action of *Nana* turns on the lemming-like drive of upper-class men to ruin through their response to the powerful sexuality of the title character. Nana's main victim, the Count de Muffat, chamberlain to the Empress, is only the most flagrant and pathetic example of the many men in the novel destroyed by an appetite that Zola constructs Nana as provoking and the men themselves as having the power and the will to indulge. It follows that *Nana* is a novel not of female adultery but of prostitution. The distinction is important, for, as I have argued in Chapter 1, the prostitute is defined by the fact that she has sex for money, while her own marital status and that of her partners are secondary.[48] Intent on his main theme, Zola keeps in the background the adultery of Muffat's wife, though she has at least two illicit liaisons. Instead, three main concerns drive the novel forward. First, it indicts the corruption, hypocrisy and debauchery that for him characterized the Second Empire and explained its humiliating collapse to Prussia ten years before the novel was published. The indictment has several strands, including his fierce anti-clericalism and his contempt for what he saw as a decadent upper class on the one hand and a debased fashion in music and theatre on the other. Second, it presents a kind of class-revenge. As Roland Barthes puts it, 'Nana, the working-class girl, corrupts the bourgeoisie, destroys it – and destroys herself in the process'.[49] But this revenge is not calculated, despite the disgust that Nana and her fellow prostitutes are often depicted as feeling towards their upper-class clients. It results instead from female sexuality, which Zola constructs as a danger. This is the novel's third main theme, and it often appears in its imagery – as when Nana is described as 'penetrating and corrupting this society with the ferment of her scent as it hung in the warm air' (XII.406; 1430).[50]

Although Zola shapes his heroine in part as an instrument of retribution on a society he presents as rotten to the core, she also conveys masculine phobias about the female. Misogynism and anti-clericalism join in unholy alliance when the narrator remarks that Muffat 'would disappear shudderingly in the omnipotence of sex, just as he would dissolve before the mysterious power of mighty heaven' (XIII.440, TM; 1459). This submerged image of a *vagina dentata* becomes even more menacing when the narrator develops the idea of an avenging 'Golden Fly' (VII.221; 1269) introduced earlier in the novel through an article by the journalist Fauchery:

She had finished her labour of ruin and death. The fly that had come from the dungheap of the slums, carrying the ferment of social decay, had poisoned all these men simply by alighting on them. It was fitting and just. She had avenged the beggars and outcasts of her world. And while her sex rose in a halo of glory and shone down on her victims laid out below, like a rising sun that lights up a field of carnage, she remained as unconscious of her actions as a splendid animal, ignorant of the havoc she had caused, still the good-natured slut. (XIII.452–3, TM; 1470)

Zola's portrayal of monstrous female sexuality in his heroine is so compulsive and excessive that it threatens to overwhelm the novel's entire critique of Empire society. This is clearest at the end, when Nana dies of smallpox as the crowds outside, heralding the Franco-Prussian War, shout 'To Berlin!' Here the narrator seems to attribute the coming disaster not to social or political but to female sexual corruption, through the metaphor of Nana's fatal disease: 'It was as if the germ she had picked up in the gutters, from the carcases left to rot there, that ferment with which she had poisoned a whole people, had risen to her face and rotted it' (XIV.470, TM; 1485). This comes close to indicting Nana for the downfall of the Second Empire, not least because smallpox stands in for syphilis.[51] The fact that Nana has caught smallpox not from the gutter but from her son only widens the charge, blaming her for tainted offspring as well as inadequate mothering.

In his presentation not only of Nana but of other female figures in the novel Zola draws on a range of misogynistic myths as well as that of the *vagina dentata*. If he describes Nana as corrupting Paris 'just as women, every month, curdle milk' (VII.221; 1269–70), he later links Sabine de Muffat's excesses with the menopause: 'Suffering from the restless feverishness of a woman in her forties, she was always hysterically nervous, filling the house with the maddening whirl of her life' (XIII.428; 1449). Similarly, while the novel shows tolerance for male homosexuality through the figure of Labordette, emphasizing his courage, good humour and skill with people and money rather than his sexual orientation, it portrays lesbianism as a perversion. When Nana has her lesbian friend Satin move in with her, the narrator remarks that 'Satin became her vice' (X.326; 1360); and the role of Mme Robert has no other effect than to suggest that even the demimonde has a side still seamier.

Given the hysterical presentation of female sexuality in *Nana*, it may seem odd that Zola makes his central character the instrument rather than the agent of social collapse. Nana is a kind of moral innocent, and a myth rather than a monster; in different ways, it is revealing that Beatrice Chitnis can celebrate her as an icon of female autonomy,[52] and that the novel never describes her in detail, though Zola did so in his working notes.[53] What helps resolve the apparent anomaly is Zola's attitude to the upper and lower classes. In her essay on *La Bête humaine* Nelly Wilson addresses this question in a way that is also relevant to *Nana*, for example when she observes:

> In Zola's view of things, only the *peuple*, provided their natural vitality is not drained away by alcoholism or the daily struggle for economic survival, as debilitating as excessive wealth and food, have the necessary raw energies, uncorrupted and untamed by civilisation, to commit simple crimes of passion. Furthermore, since they lack the intellectual capacity to rationalise or sublimate and since they have no clear sense of wrong-doing, an acquired moral sentiment alien to innocents and animals, they cannot subsequently disown their acts, at least to themselves.[54]

It is on the basis of such patronizing assumptions as these that Zola can portray a woman who does so much wrong as essentially a *bonne fille* to the last. The other side of those assumptions is his characterization of the bourgeoisie and upper classes as venal on the one hand and sexually corrupt on the other.

Of these two vices attributed by Zola to Second Empire society, corrupt and hypocritical sexuality is the more explicit. Thus Nana's friend Satin finds that 'the most distinguished-looking men were the dirtiest. The varnish cracked, and the beast showed itself, exacting in its monstrous tastes, subtle in its perversions' (VIII.272, TM; 1313–14). Similarly, at Nana's party early in the novel the narrator drily comments that 'for a moment it was like being back in the Muffats' drawing-room; only the ladies were different' (IV.114, TM; 1178); and Fauchery twice notices that Sabine has exactly the same mole on her neck as Nana (III.81, 96; 1150, 1163). The novel suggests that the demimonde apes both the perversion and the hypocrisy – so that Mme Robert, first introduced as 'a respectable woman who had only one lover at a time, and that always a respectable man' (I.43; 1117), turns out to be an unbridled lesbian. Its most glaring example, however, is Sabine's father, the

Marquis de Chouard, who deplores 'the disintegration of the governing classes through the shameful compromises of modern debauchery' (XII.400, TM; 1424), but who lurks on the novel's seediest margins throughout till his son-in-law, Muffat, finds him in bed with his own mistress Nana.

The venality for which Zola criticizes the bourgeoisie is clearest in his presentation of marriage as a socially approved form of prostitution. Ironically, the only marriage that the novel presents as functional and even happy is one in which such an arrangement is hardly disguised: Mignon pimps prudently and on the whole with good humour for his actress wife. Zola upstages Flaubert's famous remark about Emma rediscovering in adultery all the platitudes of marriage by showing how the Mignons keep their marriage contented through a succession of paying lovers: 'You couldn't have found a more middle-class or a more united couple' (IV.110, TM; 1174). By the end, the last of the lovers is treated by Rose 'like a husband indeed' (XIII.436, TM; 1456), and Mignon himself has found 'very many advantages in having a husband about for his wife' (XIII.447; 1465).

This sardonic variation on bourgeois marriage is flanked on the one side by Nana's disastrous cohabitation with the actor Fontan and on the other by the home life of the Muffats. After a short-lived period of happiness, Fontan starts beating Nana and living off what she can earn on the streets. Far from helping her achieve the dream of bourgeois respectability that she briefly indulges, her bedfellow becomes 'a vice she paid for' (VIII.277; 1317) until he throws her out for another. In his portrayal of the Muffats, at the other end of the social scale, Zola leaves even less room for mutual contentment. Sabine de Muffat, child of 'a divided family' (III.81; 1150), had married very young when her mother died; her husband, a virgin on their wedding night, has never learned how to satisfy her. Muffat is violently jealous when he learns of Sabine's affair with Fauchery, but the debts incurred by both spouses in pursuing their liaisons bring them to agree tacitly 'that they should both retain their freedom' (XII.406; 1430). In the way that they relate sex and money, lower-class cohabitation and upper-class adultery contrast both with each other and with the bourgeois *ménage à trois*. On the one hand, Nana's passion for Fontan is described as 'all the blinder now that she was paying' (VIII.269, TM; 1311); on the other, Muffat is reminded sorely of his wife's adultery when, to pay debts resulting from his own sexual abandon, he has to obtain her signature to sell some of her property (XII.392; 1418). While sex overwhelms money for Nana, and the Muffats reconcile them only with difficulty, for the bourgeois couple money comes an easy first.

Within the ten-year period from the mid-1870s to the mid-1880s, there first appeared not only *Nana* but *Anna Karenina, Cousin Bazilio* and *La Regenta*. However, whereas Tolstoy, Eça de Queirós and Alas all used the novel of wifely adultery as a means of critiquing the contemporary social orders of Russia, Portugal and Spain respectively, Zola chose for a similar purpose a novel centred on prostitution. The contrast cannot be explained simply by the fact that *Nana* depicts a social order that had already collapsed and been utterly discredited. It also reflects at least three further differences: that the novel of wifely adultery was already a moribund form in France, where it had developed earlier; that the constraints on what could be published in France were fewer; and that Naturalist assumptions about human behaviour and its representation were already well established there – thanks largely, of course, to the work of Zola himself. All this helps account for the excessiveness of Zola's novel, which seems to find no human value at any level of Empire society, figuring the upper classes as effete and corrupt, the proletariat as open to degradation and brutality, and bourgeois customs as laughably stereotyped. It also illuminates why the satire goes so far in Zola's most comprehensive variation on the novel of female adultery, *Pot Luck*.

Although *Pot Luck* is one of the two novels by Zola that come closest to the novel of wifely adultery, it departs in several respects from the dominant conventions. In particular, its main figure, Octave Mouret, is an unmarried man; and the story focuses not on a single adulterous liaison, but on a proliferation of adulteries, involving most of the main characters. As Robert Lethbridge points out, *Pot Luck* is not only 'written in the shadow of other texts', all of them novels of adultery, but 'also more deliberately *shadows* other texts', including Balzac's *Cousin Bette* and Flaubert's *Sentimental Education* as well as *Madame Bovary* itself.[55] Its action, however, both follows and parodies another nineteenth-century narrative tradition, that of the *Bildungsroman*. In *Pot Luck*, Octave Mouret is a Rastignac *manqué*. Like his predecessor, he is a young man from the provinces aspiring to conquer Paris; and, as in *Le Père Goriot* (1835), much of the action centres on the house in which he lives – though, in keeping with forty-odd years of social and economic change, this is an apartment house rather than a lodging house. The fact that Octave's story resembles Rastignac's – while, at the same time, burlesquing it – helps explain some of the differences between *Pot Luck* and classic novels of wifely adultery. The theme of a male character's education gives the narrative its main organizing principle, and the female characters with whom he tries but sometimes fails to have sex furnish a gallery of female types.

In Zola's first detailed plan for the novel, he set out his aim 'To show the bourgeoisie naked, after having exposed the populace, and to show it as more detestable for its claims to order and respectability'.[56] Lethbridge suggests that he meant his novel 'as complementary to both *L'Assommoir* [1877] and *Nana* (1880), and designed to explode the impression left by such works that misery and promiscuity might be the preserve of the proletariat'.[57] The relation between the three novels is closer still, however, since *Nana* deals as much with misery and promiscuity among the upper classes as among the lower. In accordance with Zola's campaign against the middle classes, the point of departure for *Pot Luck* can, Henri Mitterand has shown, be dated from February 1881 when he published an article in *Le Figaro* entitled 'Adultery among the Bourgeoisie'.[58] Here he defines three types of bourgeois adulteress: the hysteric, the man-seeker, and the sentimental innocent. His outline for the novel shows that it was on these types that he based three of his female characters;[59] and, as Lethbridge makes clear, the article also provides the social and economic interpretation by which Zola sought to explain their behaviour:

> he analyses three forms of upbringing: the neurotic effect of spatial enclosure on incipient degeneracy seeking a sexual outlet; mothers' roles in instructing their daughters, perverted to the extent that the goal of 'catching a man' both makes marriage synonymous with legalised prostitution and encourages subsequent adultery in exchange for further material reward; and the perpetuation of girlhood innocence *within* marriage, thus encouraging the most prevalent of adulterous escapisms, driven less by frustrated physical needs than by the attractions of living out amorous illusions fostered by an educational diet of romantic novels.[60]

In this way Valérie Vabre corresponds to the type of woman that 'falls into the arms of a lover not because she is pushed there by the slightest sensual appetite, but because she is ill, because she is unbalanced'; Berthe Vabre, who becomes Valérie's sister-in-law, to the type that, taught to trap men by her mother, starts hunting once she is married 'no longer for a husband, but for a lover'; and Marie Pichon to the type that displays 'adultery through stupidity', with her 'false sentimentality' supposedly shown by her liking for novels by George Sand.[61]

But this is hardly the 'taxonomy of female adultery' that Lethbridge calls it.[62] Not only is it limited to bourgeois wives, but it also omits other forms of female adultery that Zola portrays elsewhere. Brian Nelson notes further causes of bourgeois wifely adultery in Zola's fiction as '*désoeuvrement* [idleness] and socially-inspired curiosity', citing as examples 'Renée Saccard (*La Curée*), Juliette Deberle (*Une Page d'amour*), Mme Desforges (*Au Bonheur des Dames*), Mme Hennebeau (*Germinal*) and Gilberte Delaherche (*La Débâcle*)'.[63] But this list includes only adulterous wives (potentially adulterous in the case of Juliette Deberle); it excludes sexual passion as a motive for adultery (as in *Thérèse Raquin* and *La Bête humaine*, to name only two examples); and its inclusion of Mme Hennebeau is misleading, because *Germinal* presents her adultery as the product of her own depravity and her resentment of her husband. Zola's *Figaro* article is therefore a blueprint for *Pot Luck*, in some ways as 'Un mariage d'amour' had been for *Thérèse Raquin*, and not an outline of his views in general about adultery.

What is much more significant is that the article labels adultery as a specifically bourgeois vice. This it does in its opening sentence, which begins with an equally tendentious assumption – that, also as a result of environment and education, the vice of working-class women is prostitution.[64] Furthermore, through the examples the article offers, it suggests that what is at issue is not adultery as such, but the adultery of the wife. *Pot Luck* bears out this presupposition to the extent that its action centres on the three types of adulteress Zola had discussed in his article – Octave having affairs with two of them and failing only with the hysterical Valérie, who has other lovers. But this is the story only in part. First, there is the role of Octave, which Nicholas White has read as that of a Don Giovanni.[65] The problem with such an interpretation is not only that Octave is much less successful than his avatar but that the novel is much more interested in female sexuality and its aberrations than male. For example, it goes near to suggesting that adultery by bourgeois husbands may be explained as a response to sexual dysfunctions on the part of their wives. Rose Campardon, who suffers from some form of vaginal constriction, tolerates her husband's affair with his first love, Gasparine, to whom he returns after several years of marriage, even hinting at and then happily accepting the mistress's installation in the family home; while Clotilde Duveyrier connives at her husband keeping a mistress because of her own sexual repugnance for him and, implicitly, her frigidity. Other female figures are Mme Josserand, who tyrannizes over her mild-mannered, decent, husband; Mme Juzeur, left by her husband after ten days of marriage and nicknamed by the men she frustrates 'anything-but-that'; and Mme Dambreville, maligned because she still wants sex at 50, and who, despairing that her younger lover will marry and leave her, finds him a wife in her niece and later resumes their affair.

All the same, it is not quite true that, as Brian Nelson has argued, 'The adulteries of the men in the novel, such as Campardon and Duveyrier, are blamed on the mysterious maladies and hysterical natures of their wives'.[66] Although such an inference is tempting, not only is there at least one example of the reverse case, in that Valérie's husband is impotent, but, much more important, Zola invites no sympathy for male sexual transgression either. Without a single exception, *Pot Luck* presents sex as nasty, brutish, and short. Zola stressed in his first detailed plan for the novel that the three central adulteries would be *'without sexual passion'*;[67] and this he followed through to the letter. Octave's affair with Marie Pichon is as joyless as its origin when he rapes her on her kitchen table; Valérie, whom he fails to seduce, is constantly anxious lest her affairs be discovered; and his success with Berthe not only drains his pocket through her luxurious tastes, and frustrates him through her caprice, but leads to her humiliation when, in the middle of the night, her husband bursts into Octave's room and she flees in panic in her chemise. The heavy ironies in this scene reinforce the point that adultery, worse even than marriage, brings many pains and no pleasures. Having succeeded after lengthy persuasion in getting his mistress to his bedroom, Octave no longer wants her, his lust already slaked by Marie; and, far from enjoying the 'filthy tricks' imagined by the irate husband (XIV.279; 285),[68] the two are quarrelling like an old married couple when he breaks in.

Zola's presentation of sexual corruption, hypocrisy and suffering is so unremitting in *Pot Luck* that the novel seems to denounce not only adultery but sexual relations in general. The attack culminates in a gruesome account of the maid Adèle giving birth on her own at night and then ridding herself of the baby. Although this is part of Zola's assault on the bourgeoisie – the baby's father is Appeal Court counsellor Duveyrier – the focus on messy, painful labour and child-murder is revealing. Such, the novel suggests, is the fruit of sex from sheer lust, with no aim of reproduction. What it proposes instead is the kind of marriage Octave enters at the end, based not on sex but on business and a kind of respectful affection. Zola prepares his hero for such a marriage through his unhappy experience of adultery: 'Still sore about his ridiculous love affair with Berthe, he now no longer thought of women; he even feared them' (XVII.332, TM; 339). Having rebuffed him previously when he had tried to seduce her, Mme Hédouin completes his reformation, proposing that they marry because she cannot run her shop on her own, and restricting physical contact between them. One reason why this is significant is that it appears to correct Octave's misogynism. Zola speaks twice of 'the ferocious disdain he had for women' (I.20, TM; 21, and XII.241; 245), and this Mme Hédouin seems to have tamed by removing sex from their relationship. But the matter is not quite so simple. First, Octave has to repeat his education in *The Ladies' Paradise* (1883), the next novel of the series, for Zola has Mme Hédouin die to be succeeded by a wife who is an even better model of decency and restraint, Denise Baudu. Second, the fact that the novel itself is scarcely free of misogynism suggests that what is really at issue may be different.

The misogynism of *Pot Luck* not only shows in the precedence it gives to adultery by women, especially wives, over adultery by men, whether or not they are husbands. It is also clear from the narrator's concern with female physical appearance and from his prurience over female bodily functions. In this remorselessly anti-sexual text, women are often portrayed in sexual terms. Part of the reason for this is that the main point of view is the womanizing Octave's. In the first chapter he sizes up each woman he encounters – not only Marie, Mme Hédouin, Valérie, and Berthe, but also his cousin Mme Campardon: 'she had ripened at about thirty, gaining a sweet savour, a pleasant, fresh odour as of autumn fruit' (I.11; 11). But not all such images are assigned to Octave. It is the narrator who focalizes the Josserand daughters when he observes: 'They went on eating, their dressing-gowns unbuttoned and showing their shoulders, gently rubbing their bare skin against the warm earthenware of the stove. They looked charming in this undress, with their youth and healthy appetites, and their eyes heavy with sleep' (II.31; 33). Later on, in an act of double voyeurism, it is another male character who focalizes a woman's exposure: 'Campardon took the liberty of putting his head round the door. He saw his daughter standing by the couch staring in fascination at Valérie, whose breasts, shaken by spasms, had broken loose from her unhooked bodice' (VIII.153; 155). Similarly, Mme Josserand is focalized by the narrator before he presents her husband's view of her: 'She looked enormous, though her shoulders were still shapely, and resembled the shining flanks of a mare. [. . .] His wife positively overwhelmed him when she displayed that mammoth bosom; it seemed as if he could feel its weight crushing the back of his neck' (II.23; 23, 24). Zola is careful to motivate the display of Berthe's half-naked body when she flees in panic from Octave's room, and he highlights the interest Campardon cannot resist showing in her exposed breasts and legs: all this, implicitly, is part of the price of adultery. Elsewhere, however, the attention given to the female body and to female bodily functions is gratuitous, for example when the narrator mentions that 'As the ladies passed over the broad gratings of the heating apparatus a warm breath penetrated their skirts' (VIII.142; 145), and when he has Octave 'hear the sounds of women undressing and relieving themselves', a sound he renders more explicit a few pages later: 'then splashing as of a fountain resounded along the floor' (XIII.256, 259; 261, 264–5).

I have documented this aspect of the novel because it passes without notice among Zola's recent critics – unlike those of his own period. To some extent it can be explained as Naturalist convention, to some extent by Zola's situation and psychology;[69] and, within the novel, to some degree too by the lesson Octave has to learn about sex. The trouble is that this lesson is also about women: that the best of them keep their sexuality and their physicality under constraint. In this way Octave sheds one type of misogynism, based on exploiting women sexually, only to inherit another that is more subtle. This consists in the idea that women are more sexual and more physical than men, and therefore need to control themselves better. Thus Zola's assault on bourgeois corruption and hypocrisy is rooted in a thoroughly bourgeois code of sexual and other self-discipline. The paradox may be explained by the close association, in the dominant ideology of late nineteenth-century France, between women and proletariat. Citing the work of Susanna Barrows, Janet

Beizer points out that, in that ideology, the proletariat 'is consistently feminized (seen as uncontrollable, capricious, uncivilized, closer to nature and the body). Correlatively, proletarian women are represented as hyperfemale, hypernatural'.[70] As Beizer also remarks, Zola's title suggests a melting-pot, a hotchpotch in which distinctions are lost, and his novel works to reinscribe the key distinction between bourgeoisie and proletariat:

> When we look at the signifying structure of the novel, we can easily recognize the maids in their kitchens as signifier of bourgeois moral turpitude. This sign is ambiguous, however, because the equation of domestic abjection and bourgeois turpitude would not be possible if maids and masters were equal. The equation upon which the sign depends works only because there is, in the imaginary of Second Empire France, a radical disjunction between the people and the bourgeoisie. In other words, the initial sign assimilating the two classes also signifies something quite different: the reassuring survival of the class system.[71]

In turn, the underlying wish to preserve that class system helps explain why, despite denouncing the bourgeoisie, the novel is, as Brian Nelson argues, complicit with the patriarchal bourgeois ideology that underwrites the novel of adultery. Developing the theory put forward by Tony Tanner, Nelson claims that 'The infidelities of the bourgeoisie were much more significant than those of the working class because, as transgressors of their own law, the bourgeoisie put at risk an order of civilization structured precisely to sustain their own privileged position.'[72]

It is therefore not true to say, with Robert Lethbridge, that *Pot Luck* 'positions itself *against*' the tradition of adultery fiction; or, with Nicholas White, that it is 'both inside and outside the novel of adultery'.[73] Instead, the novel is better understood as an example of the tradition writ large, pushing it to an ironic, disgusted extremity.

The second of the two novels by Zola that come closest to the conventional novel of wifely adultery is *A Love Affair*. Published in 1878, between *L'Assommoir* and *Nana*, *A Love Affair* bears out in a different way from *Pot Luck* the extent to which his work is written within the dominant assumptions of nineteenth-century French adultery fiction. This is despite the fact that Zola wrote in his notes that his aim was 'to study passion as no one else has studied it',[74] and that the novel departs in three striking respects from canonical examples of the form. First, the heroine, Hélène Grandjean, is unmarried – she is a widow who has a fleetingly consummated affair with a married man, Henri Deberle. Second, apart from her lapse the heroine is virtuous: the novel endows her with an integrity that it attributes to her modest upbringing in the provinces, and it contrasts her with the Parisian women around her who have casual affairs. Third, and crucially, the 'passion' Zola set out to study was that not only of woman and man but child. It is Hélène's daughter Jeanne who is instrumental both in bringing the lovers together and in forcing them apart as soon as they have consummated their affair. The lovers first meet in the opening chapter when Jeanne is seriously ill and the doctor found in panic by Hélène is Henri; and, after their sole act of coition, it is Jeanne's final illness and death that part them permanently.

It is clear that Zola wrote *A Love Affair* in light of the form from which it diverges. Following Balzac's famous example, he made his heroine a woman of thirty;[75] he has a romance, Scott's *Ivanhoe*, give her dangerous thoughts about love;[76] and, when she goes on the mission that takes her to her lover, he associates her with the imagery of liquidity and dissolution that Janet Beizer has identified in medical and fictional discourse of the period about women.[77] However, as the title suggests, passion in Zola's novel overwhelms its heroine only temporarily. The title *Une Page d'amour* might better be translated as 'A Brief Affair', for in a letter of 1892 Zola glossed it as meaning 'one page in a work, one day in a life'.[78] This suggests that wifely adultery may be contained and neutralized. The page of Hélène's life stained by her transgression is preceded by her childhood, twelve placid years of marriage, and two otherwise unblemished years as a widow; and it is succeeded by a second marriage as sensible and passionless on her part as her first. In his outline for the novel, Zola also set out his intention to write what he called 'the *general history* of love in our time, without the lies of the poet or the bias of the realist'. As Henri Mitterand points out, this is to reject both romantic idealization and naturalist reductiveness.[79] It is also to imply a decidedly sober view of what constitutes 'love in our time' – especially for women.

A Love Affair conveys such a view by subordinating love to motherhood, and it is in this respect that it gives a further twist to the novel of female adultery. Although, unlike other novels in the tradition, it turns on the adultery of a woman who is not a wife, there are two strong reasons why it belongs with them. The first is that, as the tradition developed, it brought more and more into play the adulteress's child.[80] The second is that Zola gave the heroine's daughter part of the role attributed to her husband by other novelists in the tradition. F. W. J. Hemmings draws attention to a revealing slip in his notes when he wrote of his aim 'To study these three figures in the household: the wife, the lover, the husband, the child.'[81] The slip consists in counting husband as well as child – even though, because he dies before the action starts, and does not influence it posthumously, the novel elides the husband's role entirely. By substituting child for husband, by making her female, and by placing her on the edge of puberty, Zola greatly increased his novel's dramatic and ideological potential. At the same time he set in relief the assumptions about love, marriage and motherhood to which his fiction subscribed.

Those assumptions are in harmony with the ones Rousseau built into *Julie* over a century before: marriage is best founded on rational affection, and the role of the wife best centred on home and children. Both Hélène's marriages obey these rules, even though – indeed, in part because – she feels no passion for either husband. The conflict she experiences is therefore clear-cut. It is, as Zola puts it, a 'struggle between passion and mother-love' (III.iii.166; 948). Although passion briefly overwhelms her, so that for a short while she puts her own needs before her child's, Jeanne's relapse and death present themselves not only as punishments for her sin but as reminders of her duty. The novel's narrative structure endorses such a message through ellipsis and emphatic closure. It cuts straight from the scene of Jeanne's burial to Hélène's visit two years later to her daughter's snow-covered grave, after she has resettled in her native Provence and married the good but stolid man, 15 years older than herself, whom she had not been able to accept previously. Hélène's decision to marry Rambaud is presented in a brief flashback almost as a foregone conclusion: 'she could find no reason for refusing. It seemed the best and wisest course' (V.v.316; 1089). Her former self now seems to her 'an utter stranger'; and the novel signals her day-to-day life resuming through the mundane topics of conversation with her husband with which it closes.

Although *A Love Affair* seems to offer a clear didactic message through its whole action and structure, Judith Armstrong and Brian

Nelson are among the critics who have found it ambivalent. Quoting Armstrong, Nelson declares that Zola's

> depiction of Hélène's maternal devotion underlines the prestige of motherhood, while the presentation of Jeanne's mortal illness as the retributive consequence of adultery underlines the primacy of motherhood and the unacceptability of extra-marital sexuality. [. . .] The ambiguity of Zola's position is highlighted, however, by the fact that 'he finally puts his heroine in the very situation that he acknowledges leads to incompatibility and potential adultery in his other novels of the loveless marriage'.[82]

Yet such an argument fails to take account of two key facts: that Hélène is a widow when she has her affair, and that the novel gives every reason to assume she will be as chaste a wife in her second marriage as she had been in her first. The problem is rather how a woman of the integrity with which Zola credits his heroine could have succumbed at all. This problem he solved by devising a highly ingenious crisis for his plot. Since it is not possible to explore the novel's implications without detailed reference to the crisis – which Flaubert praised as 'SUBLIME' –[83] I will summarize it.

The crisis begins two-thirds of the way through the novel after Hélène's passionate attraction for Henri – presented for the most part sympathetically – has reached full pitch. Hélène hears Juliette, Henri's wife, agree to an assignation with her admirer Malignon. Angry and jealous at this, and having discovered accidentally where the two are to meet, Hélène writes an anonymous letter to inform Henri. On reflection she decides not to send it but to try and persuade Juliette not to betray her husband; but, when Juliette treats her with indifference, giving her no chance to talk seriously or to obstruct the assignation, Hélène posts the letter on impulse. Then, after further second thoughts, she rushes to the house where the assignation is to take place in order both to prevent it and to forestall discovery. She succeeds all the better because Juliette has realized her folly and is in danger of rape; but, although Juliette and Malignon get away safely, Hélène is unable to leave before Henri arrives. He assumes that the letter is her device to enable an assignation with him, she cannot undeceive him without betraying Juliette, and she is unable to avoid yielding to him.

This complex sequence of events achieves three main effects. First, it minimizes blame for Hélène while giving full value to her passionate feelings and her resulting confusion. Surprised by Henri before she can get away after warning his wife and her would-be lover, Hélène is in an impossible position, since Henri has every reason to assume she has summoned him to an assignation with her, and since she can only clear herself by inculpating Juliette. Second, Hélène saves the Deberle marriage. Because she says nothing of Juliette's assignation with Malignon, and because her intervention puts Juliette off illicit liaisons for good, Hélène enables the marriage to survive. It is worth noting, however, that this depends on, and ratifies, the double standard of sexual morality; while discovery would threaten Juliette's position as a wife (and, under French law of the period, even her life and that of her lover), a parallel exposure would have little impact on Henri's position as a husband. Third, Hélène's absence precipitates her daughter's final and fatal illness. Zola gives Jeanne a dependence on her mother so intense that she not only feels betrayed by Hélène's abrupt departure and prolonged, unexplained absence, but even senses the moment of sexual transgression: 'from the depths of her being, from her sexuality of an awakened woman, a sharp pain sprang up, like a blow received from afar' (IV.v.254, TM; 1031). This disturbing suggestion that Henri violates Jeanne in having sex with her mother is echoed by Jeanne's refusal to let Henri treat her on her deathbed: 'the twelve-year-old child was mature enough to understand that this man must not touch her, must not touch her mother's body through hers' (V.iii.287; 1062). Not for nothing does Hélène tell Henri: 'You see we've killed her.'

It is not, therefore, possible to endorse Brian Nelson's view that *A Love Affair* has a 'profound ambivalence' at its centre.[84] Instead, although Zola took pains to dramatize Hélène's passionate feelings, he in no way suggested she was right to gratify them. The narrator offers a rare but explicit judgement when, after the affair has been consummated, he remarks that Hélène 'was weakly indulging in the pleasure of telling herself that nothing was forbidden' (V.ii.278; 1054), and, even apart from the role of Jeanne, much further textual evidence points the same way. For example, if there is any doubt over how to read the 'delicious annihilation of her whole being' to which Hélène succumbs in Henri's presence (IV.iv.244; 1021), the novel clearly presents this as both dangerous and self-defeating. After the two have had sex, Hélène says to herself 'that they had never loved one another less than that day' (IV.iv.246; 1024); and she is shown feeling 'a tremendous unsatisfied desire' (V.i.270; 1046) a few hours later. This suggestion that, once awakened, female desire is excessive and unappeasable goes along with Hélène's moral lapse in lying adroitly to Juliette, feeling none of 'those scruples of conscience that had tortured her formerly' (V.ii.271; 1047). Nor does the novel invite confidence in Henri as lover or consort for Hélène. The narrator remarks that his love 'flared up again all the more violently because he had recently begun to forget her' (IV.iv.242; 1020), and calls his final words in the novel, on Jeanne's death, 'foolish and pathetic' (V.iii.297; 1071). Furthermore, it is implied in the final chapter that he has had other liaisons; Hélène realizes that she has never really known him; and the news that he and Juliette have had a child, conceived just after his affair with Hélène has ended, not only suggests the marriage has revived but reinforces the sense of closure produced by Hélène's own remarriage.

The daughter born to the Deberles also contrasts only too legibly with the daughter lost to Hélène. However, the role played in the novel by Jeanne goes beyond that of a breathing (and expiring) embodiment of a mother's duty. By placing her on the threshold of puberty, Zola is able to give her adult as well as childish jealousy; by making her female, he is able to exploit the role not only of sensitive child but also of deserted mistress. Zola has Jeanne veer between different positions, in all of which she resents feared or actual rejection. She shifts from rebuffing Rambaud as a prospective stepfather to accepting him when it becomes clear that Henri is her true rival in her mother's love; and she moves from jealousy on behalf of Hélène, when her mother is hurt by a display of affection between Henri and Juliette, to jealousy over her. On each of these occasions Zola draws on the same kind of imagery. Jeanne is given 'the burning look of a deserted mistress' (III.iv.182; 963), 'the faded eyes of some aged spinster, never to be loved' (V.i.264; 1040), and, in death, 'the haggard mask of a jealous woman' (V.iii.296; 1071). In these ways Jeanne's role goes beyond warning, and ultimately punishing, the mother who seeks sexual pleasure to endorse an idea of femininity itself as characteristically nervous, easily excited, and over-demanding.

Zola's switch of child for husband in the traditional adulterous triangle was a brilliant ideological stroke. It enabled him to portray the adulteress sympathetically, promoting motherly devotion; and to avoid both the old formula of jealous husband and the new one of neurotic female sexuality by displacing jealousy and neurosis on to the child. Presenting the woman who succumbs as essentially virtuous was also highly adroit. It gave Zola a further standpoint from which to criticize the casual adultery he thought widespread among women of the Parisian bourgeoisie, and it allowed him both to depict and to discourage her sexual excitement – providing her with the safe solution of a second passionless marriage afterwards. Not least, the device also offered an extra frisson to its readers while reaffirming conventional marital values. This Flaubert revealed when he wrote, in the same letter quoted above: 'Despite my great age, the novel disturbed and *excited* me. One feels inordinate desire for Hélène and one understands your doctor very well.'[85] Brian Nelson argues that this remark points to 'a totally equivocal stance' on Zola's part 'towards both libidinal sexuality and bourgeois marriage'.[86] But the stance is not equivocal at all if it is male sexuality that is gratified at the expense of female.

A Love Affair leaves no doubt that, however exciting female desire may be for a reader, women's sexual pleasure is out of bounds. This idea is reinforced not only by the novel's structure and action but by its long descriptive passages and by a curious repeated motif. The descriptions are of Paris, which Hélène and Jeanne survey from the suburban heights where they live, knowing few of the features named by the narrator and rarely venturing down. Paris represents a life from which they are excluded, inviting at times but menacing, as when Jeanne watches a storm break while her mother yields to Henri. As Nelson points out, the sexual symbolism of such scenes is obvious; indeed, Hélène rushes down through the rain to her 'fall'.[87] But the descriptions of the city also imply that it is a world that women had best avoid, full of life but dangerously turbulent. The same idea underlies the repeated motif in which both of Hélène's husbands and her lover kiss 'her feet of marble' (I.v.61, TM; 848; also IV.iv.245, 247; 1022, 1023, and V.v.316; 1089). This makes male sexuality active, female passive, indulging passion in men, withholding it from women. As Naomi Schor suggests in an essay on the same novel, 'in Zola's works mothers are forbidden to experience sexual bliss'.[88] Although ostensibly an image of male adoration, the statue signifies woman's subjection to male desire, her sexuality rendered frigid and powerless. The point is the same if, in accordance with Freudian theory, the woman's foot is read as a fetish for her genitalia. It is even stronger if, through a refinement of the same thinking, it is read as a symbol of her absent phallus. In these and other ways, Zola's novels of female adultery not only develop the form but strengthen its inherent misogynism.

8

Parody, Entropy, Eclipse: Huysmans, Céard, Maupassant

The previous chapter has shown how, through most of his career as a novelist, Zola kept returning to the novel of adultery, extending, parodying and renewing its basic conventions. In the middle of that career, after he had published *Thérèse Raquin*, *A Love Affair* and *Nana*, but before he had started work on *Pot Luck*, two of his Naturalist colleagues published novels that turn in unusual ways on the question of wifely adultery. The colleagues were Joris-Karl Huysmans (1848–1907) and Henry Céard (1851–1924), the novels were *Living Together* and *A Lovely Day*, and they appeared in the same year, 1881. Both cast further light not only on how Naturalism affected adultery fiction but also on the decline of the form and, in the case of *Living Together*, its characteristic misogynism.

There are several further reasons why the 1880s were significant years for French adultery fiction. First, the decade began with the death of Flaubert in 1880 and with the 'rewriting of the Flaubertian novel', as Nicholas White puts it, that followed.[1] Examples of that rewriting are not only *Living Together*, *A Lovely Day*, and Zola's *Pot Luck*, but also *L'Accident de Monsieur Hébert* (1883) by their fellow Naturalist Léon Hennique (1851–1935). White raises the question how far 'the clutch of novels of adultery written in the wake of Flaubert's death' was 'a coherent project', and suggests that they might better be analysed in terms of rivalry.[2] Such a view certainly helps explain the extent to which these works try to go one better than their predecessors. *Living Together* is an unrelievedly sordid account of marriage, adultery and concubinage; *A Lovely Day* represents, in David Baguley's phrase, 'an attempt to rewrite *Madame Bovary* in the mode of *L'Education sentimentale*'; and, as White observes, *Pot Luck* 'was apparently intended as a novel of adultery to end all novels of adultery'.[3]

A second reason why the 1880s are significant is that in France it was in these years that, socially as well as culturally, wifely adultery was losing its status as the cardinal sexual transgression. At the end of an article summarizing her research on family life under the Third Republic, Anne-Marie Sohn goes so far as to say: 'Psychologically, though not legally, adultery stopped being a crime between 1880 and 1900.'[4] Part of the evidence for this claim is a striking decline in the number of murders motivated by adultery: 'Between 1840 and 1860, in more than one out of five homicides the motive was adultery; the numbers fell to 15 per cent in 1871, 7 per cent in 1876, and 5 per cent from 1893 onward'.[5] It is not a coincidence that divorce had been re-established in 1884; on the contrary, it was the period during which French law had no provisions for divorce that witnessed the heyday of the novel of wifely adultery. Zola's tongue was not entirely in his cheek when, in an article of 1881, he predicted that divorce would affect the whole of French literature, existing and to come: 'There will be two repertoires: the repertoire before divorce and the one after; and the first will be scarcely more than a dramatic museum, where one goes to see bygone social behaviour, just as one goes to see works of art from the past at the Louvre.'[6] On the other hand, in keeping with his forecast that divorce would also 'modify works yet to be written', his friend Maupassant was one of the first to capitalize, showing the protagonist of *Bel-Ami* (1885) exploiting the new law to escape an inconvenient marriage. Maupassant had already published an article on the new literary possibilities introduced by divorce,[7] and he was so keen to take advantage of them in his novel that he paid the price of anachronism – the novel was published the year after the law was passed, but, according to its chronology, Duroy's divorce takes place the year before.[8]

Maupassant's own contribution to the novel of adultery is a third reason why the 1880s is a crucial period for the form in France. As David Baguley remarks, adultery 'is an obsessive theme in the works of Maupassant'.[9] It features repeatedly and often centrally in his short stories and in five of his six completed novels, and he wrote an article on the subject as publicity for Zola's *Pot Luck*, printed alongside the novel's first serial instalment in *Le Gaulois*. But Maupassant is also an important figure in the tradition of French adultery fiction because his later works show him moving away from the theme and then dropping it completely. This chapter therefore ends with a discussion of his novels and how they illustrate the demise in France of the novel of wifely adultery. It begins, however, by considering the different contributions of Huysmans, Céard and, briefly, Hennique.

Living Together and *A Lovely Day* are less examples of the form than more or less caustic parodies. In Céard's novel the act of adultery does not even take place, whereas Huysmans flouts convention by starting with the wife's adultery and ending with her reconciliation to her husband. This, too, is ironic, for living together is merely a lesser evil – for him than living alone, for her than residing with relatives. Although both novels look askance at the novel of wifely adultery, *Living Together* is more biting in its irony. Nevertheless, despite the differences in tone and action, both promote the stock Naturalist themes of disillusionment, boredom, entropy.[10] Since they were written in the heyday of the Médan group, it is not surprising that each has links with a novel by its leader Zola. *A Lovely Day* looks back to *A Love Affair*. The action both of Céard's novel and of Zola's hinges on a rainstorm, reinforced by descriptions of Paris both panoramic and from the street; though, in contrast to Zola's heroine, Céard's is a wife not a widow, and her virtue remains unimpugned. *Living Together*, on the other hand, as Lucien Descaves remarked long ago, points forward to *Pot Luck*: it was after reading it that Zola wrote the essay 'Adultery among the Bourgeoisie' that paved the way for his novel,[11] and he may even have borrowed the name Berthe for his principal adulteress from that of the adulterous wife in Huysmans.

The key question of *Living Together* is not, however, adultery but the choice, for a man, between marriage and various forms of living in sin. David Baguley suggests that 'the novel reads like a bachelor's handbook, or, in more Balzacian terms, a "Physiology of Alternatives to Marriage"';[12] but it offers only negative guidance, for the alternatives prove even less satisfactory than marriage itself. The novel's opening chapter sets its agenda clearly. André and Cyprien, the two main characters, discuss whether it is in the interests of men like themselves to marry. While Cyprien sourly foresees that he will sooner or later succumb, André, who has done so already, argues that marriage is 'the better folly' (18; 11).[13] The two conduct their argument entirely in terms of personal comfort or its lack. Thus, while Cyprien shrinks from 'the misery of sleeping two to a bed, the insomnia or snores of another person, the blows of elbows or feet, the strain of exacted caresses, the tedium of expected kisses' (17, TM; 10), André has found it even worse to eat poor food, go with shirt-buttons missing or without a clean handkerchief, and either 'to feel continually sickened by the dirty skins of prostitutes' or depend on unpredictable liaisons with mistresses (17–18; 10–11). Such a defence of marriage is scarcely inspiring, but it is in keeping with the materialist assumptions of Naturalism. According to those assumptions, people are driven by biological appetites that demand satisfaction, and social institutions such as marriage that seek to constrain these are fundamentally arbitrary. André claims that marriage provides an acceptable way of meeting his sexual and domestic needs. Huysmans, however, turns the tables neatly by having him return home to find his wife in bed with another man and leave her next day from vexation.

This deft if dispiriting exposition pins André on the other horn of his marital dilemma: for most of the novel's action, Huysmans has him try whether the tribulations of bachelorhood are less irksome. André tries to meet his domestic needs by renting a flat and hiring a servant he thinks he can trust, and his sexual needs first with prostitutes, then with mistresses. However, although he has periods of relative comfort, his experience merely bears out the account he has already given of the sexual side of bachelorhood. He finds sex with prostitutes to be like a drug that requires increased doses until it begins to aggravate the condition it is meant to cure; he takes a part-time mistress only to rediscover the inconvenience of the arrangement and the awkwardness of sharing her with others; and he takes up once more with a former mistress who goes to live with him till she loses her job, after which he cannot afford to keep her and she leaves for work elsewhere. It is not, then, surprising that after a little prompting André ends up again with his wife. Cyprien offers the only apparent alternative, settling into snug domesticity with an amiable lower-class concubine. In the process the two cease to work seriously as artists, and Cyprien ironically concludes: 'Basically, concubinage and marriage are the same since they have rid us of our artistic preoccupations and our carnal distress. No more talent and better health, what a dream!' (203–4, TM; 386).

The chief difference between *Living Together* and the fiction of wifely adultery is therefore that Huysmans gives little attention to the adulterous wife and no respect to marriage. These facts indicate how far, at least in France, the ideological assumptions behind the tradition were already fading. Nevertheless, while Huysmans's novel is centred very conspicuously on male experience and what it defines as male problems, its construction of the transgressive wife is also revealing. Although Berthe appears in the opening chapter when André finds her with her lover, her point of view is not given and she is not even named. Instead, Huysmans reserves Chapter IV for her side of the story, which he presents in flashback. In this way he separates it from the rest of his narrative, an effect he compounds by framing it within an account of a bourgeois household and by offering no explicit information to orient the reader until, several pages in, the narrator mentions André. The impact of these distancing devices is to emphasize the gap between conventional bourgeois life and that of the two main characters, and to keep most of the narrative focus on them while offering an explanation of what is wrong not only with André's marriage, but, implicitly, with bourgeois marriage in general. It is in this latter respect that the presentation of Berthe has its main interest.

First, bourgeois life is characterized as insipid, narrow-minded, and penny-pinching. Second, it is suggested that these features help account for an aggressive reaction on the part of bourgeois women. Huysmans models Berthe's story as an aggravated form of that reaction. The narrator points out that she has been, 'like most young girls who have lost their mother at an early age, very badly brought up' (55; 83); she looked on her father as 'a banker whose cash box had to provide for all her needs and her caprices'; she had learned how to manipulate him; and, finding her freedom gone when he died and she had to live with her uncle and aunt, she leapt at André's proposal, having rejected suitors previously. All this sets the stage not only for dissatisfaction and conflict with her husband but for adultery. Anticipating Zola in his representation of bourgeois wives both in his article and in *Pot Luck*, Huysmans makes Berthe frigid. He seeks to explain her affair by dislike of her husband, encouragement from her female friends, and, once she has failed to find pleasure with her lover any more than with her husband, by neurotic persistence in search of it. Most significantly, despite the unusual nature of Berthe's upbringing, he uses her as a pretext for repeated generalizations about women. For example, the dictum quoted above on girls who have lost their mothers is followed almost immediately by the remark: 'And there the eternal woman came out again; every woman, respectable or not, thinks it is natural to squeeze the man on whom she depends, be it her father or her keeper, out of as much money as she can' (55, TM; 83).

Such generalizations tend to reduce Berthe's impact as an individual character, and seek to justify the novel's cynicism about conventional marriage.

Unlike Zola in *Pot Luck*, Huysmans chose not to pursue the implications of his analysis with respect to bourgeois women. It was open to him, for instance, to criticize their typical upbringing and education, and the convention that they marry an older man. In the novel's opening dialogue he has Cyprien denounce the kind of party presented in *Pot Luck* at which bourgeois mothers attempt to find husbands for their daughters: 'Look, there they are: physically, a stall of unripe bosoms and artificial behinds; morally, an eternal dead season of ideas, a dunghill of thoughts in a pink noddle! yes, there they are, the ones who are destined for me' (17, TM; 10). But he presents this custom solely in terms of its impact on men.

Indeed, what is most striking about Huysmans's novel is its brutal candour about male attitudes to women and to sexuality. *Living Together* takes for granted that men need sex and domestic help, and that both, inside or outside marriage, can only be supplied by women. Chastity is not hinted as an option; despite the close friendship between Cyprien and André, neither, even in the most veiled terms, is homosexuality. As early as the opening chapter, before he discovers his wife's infidelity, André declares that better than either sex within marriage, or extra-marital sex as a bachelor, would be to have 'an emetic to make you bring up all the old tendernesses you have inside' (18; 11), so removing the need for any form of sexual contact. Huysmans does not present this wish as inspired by artistic vocation, for both characters are aimless and idle; it therefore seems a response to what he constructs as a general male condition of dependence and sexual irritability.

This response is rooted in part in a deep-seated misogynism that is expressed by the narrator as well as the two main characters. It is the narrator who speaks of Berthe's 'lust for enjoyment and luxury' (54; 81), generalizes about 'the eternal woman' and 'the weakness of her woman's brain' (55; 83, 84), announces the 'undeniable truth that, no matter how stupid and dense a woman may be, she will always dupe the shrewdest and most intelligent man' (57, TM; 88), and presents Berthe as rationalizing her adultery with 'the stock arguments, the reasonings prepared and dished up by entire generations of women, excuses for all their low actions and all their faults' (62, TM; 99). Later the narrator remarks that 'weariness of feminine stupidity had cured André of women' (119; 213), though the cure is not to last; and that 'women are either early or late, but never on time' (125; 226), despite the fact that André is waiting because he has arrived far too soon to meet his former mistress from work, which she leaves at exactly the time she has specified. Though the last example invites the surmise that it is André who is being criticized, the text does not bear this out. Instead, while it shows the misogynism both of André and Cyprien, it does nothing to distinguish its own attitudes to women from theirs.

Huysmans's own misogynism is well known. As Annette Kahn remarks, many of his works 'do not contain a female character of any consequence', and 'this very omission reinforces the fact that Huysmans was scared of women, was disgusted by what he considered their stupidity, often despised them for the power they exerted over him, experienced trouble relating to them, and tried hard to live without them'.[14] In keeping with attitudes such as these, what the narrator of *Living Together* calls 'the only happiness which is perhaps complete on earth' consists of 'being warm, in a solitary bed, at home, free to smoke, free to read, without any sort of discomfort and without the obligation to listen and answer' (110, TM; 196). But a solitary bed leaves sexual frustration unappeased, so compounding the misogynism. For 'this indescribable discomfort which had to end in carnal relaxation' (198; 376), as the narrator terms it, produces a dynamic in which the man despises the woman who provides relief. It is such a dynamic that both accounts for the phrase 'petticoat crisis' that the narrator applies to André's periods of frustration, and uses their under-garments to represent his lust. Thus André says that, 'having studied women', he has 'acquired a confounded contempt for them' (20, TM; 16); and thus, on the other hand, Cyprien's 'exemplary concubinage' with Mélie is 'a union where the senses were exhausted' (171; 322). Provider of basic comforts, Mélie seems less a concubine than a compound of mother and wet-nurse, Cyprien describing her as 'mature, calm, devoted, without amorous needs, without coyness and without affectation; in a word, a powerful and pacific cow' (180; 338).

Living Together may be understood as a display of impotent resentment from an alienated male intellectual. Anticipating Zola in his essay 'Adultery among the Bourgeoisie' and in *Pot Luck*, the novel presents bourgeois women as frigid; and it suggests that lower-class women are more likely to provide domestic as well as sexual comfort, however unsuitable they may be considered in other respects as wives for bourgeois men. In this way Huysmans turns the novel of wifely adultery inside out, focusing on male desire, not female, and on the cuckolded but promiscuous husband rather than his erring but passionless wife. Robert E. Ziegler has argued that 'Huysmans's pessimistic works are less concerned with repellent mistresses and meals than they are overwhelmed by their own content, glutted with a feminised or alimentary reality no longer susceptible of sublimation into literature'.[15] Yet literature is what they are, and what they represent is not so much a 'feminised or alimentary reality' as an ideological paradigm based on assumptions about women, male biological needs and social class. *Living Together* is more accurately described in one of Ziegler's concluding phrases as a 'self-autopsying book auguring the death of the literary movement it exemplifies'.[16] If, however, the novel foreshadows the end of the Realist and Naturalist movements, and with them that of the novel of wifely adultery, it does so not, as Ziegler suggests, because of some 'intuitive understanding that interaction with others in the context of the real is incompatible with writing',[17] but because the assumptions behind their construction of 'the real' were in process of collapse. Indeed, Huysmans himself was already on the verge of his successive transformations into decadent, symbolist, and Catholic.

Henry Céard's reversal of the conventions of adultery fiction in *A Lovely Day* complements Huysmans's in *Living Together*. Céard's approach is more direct in that he begins by raising stock expectations. His central character, styled throughout as Madame Duhamain, is 'scarcely thirty', the age of wifely adultery defined by Balzac's eponymous heroine;[18] and the opening sentence sets her up for a fall by declaring that her 'virtue was established above suspicion' (9; 3).[19] Further clues are that she is dissatisfied with both marriage and spouse (e.g., 15–16; 13–15); and that the latter has 'read Balzac' (14; 11) – implicitly *The Physiology of Marriage*, that manual for the suspicious husband.[20] Through an early description of the heroine, the text even offers a mildly erotic suggestion of future pleasures:

> She had just washed, and from the handkerchief pulled out to stifle a little cough, from her sky-blue dressing-gown, which fitted her perfectly and emphasized the outline of her hips and the soft lines of her uncorseted body, from her mouth, from her

freshly washed hands – from every part of her plump little person there emanated a disturbing perfume. It was an odour of jasmine, an expensive perfume to which, in spite of her husband, the surviving coquetry of Madame Duhamain clung. As she stood there, her face pink with emotion, with all the shyness of a boarding-school miss and the ripe graces of a mature woman, she was enormously desirable. (20, TM; 22–3)

The novel's action (such as it is) is narrated in flashback – formally, its most unconventional feature. Nevertheless, Céard keeps open the expectations he has invited, for the phrase 'her adventure, a very brief little romance' (10; 5) leaves in suspense the question whether it is to seduction that Madame Duhamain will have yielded by the end. The omens seem propitious when she attends a ball at which she is irritated by her husband and responds to the advances of Trudon, a womanizing neighbour, so far as to grant him an assignation, especially when she accompanies him to a private room in a restaurant redolent with 'the week's accumulated odours of wedding-parties and love-affairs' (70; 112). Even before the two arrive, the narrator suggests she is succumbing with the remark: 'Like a woman fallen into the water, whose skirts weigh her down and whose strength is exhausted, she did not struggle but let herself sink into this stream of soft words' (56, TM; 87). And although, ironically, the private room does not help Trudon's designs, the question whether she will yield is not closed till the end of the novel; it is even briefly revived as they leave in one of those vehicles notorious for illicit sex, a hackney cab.

However, there are signs that Céard is not so much following as playing with the conventions almost from the start. The meeting that first inspires the two with desire stems from an incident that is both unromantic and slyly symbolic: one of Trudon's flower-boxes in his flat above leaks water, 'perhaps because of an invisible crack in one of the pots' (19; 20) – the cracked vessel being a familiar image of broken chastity.[21] Other images give further evidence of playfulness, as when the narrator observes that Madame Duhamain has 'a flavour of her husband about her comparable to the flavour of cork which certain wines have' (63; 100). The discreet salacity of the comparison both alludes to and, through its comic innuendo, distances itself from libertine connoisseurship. But the central joke of Céard's novel is, of course, that its suggestiveness is only play and leads to no action. Whereas Flaubert has Madame Bovary rediscover 'in adultery all the platitudes of marriage',[22] Céard has his heroine make a further cognitive step without even having taken the sexual one: 'whatever way she turned, marriage and adultery alike offered her the same prospect of stupidity [. . .]. When it came to a choice of banality, she preferred the legal platitude' (94; 153).

From a literary point of view, the furthest variation that could be played on the theme of wifely transgression was to have the heroine learn the emptiness of adultery without it even having taken place. It is in this sense that, as David Baguley suggests in a remark I have already quoted, the novel represents 'an attempt to rewrite *Madame Bovary* in the mode of *L'Education sentimentale'*.[23] But the remark should not be taken to imply that *A Lovely Day* is merely a travesty or a jeu d'esprit. First, Céard's novel, like the two by Flaubert, is part of the nineteenth-century French intelligentsia's long-running offensive against the bourgeoisie. Céard's plot is itself an affront to bourgeois decencies, presenting as it does all the paraphernalia of adultery fiction but without so much as giving its heroine a moral reason for defeating temptation. The novel shows its cynicism when Trudon is described as pouring forth 'all the usual twaddle of love, the imbecile declarations, exhausting the formulae beneath which brutal desire is concealed by gallant phraseology' (36; 52); and it displays its Naturalist credentials in such images as that which describes the Seine as 'green as a stream of pus' (121; 201). Céard puts to especially adept use the long hours in which his adulterous couple *manqué* have to wait in their private room for the rain to stop. The newspapers with which they try to relieve their boredom allow him to ridicule contemporary journalism and its readers: he parodies an obituary, providing a farcically gnomic mock-quotation from Victor Hugo (155–6; 264–6), and he paints a sketch of 'a local conservative' who pays half-price for his daily once the restaurant has finished with it and reads it to his family who, the narrator adds, 'all thought highly of the paper which provided them with pretentious formulae in which to express the innate poverty of their ideas' (133; 224, 225). Most of all, the boredom that engulfs an assignation that should, by convention, be full of excitement reinforces the novel's display of bourgeois tedium and inanity.

At the same time, however, there is more at stake. In particular, as Baguley and others have pointed out, *A Lovely Day* conveys a sense of disillusionment and existential emptiness that Céard and several of his colleagues had found expressed by Schopenhauer, though in a different key.[24] The theme is most explicit near the end

when the narrator remarks that Madame Duhamain 'became
obscurely aware of certain philosophical reflections':

> She realized that the heart is sad, not as a result of the continual
> sorrows that wound it, but of its attempts at escaping its
> condition. The ideal it demands as a release shows itself even
> more murderous than the vulgarities it tries to evade. [. . .] She
> divined what depths of folly are manifest in constant rebellion
> against this law of universal mediocrity which presses upon the
> world as despotically as the law of gravitation and bends it to its
> will, and she saw the necessity of staying in one's place and of
> trying to make oneself as inconspicuous as possible, in order to
> lessen the risk of adventures, and to provoke as little as possible
> the disconcerting unleashings of fate. (194–5, TM; 338–9)

It is significant that it is a woman to whom Céard assigns the
novel's key intuition. In contrast, he portrays the husband as crass
and allows the lover only basic awareness, as when he describes
Trudon as 'dumbfounded by the difference that he had discovered
between the exaltation of literature and the platitude of life' (82,
TM; 131). Trudon is able to recognize what the narrator calls 'the
uniformity of all manifestations of sexual pleasure' (147, TM; 250).
But this does not prevent him from finding a woman more
compliant than Madame Duhamain on his return; and, though he
has no shame about sex, he is conventional enough for repulsion at
a different physical function that his companion has to discharge
before they leave the restaurant: 'He could not pardon women for
publicly satisfying needs which he regarded as vulgar and entirely
destructive of romance' (164; 282).

The narrator's scorn for prudery over female physical functions is
in keeping with the novel's frank materialism. More important, the
fact that it is only the heroine who grasps the narrator's philosophy
distinguishes *A Lovely Day* not only from *Madame Bovary* but from
the misogynism that is implicit and sometimes explicit in other
fiction of wifely adultery – as Huysmans's *Living Together* only too
fully witnesses. In this respect the novel points beyond that
tradition, and in further ways beyond Naturalism itself. On the one
hand, as Baguley shows, *A Lovely Day* is 'a key naturalist text';[25]
on the other, as he indicates in an essay published in the same year as
his book, others have claimed it as 'a work ahead of its time'.
Indeed, they have gone so far as to compare its thematic and formal

experiments to 'Beckett, Ionesco, and the *nouveau roman*', 'Dujardin's *Les Lauriers sont coupés* or the stream of consciousness of *Ulysses*', 'the contemporary novel', with its 'minute description, the banal characters and situations, the use of *conversation* and *sous-conversation*', and 'the circadian or "one-day" novel'.[26]

Another motif, the importance of dreaming, takes the novel in a different direction still, and again Céard grants a crucial intuition to his heroine: 'The ideal love which she had tried to achieve seemed less remote; through the gross stupidity of the individual she could discern it just as she could see the lights in the distance through the fog' (176; 304). This evokes a Platonic ideal world behind that of appearance, and one that, surprisingly, the novel's Naturalist attack on illusions does not dispel. Instead, irony yields to a pathos hardly characteristic of Naturalism as the two main figures recognize their defeat: 'both Trudon and Madame Duhamain, separated by reality, were brought together by a similar expansion of their whole being, by an identical aspiration after inaccessible loves, and the thought of leaving each other was painful not so much because it meant physical separation as because it put an end to their dreams' (179–80; 310). The notion that dreaming has value even survives the narrator's remark that, 'Too preoccupied in achieving the ideal, perhaps they had missed a happiness that no power of will or circumstance could ever bring back to them' (186, TM; 322). Not only does this leave the existence of the ideal unquestioned, but it recalls the novel's single idyllic sequence, in which the two would-be lovers imagine a day in the country together (56–8; 87–90). The sequence begins with the first use in the novel of the phrase Céard took for his title, 'A lovely day'. It is, of course, Madame Duhamain who utters it, and, although it is ironized repeatedly in what follows, the novel does not discount the value of their dream.

In allowing a space for the ideal, *A Lovely Day* looks forward not only to the developments summarized by Baguley but to Symbolism as well. Nevertheless, the facts that the novel is centred on a woman and that it encourages containment of her desire show its links with the tradition it parodies. *A Lovely Day* goes beyond a feminine reprise of *Sentimental Education* to offer, quite literally, a chastening.

Hennique's *L'Accident de Monsieur Hébert* is a more stereotypically Naturalist text – it is significant that, though first published two years after Céard's novel, a letter from Zola to Hennique shows that it was conceived as early as 1878.[27] As O. R. Morgan points out,

Hennique pays homage to Flaubert and Zola respectively by producing his own versions of the scene at the agricultural show in *Madame Bovary* and of the maid Adèle's messy and painful labour in *Pot Luck*.[28] Indeed, he goes one better than Zola not only in the repulsiveness of his account but in making the labour abortive; and there is a further echo of *Pot Luck* in that, like Marie Pichon's affair with Octave, Gabrielle Hébert's with Ventujol begins, as Nicholas White has emphasized, with rape.[29] Unlike Céard, Hennique leaves no space for dreams: Gabrielle's *bovarysme* is almost ludicrously banal, and the *fête champêtre* pictured fondly in advance by the bourgeois characters ends as a rout.[30] *L'Accident de Monsieur Hébert* is much closer to Huysmans's *Living Together* in its misogynism and also in its ending, which simply reinstates the marriage from which the heroine tries to escape. The laconic title, which refers to a wife's adultery as an 'accident' – and one that, moreover, happens not to her but to her husband – is of a piece with this downbeat closure. However, it is questionable whether as White argues, the novel's parodic treatment of adultery goes so far as to suggest 'a decaying society in which the order of signs and things is radically confused'.[31] The more likely implication of *L'Accident de Monsieur Hébert* is that, at least in fiction, wifely adultery no longer signifies.

If, as I argue in Chapter 7, Zola's work develops the novel of female adultery, and if the examples by Huysmans, Céard and Hennique point beyond it, the work of a fifth member of the Médan group, Guy de Maupassant (1850–93), epitomizes most fully the tradition's demise in France. Maupassant often addressed the questions of marriage and adultery in his journalism, and five of his six novels, along with many of his 300 or so short stories, either turn on or feature an adultery plot. Most of these plots are of female, indeed wifely, adultery; yet in several ways they represent a development beyond the adultery fiction of Zola, Huysmans, Céard and Hennique. Because this book is mainly about the novel of wifely adultery, and because space is limited, the following discussion focuses on Maupassant's longer fiction. However, two short pieces written early in his career show his interest in the subject and lay down some of the attitudes behind it.

As Louis Forestier notes, Maupassant might have given his sketch 'In Times Past' ('Jadis', 1880; 1883; 1900) Diderot's title 'This Is Not a Story'.[32] It consists less of a narrative than a dialogue between a young girl and her grandmother, centred on the difference between love in the present and the past. Two newspaper articles read out by the girl typify love in the present: one about a wife revenging herself with vitriol on her husband's mistress, the other about a jilted spinster shooting her unfaithful lover. These contrast only too sharply with the grandmother's nostalgic memories of Old Regime gallantry. In the longest speech in the dialogue the grandmother puts forward an Enlightenment view of the matter:

> Marriage and love have nothing in common. We marry to found a family, and we form families in order to constitute society. Society cannot dispense with marriage. [. . .] We marry only once, my child, because the world requires us to do so, but we may love twenty times in one lifetime because nature has made us able to do this. Marriage, you see, is a law, and love is an instinct, which pushes us sometimes to the right, sometimes to the left. Laws have been made to combat our instincts – it was necessary to make them; but our instincts are always stronger, and we ought not to resist them too much, because they come from God, while laws only come from men. (V, 12, TM; I, 183)[33]

The impersonal narrator does not leave this position unqualified, as he calls the grandmother one of 'those people who did not believe that they were of the same clay as others, and who lived as grandees for whom common beliefs were not made' (V, 13, TM; I, 184). Nevertheless, he credits her with 'that charming, healthy logic with which the gallant philosophers seasoned the eighteenth century', and she has the last word, responding to the girl's wish for 'a single eternal passion, according to the dream of modern poets' with the remark: 'If you believe in such follies as that, you will be very unhappy' (V, 14, TM; I, 184–5). In this way Maupassant uses a female figure to finesse encouragement for wifely adultery.

As Edward D. Sullivan remarks, 'Maupassant, following the lead of the Goncourts, frequently expressed a definite nostalgia for the eighteenth century'.[34] Forestier points out that the grandmother's account of love under the Old Regime evokes the Goncourts' *Woman in the Eighteenth Century* (*La Femme au dix-huitième siècle*, 1862), and he quotes Maupassant's praise of the work as 'the most admirable that I know that deals with the art of being a woman'.[35] In January 1882 Maupassant quoted a lengthy passage from the same book in an essay on adultery that he published in *Le Gaulois* to coincide with the first instalment in the same paper of Zola's *Pot Luck*. The essay is more than a puff for his friend's novel, of which he says in his opening sentence that he knows almost nothing. Instead, it gives evidence of an informed, sceptical curiosity about the institution of marriage and the practice of adultery, especially in its awareness of how attitudes towards both vary historically and between different classes. Maupassant strikes the detached, ironical keynote of his essay when he reflects that, though the topic is scarcely new, 'it would make a very intriguing study to investigate in what way, now humorous, now tragic, successive generations have judged the deficiencies to this legal coupling that is called marriage'.[36] His quotation from the Goncourts supports his claim that adultery was often condoned in the past; he contrasts bourgeois condemnation with the much greater tolerance he finds in the upper and lower classes; and he speculates about a question he was often to address in his fiction, that of the *ménage à trois*.

In his first two novels, *A Life* (*Une Vie*, 1883) and *Bel-Ami* (1885), Maupassant addresses the subject of adultery by, as it were, going back in order to go forward. As Forestier observes, *A Life* is the only novel by Maupassant that does not have a contemporary setting,[37] and David Baguley, quoting Lukács, claims that it is typical of Naturalism in dissociating private from public life: 'the essential action of the novel is quite "timeless"; the Restoration, the July Revolution, the July Monarchy etc., events which objectively must make an extremely deep impression upon the daily life of an aristocratic *milieu*, play practically no part'.[38] Although in most respects this statement is valid, it does not take account of the extent to which the novel historicizes its presentation of adultery. *A Life* reverses the novel of female adultery by telling the story of a wife and mother whose life is determined not only by her marriage, as the form requires, but, wholly unconventionally, by adultery on the part of her husband, not herself. At the same time, by showing the behaviour of three generations, it offers an historical perspective on attitudes to adultery.

Julien de Lamare, husband of the heroine Jeanne, has two affairs soon after marrying her. First, he seduces their maid straight after returning from honeymoon and has a child by her, born shortly before the child Jeanne bears him. She is given no choice but to overlook his betrayal, though she cannot accept it emotionally: even the priest urges her to forgive him, and her father, outraged at first, has to admit to the priest that he has himself had affairs, including with female servants. The priest gets the maid married off to a man from her own class with the help of a dowry provided by Jeanne's father, leaving Jeanne – as Maupassant defines it – the only victim. Since the period is the early nineteenth century, and since all the characters except the maid and priest are from the minor nobility, the episode recalls the attitudes to adultery that Maupassant attributes in his essay in *Le Gaulois* to the old aristocracy and to the lower classes. But Julien's second affair is with a married neighbour of the same social rank, and Maupassant has it coincide with the ministry of a new priest who is fanatically puritan. Having found that Jeanne knows of the liaison, and having tried and failed to force her to confront Julien, the priest informs the betrayed husband, who, finding the adulterous couple in the caravan where they have been making love, pushes it over a cliff and kills them.

The contrasting outcomes of Julien's two adulterous affairs not only register the obvious point that it is much more dangerous for him to take as his lover a married woman from his own social class than an unmarried servant. They also suggest, through the new priest's violent reaction as well as the betrayed husband's, that in Maupassant's view the relaxed attitude to adultery characteristic of the old aristocracy was giving way to intolerance in the 1820s when these events are set. The point is reinforced by Jeanne's response, especially because, between her discovery of the affair and its fatal conclusion, she discovers that her mother, who dies suddenly, has had a secret affair with a family friend. Her triple shock – at both of Julien's affairs and her mother's – provides the novel's turning-point. Yet, although Maupassant presents her as capable of sensual and sexual responsiveness, and although she is fond of the Count whose wife her husband seduces, infidelity never tempts her. The contrast with her mother suggests, again, that adultery was becoming much less acceptable, especially for women. Distanced historically both from the period it represents and from the heyday of the novel of wifely adultery, *A Life* looks back to the years during which the attitudes that produced the form were cohering.

Nevertheless, the most striking difference between Maupassant's first novel and the novel of wifely adultery is its representation of motherhood. Channelling all her affection to her son Paul after her husband's betrayal, Jeanne over-indulges him, with the result that he runs off with his mistress and spends all his inheritance. Worse still, the daughter Jeanne has after foiling her husband's efforts at contraception is stillborn, as if figuring the marriage's emptiness. In contrast, the illegitimate son of the maid Rosalie turns out well. These outcomes question the conventional wisdom that a woman's vocation is to be a faithful wife and mother: Jeanne is both, but to little avail; while Rosalie's marriage, albeit arranged when she is pregnant by another man, is successful, and her only child, though adulterine, in no way suffers from her transgression. In these ways *A Life* steps outside and beyond the fiction of wifely adultery, though it echoes other texts of its period, like Céard's *A Lovely Day*, through its theme of ever-renewed hope and disillusionment, and through the choice of a female character as its vehicle.

In his second novel Maupassant returned to the past in a different way. As Robert Lethbridge remarks, the originality of *Bel-Ami* 'lies in its reconfiguration of the themes and structures of the classic nineteenth-century realist novel'. But it is not just, as Lethbridge shows, that the novel pays homage to Flaubert and Zola and ironic acknowledgement to Balzac, while playing a further variation on the theme of the young man from the provinces that goes as far back as Marivaux.[39] In presenting the rise of Georges Duroy from a menial of government to one of its masters, the novel also refocuses the theme of wifely adultery. It centres not on any of the three women whose adultery is pivotal to its action but on the man who exploits them entirely to his own advantage. In doing so, however, it does not so much celebrate male supremacy as betray a growing anxiety about female power.

There are instructive contrasts between *Bel-Ami* and two of the novels from the period immediately before the rise of the novel of wifely adultery on which it draws. Stendhal's *The Red and the Black* and Balzac's *Le Père Goriot* chart the progress of ambitious but penniless provincials through the help of socially superior women. Like Julien Sorel, though unlike Eugène de Rastignac, Duroy is of plebeian stock despite his ironically regal surname. But there are two marked differences. First, Maupassant's hero has no moral scruples to shed. This is unlike not only Rastignac, who loses his during the course of the story, but, more strikingly, Sorel, who commits a crime that condemns him to death rather than brook the suspicion that he owes his success to strategic seductions. Maupassant's presentation of his hero is therefore much more ambivalent, especially because at the same time the novel invites criticism of the world he typifies. The second difference is that, though all three texts centre not on sexually transgressive women but on sexually and (in two cases) socially transgressive men, only

Maupassant's displays the stereotypes of femininity and female sexuality that define the novel of wifely adultery. Although *Bel-Ami* shows it has assimilated those stereotypes, it also starts to move beyond them; but this movement is complicated by the ambivalent presentation of the hero.

In order of their relationships with Duroy, the novel's main female characters are Clotilde de Marelle, who becomes his mistress and forgives his repeated betrayals; Madeleine Forestier, who rejects his advances but marries him after the death of her husband, only to cuckold him as she had his predecessor; and Mme Walter, a middle-aged woman noted for her chastity who falls for him head over heels. Each of these is a different type of adulterous wife. Clotilde is a high-class slut: despite the 'fastidious, refined elegance' (I.v.61; 254)[40] of her person, her home is neglected and she has Duroy take her slumming in working-class bars. Madeleine, on the other hand, is a woman whose sexuality is bound up with an appetite for power. The fact that she hides her desire for Duroy 'as though it were a weakness' (II.i.156; 349) shows that it is both strong and highly controlled, and, though she meets her match in him, she is adept at managing powerful men. She provides inside information and copy for both her journalist husbands, and she has affairs with the Comte de Vaudrec, who dies and leaves her all his money, and the politician Laroche-Mathieu from whom she obtains financial and political secrets. In terms of the dominant fictional codes, Mme Walter is the most conventional adulteress of the three, a bourgeois wife who has never known sexual passion or fulfilment and whose liaison with Duroy unhinges, abases and prematurely ages her.

These three types of adulterous wife suggest how far Maupassant had absorbed the themes of the novel of female adultery. They are, however, quite different from the taxonomy put forward by Zola in his essay 'Adultery among the Bourgeoisie' and in *Pot Luck*. Their sexuality is presented as natural, not pathological, and Maupassant gives them a larger role in the narrative economy. Although the narrative voice of *Bel-Ami* is impersonal and the hero is the main character-focalizer, Maupassant also allows each of the main female characters to focalize. The effect is to highlight their dominant traits and so to distinguish them further. Clotilde. is presented as swallowing brandied cherries with 'the feeling of committing a sin', every drop giving her 'the pleasure of a wicked, forbidden gratification' (I.v.77; 271); whereas Madeleine's need to control is emphasized by contrast when she is out of her depth on a visit to Duroy's parents: 'it seemed to her that she was lost, overwhelmed, surrounded by dangers, abandoned by everyone, alone, alone in the world, beneath this living canopy which rustled high up above' (II.i.168; 362). There is a similar pathos in Maupassant's presentation of Mme Walter's feelings when she is struggling with her desire for Duroy – 'And now, in this church, very close to God, she felt herself weaker, more forsaken, more lost even than in her own home' (II.iv.205; 398) – and later when she is betrayed by him: 'She was overcome by a kind of inertia which fettered her limbs and left only her mind alert, although this was haunted and tormented by frightful, unreal, fanciful images' (II.ix.279; 470). Only to Mme Walter's daughter Suzanne does Maupassant grant the kind of imagination that Flaubert had given Emma Bovary, as she dreams of 'never-ending highways bathed in eternal moonlight, dark forests traversed, roadside inns, and ostlers hurrying to bring fresh horses' (II.ix.273; 463).[41] Ironically, however, Suzanne's fantasy comes true, and she elopes not for adultery but marriage.

Given the sharp differences between these characters, it is striking that Maupassant uses them all as pretexts for generalizations about femininity. Describing Clotilde's behaviour, the narrator refers to 'the way women smile in offering their desire, their consent, their readiness to surrender' (I.v.68; 262), and to 'one of those feminine hesitations so transient as to be barely noticeable' (I.v.75–6; 269). Similarly, he observes that Madeleine is gratified by a remark from Duroy 'as women are by compliments that speak directly to their heart' (I.vi.90; 284); he comments in a very different context that she is shocked by the word cuckold, 'as are all women' (II.ii.179; 373); and, when she is disappointed by their visit to his parents, he exclaims: 'As if women do not always hope for something other than what actually is!' (II.i.166; 360). The generalizations about Mme Walter are more demeaning. About to yield to Duroy, she has what the narrator calls 'one of those attacks of hysteria that fling women to the ground, quivering, howling, and writhing' (II.iv.205; 398); and the same voice later ascribes to her 'one of those superstitious notions that in women often take the place of reasoning' (II.v.225; 417). In these ways the novel rehearses a familiar discourse of woman as easily subject to her emotions and her sexuality, even though the behaviour of individual characters – especially Madeleine – does not always confirm and sometimes even contradicts this.

The novel's discourse on woman is in keeping with its overtly masculine tenor. Despite the doctrine of objectivity that Maupassant had learned from Flaubert, and despite there being many women among his readers, both the narrator and the position he constructs for the reader are masculine. The most explicit example is the way a phrase quoted above continues: 'and she gave him one of those rapid, grateful glances that makes us their slaves' (I.vi.90; 284); but all the generalizations have the same effect. Maupassant employs the old realist trick of flattering the reader into collusive agreement, as with the phrase 'one of those' to introduce a generalization, that appears in three of the examples quoted. Similarly, his descriptions of women invite a masculine sexual gaze, as with Madeleine, who wears 'a gown of pale blue cashmere which showed off her supple figure and full breasts to advantage' (I.ii.19; 212); Clotilde, whose dress 'clung to her waist, her hips, her breasts, and her arms in a tantalizing, alluring way' (I.v.61; 254); Mme Walter, whose low-cut bodice, 'beneath the golden lace, hinted at generously rounded breasts' (II.iii.187; 380); and Suzanne, who has 'the look of a delicate blond doll, too small, but dainty, with a slender waist, shapely hips and breasts' (II.iii.184; 377). Lethbridge identifies the narrative tone aptly when he remarks that many of the novel's turns of phrase 'resemble those of a conversation between men' (Introduction, xxiii). The fact that Maupassant was able to maintain such a tone in a novel intended for a mixed readership illustrates the dominance of masculinist ideology in the France of the period.

What is more complex ideologically is the novel's presentation of its hero and his success. For Lethbridge, 'we are constantly made aware of Duroy's illusions and yet subscribe to his point of view' (xxxv), because 'the vicarious, albeit gendered, experience of domination and control' invites 'a sneaking sympathy' (xlii). Yet, although Duroy is the novel's central consciousness, and although he succeeds in dominating and controlling others, men as well as women, both the nature of his role and its presentation raise questions. His role is that of an unscrupulous seducer who exploits women for ambition as well as sex. Madeleine writes his first article for him, and he marries her after her first husband dies, relying on her in his career as political journalist both for copy and inside information, obtaining a half share of her legacy from the Comte de Vaudrec, but ultimately divorcing her when he sees that his interest lies elsewhere. He pursues that interest not only by cold-bloodedly surprising his wife with her lover to obtain the divorce, but, with rank hypocrisy, seducing Mme Walter, from whom he obtains even more privileged information and whom he discards before eloping with and marrying her daughter. His only more or less continuous relationship is with the woman who least benefits his career, Clotilde. Although he often betrays her, she always returns – indeed, the novel ends on the day of his marriage to Suzanne Walter by suggesting he is about to take her back once more.

While much less stark in its implications than this summary of Duroy's career, Maupassant's presentation of his hero is scarcely uncritical. Early in the novel, through the response of Clotilde's young daughter, he gives an example quite unrelated to the plot of Duroy's use of his charm and lack of concern for the consequences; and, when Duroy first meets Clotilde's husband, he portrays him feeling a 'very private, vicious satisfaction, the joy of a successful thief who is not suspected' (I.vi.110; 305). The chapter in which Duroy succeeds in seducing Mme Walter ends with him thinking callously, in response to her avowal that she has never had a lover, 'As if I care!' (II.iv.212; 405); Mme Walter guesses and judges correctly when, confronted by her daughter's elopement, she exclaims to herself: 'What a scoundrel, if he had planned this!' (II.ix.275; 466); and the novel ends with him 'thinking only of himself' in his euphoria on the day of his wedding – but then of Clotilde in the closing words. Elsewhere the narrator distances himself from Duroy by pointing to the 'innate heedlessness' (II.i.153; 346) that helps him survive and that links him to the courtesan (I.vi.109; 304) or gypsy (II.v.220; 412). It is this incapacity for reflection that both enables his success and limits him, as when, inspired to 'vast conjectures' by the silence of the church in which he has gone to meet Mme Walter, he 'disposed of the Creation in a single thought, muttering: "How stupid all that is"' (II.iv.202; 395); or when, after the narrator has described a painting of Christ walking on the water as 'one of those works that turn your ideas upside down, and linger in the mind for years', Duroy's sole comment, 'after gazing at it from some time', is: 'Nice to be able to treat yourself to baubles like that' (II.vii.248; 439).

Although examples such as these invite criticism rather than give it directly, their cumulative impact would be considerable if it were not for a fact that, once more, distinguishes *Bel-Ami* from novels of wifely adultery. Because, as a male, Duroy has access to the public sphere of finance and politics, he can function as the main vehicle for a critique of contemporary commerce and politics in a way that a female character could not; and for this reason his ruthlessness and immorality are less significant for what they tell about him as a character than for what they show about the system in which men such as he can triumph. All the same, the terms in which Lethbridge suggests the reader is invited to sympathize with Duroy are also significant. There is a logical though not necessarily an imaginative or ideological contradiction between the critique offered by the novel and what Lethbridge calls a 'vicarious, albeit gendered, experience of domination and control'. At the ideological level this contradiction may be resolved by asking over whom the reader is encouraged to feel dominant. The novel provides two main answers: not only women, but also male rivals. Duroy succeeds by replacing or defeating Forestier, Madeleine's first husband; de Marelle, Clotilde's civil servant husband who is usually away on business; the Comte de Vaudrec, Madeleine's rich lover; Laroche-Mathieu, the politician lover with whom he finds her in bed; and Walter, the financier who runs the newspaper for which he works. By identifying as the protagonist's male victims such popular butts of the period as a civil servant, an aristocrat, a lawyer turned politician and a Jewish financier, Maupassant encouraged ordinary readers and disaffected intellectuals like himself to take Duroy's side. He also increased Duroy's appeal for masculine readers by having him succeed through his ability to dominate women.

This appeal is heightened by two related themes that run through the novel. The first is impotence, as on the various occasions when Duroy is at a loss: when he cannot write his first article; when Clotilde publicly humiliates him on discovering he has betrayed her; when the prostitute Rachel insults him; when he propositions Madeleine and she coolly rebuffs him; when he has to accept her terms in marrying her; or when, on several occasions, 'her lively, subtle intelligence' (II.i.157; 350) disconcerts him. The second is rage, which the novel portrays him as feeling again and again: at the start against the diners who can afford as he cannot to eat and drink freely; in the first phase of his liaison with Clotilde when he runs out of money; at the rival journalist whose insults force him into fighting a duel; and above all at the success of others that for a time dwarfs his own. The link between the two themes becomes explicit when Duroy visits Walter's mansion and, unable to imagine how he could obtain such a prize, grows 'angry at his own impotence' (II.vii.247; 438). By dramatizing his protagonist's envy and resentment Maupassant extended his appeal to a mass readership, especially one with male-centred interests, and this helps explain the ambivalence of the presentation. Duroy's energy and sense of 'superhuman strength' (I.ii.25; 218) pull against his ruthlessness and lack of principle. They even look forward, when he feels at the end that he is 'becoming one of the masters of the earth' (II.x.288; 478), to Nietzsche's *Übermensch* a few years later.

The equivocal nature of Duroy's triumph is significant because, as Lethbridge says, his 'sexual confidence is perilously close to a fear of rejection', so that a feminist or a psychoanalytical reading might find in the novel 'less a narrative of conquest than a virility under threat and an ambiguous sexuality seeking a Don Juanesque reassurance' (xxv, xxvi). The presentation of male and female sexuality shows a similar element of ambivalence. A generalization about 'the capriciousness of female desire' (II.ii.181; 374) is followed in the next chapter by one about 'the novelty which men always want' (II.iii.198; 391); and, if Madeleine's gaze when Duroy first meets her reminds him of the prostitute he has met the night before (I.ii.19; 212–13), he not only succeeds through his own sexuality but is paid for sexual favours by both Clotilde and Mme Walter. Nevertheless, if the theme of impotent rage suggests tensions behind the narrative, Duroy's success, above all with women, offers to soothe them, reinforcing the power of the dominant male and using it to overwhelm the threat of transgressive female sexuality.

In these ways, and without centring its narrative on an adulterous woman, *Bel-Ami* both sustains the themes of the novel of wifely adultery and begins to point beyond them. It ties those themes to a critical account of a man's success in a corrupt society, recognizes them to some extent as problematic, and yet still applies them to legitimate male hegemony. The novel goes a long way beyond Feuillet's *Monsieur de Camors*, which in some ways it resembles.[42] Yet, in the same way as it does not introduce new fictional techniques but refines those of the established realist novel, it marks the end of a tradition rather than inaugurates a new one.

In his next two novels, *Mont-Oriol* (1887) and *Pierre and Jean* (1888), Maupassant addressed in opposite ways an aspect of wifely adultery he had ignored in *Bel-Ami*, that of paternity. Critics have often recognized the large role played in his work by the related questions of illegitimacy and doubtful paternity, and, according to Lethbridge, even the more sober estimates 'conclude that between thirty and forty of his texts include variations on the theme'.[43] A further motif, conspicuous in *Pierre and Jean* and often discussed by the novel's critics, is that of the Oedipus complex. In a wide-ranging essay on *A Life*, Naomi Schor puts these two issues together. First, she states what she claims is 'the great law that rules all sexual relationships in Maupassant: *the necessary separation of the pleasant and the useful*'. According to this, 'if a woman has a child by her lover, she will not have one by her husband, and vice versa'.[44] Significantly, the main exceptions to this law are among characters from the aristocracy, the class noted for more tolerant attitudes to sexual misconduct; and, as she observes, 'in the rare cases where the taboo is violated (because it is obviously a question of an interdiction), such as in *Pierre et Jean* or *Le Testament*, the lover's son is favoured by the mother at the expense of the legitimate son or sons'. Second, Schor connects the paternal and the Oedipal themes: 'in promoting the separation of the pleasant and the useful, Maupassant does little more than place an eighteenth-century aristocratic morality in the service of an oedipal fantasy, which consists of flouting the husband (the legitimate father) by making him sterile and delegating the procreative function to the lover'. What this analysis overlooks, however, is a contradiction in the position of the lover already apparent in *Bel-Ami*. For, if the lover can enjoy cuckolding a husband, he may also suffer anxiety that he is vulnerable to betrayal in turn. The Oedipal fantasy therefore works both ways, so that Duroy is tormented more by the suspicion that Madeleine betrayed her first husband than that she is betraying him. It is not only that, as Mary Donaldson-Evans argues, 'Duroy's jealousy of Forestier, his predecessor, can be seen as an almost classic manifestation of the Oedipus complex.'[45] At the same time, Duroy's jealousy on behalf of Forestier points to anxieties that, in this text, the breaking of the taboo unleashes. Maupassant explored these anxieties in *Pierre and Jean*, breaking decisively with the novel of wifely adultery; but in *Mont-Oriol* he prepared the way.

While *Mont-Oriol* conforms to the tradition of adultery fiction much more directly than *Bel-Ami*, in other respects it looks further beyond the declining form. It is typical of the tradition in that it is a male-authored text, told in an impersonal narrative voice, about the seduction of a married woman from the middle or upper classes by an unmarried man of the same class and the suffering it brings her. Nevertheless, the novel illustrates very clearly, and in two principal ways, not the persistence of the tradition but its displacement. The most obvious difference is that Christiane Andermatt's story is by no means the sole narrative interest. It runs in parallel with a story that Maupassant highlighted in his title about the development of a spa in the Auvergne, and with a subplot about how Christiane's roué brother marries for personal and commercial advantage. In this way the impact of the adultery plot is diffused, especially as the tone is often lightly satirical, and as Maupassant gives not only Christiane's viewpoint but those of other characters too. But the more important difference is that, although the narrator expresses various of the assumptions about femininity that run through nineteenth-century fiction of wifely adultery, the novel gives no intrinsic value to marriage. It is no doubt for this reason that, though Christiane is abandoned by her lover, she, unlike other heroines in the tradition, is otherwise unscathed. The affair stays secret, and Christiane continues in her marriage with the child she has been unable to conceive with her husband.

The reason why the novel gives little significance to marriage is that it defines it merely as 'a contract' (VI.117; I.vi.555).[46] Instead, and in keeping with the grandmother's doctrine in the story 'In Times Past', the only proper link it accepts between men and women is love. Christiane has married without loving her husband, a Jewish financier who develops the spa at Mont-Oriol. Presenting her state of mind after she has yielded to Paul Brétigny for the first time, the narrator comments that her realization that she is in love with him 'acquitted her before her conscience' (VII.134, TM; I.vii.565). Thus, although she recognizes her husband as 'the man who ought to be, according to human ideas of religion, of society, the other half of her – more than that, her master', she believes that 'between her and him no bond could ever exist' and feels 'no remorse' for having betrayed him (XIV.334, 335; II.vi.693). The narrator adds weight to these views by observing that 'to marry and to buy' seem to have the same meaning in her husband's mind (VII.133; I.vii.564), and by referring to him often as 'the banker'. Instead, Christiane comes to look on herself not as her lover's mistress 'but as his wife, his companion, his devotee, his worshiper, his prostrate slave, his chattel' (XI.244, TM; II.iii.636). The novel constructs her as becoming fully a woman only through sexual fulfilment and motherhood, and as essentially passive before the man who 'possessed her as easily as if he were picking a ripe fruit' (VII.126, TM; I.vii.560), or takes her body and soul 'just as a huge bird of prey with large wings swoops down on a wren' (VII.141;

I.vii.570). Nevertheless, this is not a libertine text, and it invites no particular sympathy for Brétigny. At the same time as she is giving birth to their child, he gets engaged to another woman; and, when he goes to visit Christiane, the narrator describes him as feeling 'sunk in one of those moral foulnesses which stain a man's conscience up to the hour of his death' (XIV.343; II.vi.698). It is, accordingly, Christiane who has the novel's core perception when, abandoned by Brétigny in her greatest hour of need, she understands that 'nobody has ever been able, or ever will be able, to break through that invisible barrier which places living beings as far from each other as the stars of heaven' (XIV.333; II.vi.691–2).

In sounding this note of Schopenhauerian pessimism, especially through a female character, *Mont-Oriol* is wholly of its period. However, while these features recall such contemporary work as Céard's *A Lovely Day*, Maupassant's novel, unlike his colleague's, does not parody the fiction of wifely adultery but looks beyond it. Surprisingly, it does this in part through attitudes to love and marriage that are much closer to those conveyed by George Sand in her novels of the 1830s than to those that characterize French fiction during the heyday of Naturalism 50 years later. The key principles behind these attitudes are that only mutual love can legitimate a man and a woman's union, overriding any legal or religious bond; that the woman's vulnerability calls for compassion both in a loveless marriage and in an extra-marital affair; and that a child born from an adulterous liaison is in no way blighted by it. All these principles run directly counter to the governing assumptions of the novel of wifely adultery. They may be found in novels by Sand such as *Indiana* (1832), *Valentine* (1832), or *Jacques* (1834),[47] and they re-emerge in Maupassant's fiction of the 1880s. However, to put it mildly, Maupassant was rarely in conscious agreement with Sand. The qualified support he gives for wifely adultery stems from other motives than hers and, as *Pierre and Jean* makes clear, it has quite different ramifications.

As Edward D. Sullivan has suggested, *Pierre and Jean* is 'a kind of transposed sequel' to *Mont-Oriol*, 'beginning where the earlier novel leaves off'.[48] It presents the psychological impact on a young man of discovering that his mother had a long-standing affair when he was young, and that his younger brother, Jean, is her son by her lover. Pierre finds out the secret after Jean receives an unexpected legacy, but his father never has an inkling either of the affair or of Jean's true paternity. In the scene during which Pierre obtains proof of his suspicion, the narrator lays down a generalization that marks not only the affinity but also the distance between Maupassant's novel and the fiction of wifely adultery: 'The love between man and woman is a voluntary pact in which the one who falls short is only guilty of perfidy, but when a woman has become a mother her duty is greater because nature has entrusted the human species to her' (V.113; 780).[49] The double standard invoked here is characteristic of adultery fiction, though it is rationalized differently: not by a need to protect the inheritance of property, which was the staple excuse, but according to the idea that children are a woman's responsibility. A much larger difference is that marriage is not even mentioned, only the 'voluntary pact' of love. However, what separates *Pierre and Jean* definitively from the tradition of adultery fiction is Pierre's astonishing sense that his mother is 'even more criminally guilty towards him than towards his father'. Since the adulterine son feels no resentment after his brother has told him his parentage, this is the clearest possible evidence that adultery is not the issue.

What Maupassant produced, therefore, in *Pierre and Jean* is not a novel of adultery in retrospect, but the story of an Oedipal crisis in which the mother's lover stands in for the father.[50] Although he gave the mother a speech in which, like Christiane in *Mont-Oriol*, she states that she feels no shame or regret about her affair because she considers herself the 'real wife' of the man she loved (VII.146; 807),[51] the speech is to her lover's son, and she herself plays little role in the narrative. Crucially, Maupassant presents most of the novel from the legitimate son's point of view, giving full play to the pathological hurt and anger stirred up by Oedipal tensions. The most original and forward-looking of his works, it anticipates Freud not only in its presentation of the Oedipus theme but in its awareness of 'the other man who inhabits each one of us' (II.61; 736), and of 'unmentionable, shameful' thoughts 'locked [. . .] in the unfathomable depths of the soul like stolen goods' (IV.86; 757).

Like *Pierre and Jean*, Maupassant's fifth novel, *Fort Comme la Mort* (1889), looks beyond the novel of wifely adultery quite literally in focussing not on the wife's infidelity but on its repercussions long afterwards. It concerns the impact of a long-standing affair not on child, husband or even marriage but on the adulterous couple themselves – especially the lover. The affair has lasted for twelve years when the action starts. What brings it to a crisis is not the fact or the danger of discovery – like Pierre's father, the husband is wholly unsuspicious throughout – but the woman's fear that her lover will find someone else, and its realization when he falls in love with her daughter. In a different way, then, from *Pierre and Jean*, *Fort Comme la Mort* transforms the problem of the adulteress's child discussed in Chapter 3. Like Pierre, Annette de Guilleroy is legitimate, but the key differences are her sex and Maupassant's reversal of narrative perspective, so that in both novels the problem is presented chiefly from a male point of view – in one case the child's, in the other the lover's. These emphases demonstrate once more the masculine bias that runs through Maupassant's work, despite his ability, when he wished, to represent female characters with insight and sympathy.

Annette's mother Any is another adulteress who feels no shame or remorse (I.35; I.i.860) because she believes her affair sanctioned by the love her marriage lacks.[52] Indeed, the narrator classes her as one of those women who are 'honest and straightforward in adultery as they might have been in marriage' (I.43, TM; I.i.865), and shows her lover, Olivier Bertin, wishing he were her husband (I.102; I.iii.904). Yet, although Maupassant presents Any's despair as she tries and fails to keep the looks that she believes bind Bertin to her, the novel is centred much more on his suffering than on hers. When, for example, Bertin realizes that Annette is engaged, Maupassant turns the conventions of adultery fiction upside down by comparing him to 'a deceived husband who is the witness of his wife's crime' (IX.218; II.v.982). If the implications of this parallel are accepted, *Fort Comme la Mort* becomes open, like *Pierre and Jean*, to a psychoanalytical interpretation – though in this case centred on a phenomenon that Freud notoriously played down, the father's sexual attraction to the daughter. Although the novel's most explicit themes are ageing and the fear of artistic failure, its controlling emotional emphasis is on 'the distracted love of an aged man for a young girl' (X.256; II.vi.1007). This is significant because it points to a wider loss of male confidence – already implicit in *Bel-Ami*, given a different treatment in *Pierre and Jean*, and to be developed further in Maupassant's last completed novel, *Notre Coeur* (1890).

Both *Mont-Oriol* and *Pierre and Jean* suggest that there is a further twist to what Naomi Schor formulates as 'the great law that rules all sexual relationships in Maupassant: *the necessary separation of the pleasant and the useful*'.[53] This twist is that the pleasant and useful are defined with respect to male interests alone, so that Brétigny feels repelled by Christiane as soon as she is obviously pregnant, and she is confined to maternity. Such an assumption is in keeping with the double standard about a woman's maternal duty invoked in *Pierre and Jean*, and it shows the distance between Maupassant's position and Sand's. At the same time, however, more is at issue. According to Mary Donaldson-Evans, Maupassant's fiction reveals a marked shift in the view they present of women: in the earlier work they are generally victims, essentially passive; in the later they tend to be *femmes fatales*, even *femmes castatrices*.[54] Madeleine Forestier, in *Bel-Ami*, is an early example of a woman who threatens the hero. In Christopher Lloyd's phrase, Duroy behaves most viciously towards women 'when they begin to assert their own personalities, to become subjects rather than objects'; and it is significant that, as Nicholas White observes, the speech in which she lays down her ground rules for marriage 'reflects (and perhaps stretches) many of the aspirations of conservative feminism in the *fin de siècle*'.[55] If Maupassant's work goes back to sources in his own psychology, as critics have shown, there is a social and a political context too. In 1879, as Claire Goldberg Moses puts it, 'liberal republicans took control of the Senate and the presidency: feminists' friends were now in power'.[56] The legislative rewards were, she continues, authorization of the *Société pour l'Amélioration du Sort des Femmes*, the passing of the Camille Sée education law in 1880, and the divorce law of 1884. But changes in personal and social behaviour were also important. There are examples in the incidents on which Maupassant based the newspaper stories that shock the grandmother in his sketch 'In Times Past' – incidents in which betrayed women take revenge.[57] These suggest the fear of female independence reflected in his last novel, *Notre Coeur*.

In two ways *Notre Coeur* marks a new departure in Maupassant's longer fiction. First, it is the only one of his novels that does not hinge in some way on one or more plots of adultery. Second, and relatedly, for the first time in one of his novels the power balance between the main male and the main female character is in the latter's favour. In *Fort Comme la Mort*, the mistress is more devoted to the lover than he is to her, though he falls in love with her daughter who greatly resembles her. *Notre Coeur* not only subjugates its main character to his mistress, but represents her as a new type of woman who does not accept male control. The novel does not, like *Bel-Ami*, merely imply male anxiety about female power but develops that anxiety and centres it on a modern, independent woman. In doing so, it also suggests why the fiction of wifely adultery, at least in France, had to come to an end.

Michèle de Burne is a young widow who, having been mistreated by her husband, refuses to remarry and holds court for numerous admirers without, apparently, taking any of them as a lover. André Mariolle is a leisured gentleman who is talented in many ways but has never distinguished himself in any of them. At her initiative, the two have an affair that they are able to keep secret and that survives a break caused by his chagrin that she cannot feel the passion he feels for her. Part of her power stems from her position as a rich, intelligent and attractive young widow; but part also – though the two attributes are not linked explicitly – from the fact that she is to a large extent emotionally self-sufficient. The narrator represents this as a form of narcissism, as when she admires herself in the three mirrors positioned so as to enable her to 'envelop herself in her own image' (II.31; I.ii.1049),[58] and in another way by hinting that she is lesbian.[59] Maupassant constructs Mme de Burne as a new type within a general discourse of femininity. On the one hand, she recalls stock nineteenth-century definitions of women, as when she declares: 'we look at all things through the medium of sentiment. [. . .] We are intuitive and capable of enlightenment, but changeable, impressionable, readily swayed by our surroundings' (I.24; I.i.1045). As Louis Forestier notes, it is ironic that Maupassant here puts into her mouth an idea of female sensibility promoted by Schopenhauer and Herbert Spencer.[60] On the other hand, a male member of her salon – a writer who has described similar figures in a novel entitled *Une d'Elles* – calls her one of a 'new race of women, disturbed by nerves hysterical from thinking' (I.10, TM; I.i.1036).[61] As Janet Beizer has shown, the idea of hysteria as a distinctively female quality was well established.[62] Maupassant gives it a new slant by attributing it to excessive thought, which he links in turn with the notion of modern artifice. Indeed, through an interior view of Mariolle, he suggests that it is Mme de Burne's artificiality that distinguishes her from earlier female types:

> To the romantic and dreamily passionate women of the Restoration had succeeded the gay triflers of the imperial epoch, convinced that pleasure is a reality; and now, here there was afforded to him a new development of this everlasting femininity, a woman of refinement, of indeterminate sensibility, restless, without fixed resolves, her feelings in constant turmoil [. . .]. He relished in her that flavor of an artificial nature, the sole object of whose existence was to charm and allure. (III.47–8; I.iii.1059)

These rather conventional abstractions define the role even of a new woman as that of appealing to men. Much more telling, however, is the amount of autonomy Maupassant gives her.

The novel explains Mme de Burne's independence as a reaction to five years of effectual slavery in her marriage, yet, at the same time, it presents it as characteristic of modern women. She herself claims: 'there is no such thing as a good husband, there never can be' (XIII.233; III.iii.1177); one of the male figures who comments on her declares: 'the women of to-day are incapable of loving, and they will not bear children' (VI.120; II.iii.1104); and Mariolle puts the consequences for men in a nutshell when, seeing her kiss a woman friend in a way she has never kissed him, he thinks to himself: 'These women are no longer made for us' (X.173, TM; II.vii.1136). Mme de Burne insists on dictating the terms of their affair. Instead of accepting Mariolle's absolute idea of love, which she restates as 'Everything at first, nothing afterward' (VIII.151; II.v.1123), she argues that love itself cannot survive but affectionate amity can. He therefore realizes that 'This mistress of his had made of him, not a lover, but a sort of intelligent companion of her life' (VIII.141; II.v.1116). When he has agreed to resume this role, having fled from it in despair, the narrator presents her as 'feeling in her whole body a kind of satisfied well-being that made her happy in her way, as a hawk is happy whose flight brings him down on his fascinated quarry' (XIII.234–5, TM; III.iii.1178). The simile could hardly contrast more strikingly with the one quoted above from *Mont-Oriol*, in which the lover is described as 'a huge bird of prey', and the woman he has made his mistress as a wren (I.vii.141; I.vii.570).

However, despite Mme de Burne's success in finding and then regaining a lover who suits her own requirements, *Notre Coeur* allows him compensation at the end. While trying to escape and recover from the affair in the country, Mariolle befriends and helps a waitress who falls in love with him. The two are already lovers when Mme de Burne arrives to bring him back to Paris, but he does not tell her about the liaison, and the novel ends with him promising his new mistress that he will take her with him and continue as her lover. This realizes Mariolle's wish for 'a woman who could be these two in one, who might have the affection of the one and the charm of the other' (XIII.225; III.iii.1171). From another point of view, however, the result is an equivalent of the type of marriage in which the husband keeps a mistress – the affair with Mme de Burne having quasi-marital permanence. In this way, *Notre Coeur* reasserts male infidelity in what seems an almost desperate attempt to deal with the danger to male power presented by independent, dominant women. Although the novel of adultery was not about to change gender, *Notre Coeur* is one of the texts that mark its ending.

In his edition of Maupassant's novels, Louis Forestier notes how often, especially in the last three, the writer echoes Schopenhauer's misogynism, and Mary Donaldson-Evans argues that the novels and stories alike show a 'progressive gynophobia'.[63] Since the novel of wifely adultery is an inherently misogynistic form, it is telling evidence of its demise in France that, in five of his six completed novels, and despite his growing anti-feminism, Maupassant reworked it to a point at which, in *Pierre and Jean*, it became unrecognizable before dropping it completely in the last. What remains of the two novels he left unfinished at his death, *L'Âme étrangère* and *L'Angélus*,[64] reinforces this sense of a definitive break with the tradition, for neither involves adultery. Wifely adultery would continue to figure in popular fiction; and it was still possible, in the 1890s, to centre a Naturalist novel upon it – David Baguley cites an extreme example in Paul Alexis's *Madame Meuriot* (1891) in which, he says, the heroine effectively 'dies of her female body'.[65] If, in its handling of the theme, Naturalist fiction could go no further than such a distillation of its own formulas, Maupassant's novels not only rewrite it successively but at last drop it entirely.

It is beyond the scope of this book to do more than point towards developments after the fiction of wifely adultery in France or elsewhere. By the mid-1880s the Symbolist and Decadent movements were well under way, and these focused on quite different forms of social and sexual transgression.[66] Especially significant is the fact that, for the first time in France since George Sand's controversial work of the 1830s and early 1840s, women novelists were in a position to deal explicitly with sexual themes.[67] As Jennifer Waelti-Walters has shown, a number of these novelists challenged various of the social myths of the nineteenth century, especially its central ideal of the bourgeois wife.[68] Quite apart from the fact that, except in popular fiction, the theme of wifely adultery was exhausted, such a challenge rendered it fruitless by striking at its root. The most interesting revivals of the topic rewrite it, not only by questioning the wife's role in bourgeois marriage, but by presenting the husband critically and ironically.[69] By the end of the century it was clear that, as a serious literary form, the novel of wifely adultery was defunct.

Notes

PREFACE

1. Basingstoke: Macmillan; New York: St Martin's Press.
2. Basingstoke: Macmillan; New York: St Martin's Press, 1997; Cambridge: Cambridge University Press, 1999.
3. *Novel of Female Adultery*, p. 4.
4. Oxford: Oxford University Press, 1990, p. 2.
5. Baltimore and London: Johns Hopkins University Press, 1979.
6. 'The Fallen Woman's Sexuality: Childbirth and Censure', in *Sexuality and Victorian Literature*, ed. by Don Richard Cox, Tennessee Studies in Literature, 27 (Knoxville: University of Tennessee Press, 1984), pp. 54–71; *The Adulteress's Child: Authorship and Desire in the Nineteenth-Century Novel* (Cambridge, Eng., and Cambridge, MA: Polity Press, 1992).

1   THEORIZING THE NOVEL OF WIFELY ADULTERY

1. *Adultery in the Novel*, pp. 113, 179.
2. *Adulteress's Child*, pp. 58, 61.
3. *Novel of Female Adultery*, p. 5.
4. *Novel of Female Adultery*, p. 5; *Family in Crisis in Late Nineteenth-Century French Fiction*, p. 67.
5. Trans. of *La de Bringas* by Catherine Jagoe (London: J. M. Dent; Rutland, VT: Charles E. Tuttle, 1996). This text is discussed in *Novel of Female Adultery*, pp. 212–14, where it is identified as a novel of prostitution rather than of adultery.
6. Indeed, as Nadine Bérenguier points out, 'The word "adultère" is conspicuously absent from *Les Liaisons dangereuses*.' See 'Unfortunate Couples: Adultery in Four Eighteenth-Century French Novels', *Eighteenth-Century Fiction*, 4 (1992), 331–50 (p. 340).
7. 'Men's Reading, Women's Writing: Gender and the Rise of the Novel', *Yale French Studies*, 75, *The Politics of Tradition: Placing Women in French Literature* (1988), 40–55 (pp. 44, 45).
8. Comparing *Les Liaisons dangereuses* with Claude Crébillon's *Lettres de la Marquise de M*** au Comte de R**** (1732), Bérenguier remarks that in both novels 'marriage appears only in the background adding a social dimension to the dilemma. What illicit love alters and finally destroys is not their marriage, but their identity as virtuous women' ('Unfortunate Couples', p. 342).
9. Stendhal's *The Red and the Black* is another novel in which adultery

219

occurs rather than a novel of adultery. See *Novel of Female Adultery*, pp. 5–6.

10. See *Adulteress's Child*, passim; 'Our Lady of the Flowers', in *Violetta and her Sisters: The Lady of the Camellias, Responses to the Myth*, ed. by Nicholas John (London and Boston: Faber and Faber, 1994), pp. 161–5; and *Novel of Female Adultery*, pp. 24–36, 120–8.

11. *Fanny* is discussed in *Novel of Female Adultery*, pp. 72–7, 91–4.

12. For a pioneering analysis of the geography of the novel before the twentieth century, see Franco Moretti, *Atlas of the European Novel 1800–1900* (London and New York: Verso, 1998). For discussion of an example of South American adultery fiction, see Maria Manuel Lisboa, 'Machado de Assis and the Beloved Reader: Squatters in the Text', in *Scarlet Letters*, pp. 160–73.

13. *The Novel of Adultery* (London: Macmillan, 1976), pp. 1–56 (p. 1). Subsequent page references are given in parentheses.

14. E.g., before discussing Hawthorne's *The Scarlet Letter*, she observes: 'It has not been considered essential hitherto to take into account the *forms* of the novels under discussion' (p. 101; original emphasis).

15. Tanner remarks parenthetically in his Introduction: 'The fact that it is almost inevitably the adulterous *woman* on which many nineteenth-century novels focus is itself a matter for later comment' (*Adultery in the Novel*, p. 13, his emphasis), but this comment is not forthcoming.

16. The question of childlessness is taken up in Chapter 3 below.

17. *Desire: Love Stories in Western Culture* (Oxford, Eng., and Cambridge, MA: Blackwell Publishers, 1994), p. 14. Subsequent page references are given in parentheses.

18. See, e.g., Armstrong, *Novel of Adultery*, pp. 30, 64–7, 71.

19. See *The Family, Sex and Marriage in England, 1500–1800* (London: Weidenfeld and Nicolson, 1977), especially pp. 325–404. Stone's claim remains in various ways controversial; see p. 72 below and the corresponding note. James F. Traer discusses eighteenth-century French debates on marriage, and the Revolutionary legislation to which they led, in *Marriage and the Family in Eighteenth-Century France* (Ithaca, NY, and London: Cornell University Press, 1980).

20. *Julie* is discussed below, pp. 23–33; *The Physiology of Marriage* in *Novel of Female Adultery*, pp. 15–23.

21. See *Novel of Female Adultery*, pp. 6–10.

22. On libertine writing before the Revolution, see Robert Darnton, *The Corpus of Clandestine Literature in France, 1769–89* (New York and London: W. W. Norton, 1995), and *The Forbidden Best-Sellers of Pre-Revolutionary France* (London: HarperCollins, 1996); on Merimée, Balzac, and the libertine tradition, *Novel of Female Adultery*, pp. 37–65; and, on literary censorship in France, F. W. J. Hemmings, *Culture and Society in France, 1789–1848* (Leicester: Leicester University Press, 1987), pp. 138–43, and *Culture and Society in France, 1848–1898*:

Dissidents and Philistines (London: B. T. Batsford, 1971), especially Chapter 2. The prosecution in 1857 of Flaubert and the printer and publisher of the *Revue de Paris*, in which *Madame Bovary* first appeared, was unsuccessful, in contrast to that of Charles Baudelaire for *Les Fleurs du Mal* a few months later; when the *Revue* was banned in 1858, the motive was to suppress political opposition. For a wide-ranging discussion of the *Madame Bovary* proceedings, see Dominick LaCapra, *'Madame Bovary' on Trial* (Ithaca, NY, and London: Cornell University Press, 1982).

23. 'The Double Standard', *Journal of the History of Ideas*, 20 (1959), 195–216 (p. 209). Thomas is quoting Samuel Johnson's notorious defence of the double standard.

24. 'Double Standard', p. 210; see also p. 216.

25. *Fictions of Feminine Desire: Disclosures of Heloise* (Lincoln and London: University of Nebraska Press, 1982; repr. 1987), p. 103. Kamuf's argument is considered in more detail on pp. 31–3 below.

26. *Poor and Pregnant in Paris: Strategies for Survival in the Nineteenth Century* (New Brunswick, NJ: Rutgers University Press, 1992), p. 37.

27. 'Introduction: The Present State of Affairs', in *Scarlet Letters*, pp. 1–10 (p. 4). White makes a similar case in *Family in Crisis*: 'the myth of the "end of the family" was one version of the end of history which struck a particular chord in a society based on property and inheritance and obsessed by the question of its own legitimacy' (p. 136).

28. 'Legitimation and Irony in Tolstoy and Fontane', in *Scarlet Letters*, pp. 85–97 (p. 85).

29. 'Legitimation and Irony', p. 86; Fraisse's *Reason's Muse: Sexual Difference and the Birth of Democracy*, trans. by Jane Marie Todd (Chicago and London: University of Chicago Press, 1994), is about the theorizing of sexual difference in late eighteenth-century and early nineteenth-century France.

30. See Boris Eikhenbaum, *Tolstoi in the Seventies*, trans. by Albert Kaspin (Ann Arbor, MI: Ardis, 1982), pp. 99–100, 143–6; and C. J. G. Turner, *A Karenina Companion* (Waterloo, Ont.: Wilfrid Laurier University Press, 1993), pp. 1–2, 99–101, 103. For brief accounts of the thinking of Kant, Hegel and Schopenhauer on women, see *Misogyny in the Western Philosophical Tradition: A Reader*, ed. by Beverley Clack (Basingstoke: Macmillan, 1999), pp. 144–60, 175–8, 181–92.

31. See Leonard Krieger, *The German Idea of Freedom: History of a Political Tradition* (Chicago and London: University of Chicago Press, 1957; repr. 1972), pp. 86–138 and passim; Otto Pflanze, *Bismarck and the Development of Germany: The Period of Unification, 1815–1871* (Princeton, NJ: Princeton University Press, 1963), pp. 23–7, 45–6, 326.

32. 'Legitimation and Irony', p. 94.

33. *L'Adultera* is discussed in *Novel of Female Adultery*, pp. 168–72.

34. *Culture and Adultery: The Novel, the Newspaper, and the Law, 1857–1914* (Philadelphia: University of Pennsylvania Press, 1999).
35. Leckie notes that 'French newspapers did not subscribe to the practice of printing divorce court proceedings' (*Culture and Adultery*, p. 263, n. 11).
36. For Locke, see *Two Treatises of Government* (1690), ed. by Peter Laslett, 2nd edn (Cambridge and New York: Cambridge University Press, 1988); for Astell, *The First English Feminist: 'Reflections upon Marriage' and Other Writings by Mary Astell*, ed. by Bridget Hill (Aldershot, Hants: Gower Publishing, 1986), and *Astell: Political Writings*, ed. by Patricia Springborg (Cambridge and New York: Cambridge University Press, 1996).
37. *Tender Geographies: Women and the Origins of the Novel in France* (New York: Columbia University Press, 1991), p. 106.
38. DeJean does not discuss *The Comtesse de Tende*. Terence Cave, however, notes an interesting difference between the final sentence of the accredited 1724 edition and the anonymous edition of 1718. In this sentence, which states that the Comte did not remarry but lived to an advanced age, the words 'he had a horror of women' are omitted. Cave remarks that 'The censorship exercised by the 1724 editor implies that the waters here are troubled indeed', but it is not necessary to accept his view that Lafayette's 'fictional extension of [the Comte's] life is clearly designed to emphasize the traumatic impact of his wife's infidelity'. Instead, a reading more consistent with her emphases in this text and elsewhere invites recognition of the double standard and of misogynism. See Madame de Lafayette, *The Princesse de Clèves*, trans. by Terence Cave (Oxford and New York: Oxford University Press, 1992), p. 230.
39. 'Notorious Women: Marriage and the Novel in Crisis in France 1690–1710', in *Scarlet Letters*, pp. 56–69 (p. 57). This essay is an adaptation of pp. 140–58 of *Tender Geographies*, where the remark quoted is on p. 141. DeJean notes that still another version appears as 'Notorious Women: Marriage and the Novel Crisis in France (1690–1710)', *Yale Journal of Criticism*, 4 (1991), 67–85.
40. 'Notorious Women', p. 64; see also *Tender Geographies*, p. 150.
41. 'Notorious Women', p. 65; *Tender Geographies*, p. 150.
42. 'Notorious Women', p. 66; *Tender Geographies*, p. 156.

2   TONY TANNER: *ADULTERY IN THE NOVEL*

1. *Adultery in the Novel*. All page references are given in parentheses.
2. *Road to Divorce*, pp. 232–6.
3. Leah Leneman, *Alienated Affections: The Scottish Experience of Divorce and Separation, 1684–1830* (Edinburgh: Edinburgh University Press,

1998), p. 43; Jill Harsin, *Policing Prostitution in Nineteenth-Century Paris* (Princeton, NJ, and Guildford: Princeton University Press, 1985), pp. xviii–xix; Roderick Phillips, *Putting Asunder: A History of Divorce in Western Society* (Cambridge and New York: Cambridge University Press, 1988), p. 352; Lucy A. Sponsler, 'The Status of Married Women under the Legal System of Spain', *Journal of Legal History*, 3 (1982), 125–52 (pp. 140–4).

4. Vico's misogynism is clear from the extracts cited by Tanner. For discussion of Locke and Rousseau as misogynistic thinkers, see *Misogyny in the Western Philosophical Tradition*, ed. by Beverley Clack.

5. The *Larousse* entry is discussed in *Novel of Female Adultery*, pp. 67–8.

6. For detailed argument to this effect, see *Novel of Female Adultery*, pp. 85–91.

7. *Revolution and the Form of the British Novel 1790–1825: Intercepted Letters, Interrupted Seductions* (Oxford: Clarendon Press, 1994), pp. 11–16 and passim. James H. Warner notes: 'The charge of immoral influence did not appear in the early reviews, but was frequent later.' See 'Eighteenth-Century English Reactions to the *Nouvelle Héloïse*', *PMLA*, 52 (1937), 803–19 (pp. 814–15).

8. From the extract he quotes on pp. 120–1, Tanner omits the following clause between the words 'extremely perilous' and 'Let us not deceive ourselves': 'that we are ruined if we are discovered, and that to avoid it everything must assist us'. From the extract on p. 125, he omits the end of the sentence beginning 'A certain gravity', which concludes: 'meanwhile, a tender mother, beside herself for joy, was secretly devouring this very sweet sight'. The translation Tanner uses is the abridgement by Judith H. McDowell, *La Nouvelle Héloïse: Julie, or the New Eloise* (University Park and London: Pennsylvania State University Press, 1968), pp. 121, 144.

9. *Julie, or the New Heloise: Letters of Two Lovers Who Live in a Small Town at the Foot of the Alps*, trans. by Philip Stewart and Jean Vaché (Hanover, NH, and London: University Press of New England, 1997); *Julie, ou La Nouvelle Héloïse*, ed. by Michel Launay (Paris: Garnier-Flammarion, 1967). Following Stewart and Vaché, I refer to the novel by the short title *Julie* rather than by the familiar but erroneous *La Nouvelle Héloïse*. See Stewart and Vaché's Introduction, pp. xii–xvi.

10. *Jean-Jacques Rousseau: Oeuvres complètes*, 5 vols (Paris: Gallimard, 1959–95), II (1964), ed. by Henri Coulet and Bernard Guyon, p. 1439; Peggy Kamuf, *Fictions of Feminine Desire*, pp. 109–11. Kamuf's discussion of the novel is further addressed on pp. 31–3 below, with page references in parentheses.

11. Christine Roulston, *Virtue, Gender, and the Authentic Self in Eighteenth-Century Fiction: Richardson, Rousseau, and Laclos* (Gainesville: University Press of Florida, 1998), pp. 98–9, citing Janet Todd, *Women's Friendship in Literature* (New York: Columbia University

Press), pp. 148–9. Tanner himself uses the word 'rape' in an earlier reference to the scene (p. 114).

12. *Virtue, Gender, and the Authentic Self*, p. 92.

13. See *Novel of Female Adultery*, pp. 15–23.

14. For discussions of attitudes to adultery in Sand, Jacobsen and Fontane, see *Novel of Female Adultery*, pp. 96–117, 161–7, 167–86.

15. *Oeuvres complètes*, II, p. xxxix.

16. Nadine Bérenguier, 'Unfortunate Couples: Adultery in Four Eighteenth-Century French Novels', p. 345.

17. *Desire: Love Stories in Western Culture*, p. 120.

18. The two quotations are from Rousseau's *Discourse on Political Economy* (cited by Kamuf, p. 108) and *La Nouvelle Héloïse*, p. 119.

19. William Ray goes so far as to argue that what he calls the 'ambiguity' of Rousseau's position in *Julie* 'foreshadows the more blatantly metanarrative ironies of Sterne, Diderot, and Laclos'. See *Story and History: Narrative Authority and Social Identity in the Eighteenth-Century French and English Novel* (Cambridge, MA, and Oxford, Eng.: Basil Blackwell, 1990), p. 266.

20. *Women in Western Political Thought* (Princeton, NJ: Princeton University Press, 1979), p. 176.

21. Nadine Bérenguier points out that, in *Émile et Sophie*, 'adultery is not defined by the traditional triangular structure [. . .] as a transgression of conjugal faith by a wife who aspires to a change or is submitted to the assaults of a bold suitor, but as a phenomenon destroying the couple born from the ashes of two formerly distinct persons'. This is a completely different emphasis from that of nineteenth-century adultery fiction. See 'Unfortunate Couples', pp. 346–50 (p. 348).

22. *Adultery in the Novel*, p. 179; Thomas Mann, 'Fantasy on Goethe', in *Last Essays*, trans. by Richard and Clara Winston and Tania and James Stern (London: Secker and Warburg, 1959), p. 133; 'Goethe's Career as a Man of Letters', in *Essays of Three Decades*, trans. by H. T. Lowe-Porter (London: Secker and Warburg, n.d. [1947]), p. 45; *Gesammelte Werke*, 12 vols (Oldenburg: S. Fischer Verlag, 1960), IX, 335, 748.

23. *Goethe's Die Wahlverwandtschaften: A Literary Interpretation* (Oxford: Clarendon Press, 1967), p. 201.

24. *Elective Affinities: A Novel*, trans. by David Constantine (Oxford and New York: Oxford University Press, 1994); *Die Wahlverwandtschaften*, in *Goethes Werke*, ed. by Erich Trunz and others, 14 vols (Hamburg: Christian Wegner Verlag, 1948–60), VI, 242–490.

25. In his allegorical reading of the novel, John Winkelman argues that it shows the coming together of bourgeoisie and military in Charlotte's relationship with the Captain, and adumbrates a future union between aristocracy and workers in Eduard's relationship with Ottilie. Though Winkelman claims on slender textual grounds that Charlotte represents the bourgeoisie, he has to concede that she is not

in fact from that class. See *Goethe's Elective Affinities: An Interpretation* (New York, Bern, Frankfurt am Main, Paris: Peter Lang, 1987), pp. 59–61 and passim.

26. See *Goethe's Elective Affinities*, pp. 14–15, 36–41. The novel was written in 1808–9, and, as Winkelman points out, Napoleon had not only defeated the Prussian army at Jena in 1806 but the city of Weimar had been sacked and Goethe's own house occupied (p. 40).

27. Thus, as David Constantine indicates, there was no English translation until 1854, and this remained the standard English translation until 1960. When G. H. Lewes discussed the novel in 1855, he made every effort to justify its controversial subject by arguing that 'Goethe was an Artist, not an Advocate'. See *The Life and Works of Goethe*, 2 vols (London: David Nutt), II, 372–81 (p. 375).

28. R. J. Hollingdale gives a concise account of the *Novelle* form in the Introduction to his translation of *Elective Affinities* (Harmondsworth and New York: Penguin Books, 1971), pp. 11–13. H. G. Barnes discusses the chief characteristics the novel derives from the form in *Goethe's Die Wahlverwandtschaften: A Literary Interpretation*, pp. 5–7.

29. H. Jane Plenderleith summarizes the principal terms that critics have applied to the episode in 'Sex, Lies, and *Die Wahlverwandtschaften*', *German Life and Letters: A Quarterly Review*, n.s., 47 (1994:4, special number on *Die Wahlverwandtschaften*), 407–17 (p. 407). She does not, however, refer to Tanner's term.

30. Goethe here remarkably varies an ancient belief mentioned by Paul-Gabriel Boucé who quotes from a 1749 edition of the widely circulated *Aristotle's Masterpiece*: 'The imaginative power, at the Time of Conception, which is of so much Force, that it stamps a Character of the Thing imagined upon the Child: so that the Children of an Adulteress, by the Mother's imaginative Power, may have the nearest Resemblance to her own Husband, though begotten by another Man.' The variation consists in the fact that the child resembles the beloveds of both parents rather than the adulteress's husband, so reinforcing the importance of love as well as the suggestion that male adultery is as significant as female. See 'Imagination, pregnant women, and monsters, in eighteenth-century England and France' in *Sexual Underworlds of the Enlightenment*, ed. by G. S. Rousseau and Roy Porter (Manchester: Manchester University Press, 1987, pp. 86–100 (p. 94).

31. *Goethe's Die Wahlverwandtschaften*, pp. 35, 57; 'Sex, Lies, and *Die Wahlverwandtschaften*', pp. 407–8.

32. *Goethe: Die Wahlverwandtschaften* (Oxford: Basil Blackwell, 1971), p. xliv.

33. 'Monkeys, Monuments and Miracles: Aspects of Imitation of Word and Image in *Die Wahlverwandtschaften*', *German Life and Letters*, n.s., 47 (1994), 432–48 (p. 443).

34. 'Sex, Lies, and *Die Wahlverwandtschaften*', p. 411.

35. *Novel of Female Adultery*, pp. 105–9.
36. In, for example, *Writing Degree Zero*, trans. by Annette Lavers and Colin Smith (London: Jonathan Cape, 1967).
37. See *Novel of Female Adultery*, pp. 67–8.
38. See above, pp. 15–19, 22.

3 CHILDREN AND CHILDLESSNESS IN THE NOVEL OF WIFELY ADULTERY

1. See the discussion on pp. 14–16, 18–19.
2. *Adulteress's Child.* All page references are given in parentheses. See also 'Adulteress's Children', in *Scarlet Letters*, pp. 109–22.
3. 'Introduction: Flaubert Studies 1983–96', in *New Approaches in Flaubert Studies*, ed. by Tony Williams and Mary Orr (Lewiston, NY, Queenston, Ont., and Lampeter, Wales: The Edwin Mellen Press, 1999), pp. 1–31 (p. 15).
4. 'Fallen Woman's Sexuality: Childbirth and Censure'. All page references to this essay, which is not mentioned by Segal, are given in parentheses.
5. Paris: Librairie Nouvelle, 1855 (2nd edn). The novel is discussed by Tony Williams in 'Champfleury, Flaubert and the Novel of Adultery', *Nineteenth-Century French Studies*, 20 (1991–2), 145–57; and in *Novel of Female Adultery*, pp. 68–72.
6. The Romantic confession is discussed by Naomi Segal in *Adulteress's Child* and also in 'Our Lady of the Flowers', in *Violetta and her Sisters*, pp. 161–5.
7. See Ernest Feydeau, *Fanny: Étude* (Paris: Amyot, 1858), pp. 27–8.
8. Nicholas White points out that, under provisions originated by the Napoleonic Code, the child of a married woman 'would be automatically recognized in law as the progeny of her husband even if she fell pregnant by another man' (*Family in Crisis*, p. 94). Marie Maclean discusses the theme of acceptance of adulterine children by the husband in 'The Heirs of Amphitryon: Social Fathers and Natural Fathers', in *Scarlet Letters*, pp. 13–33.
9. The phrase 'genealogical continuity' is MacPike's quotation from Tony Tanner, *Adultery in the Novel*, p. 4.
10. MacPike is incorrect in observing that Julie 'marries a man she does not love' (p. 60). The problem posed by the novel is that she marries a man she loves who is disapproved of by her father and who is soon and repeatedly unfaithful. MacPike is also mistaken in asserting that the offspring of Julie's first passionate affair is a girl. Her initial love affair is in fact unconsummated; and the first offspring of her only adulterous liaison is a boy, Charles. It is this boy who is subsequently drowned as a result of a push by his legitimate sister.

11. The contradictions in Balzac's narrative are discussed by Christopher Prendergast in *Balzac: Fiction and Melodrama* (London: Edward Arnold; New York: Holmes and Meier, 1978), pp. 132–4; in *Novel of Female Adultery*, pp. 56–60; and by D. A. Williams in 'Patriarchal Ideology and French Fictions of Adultery 1830–57', in *Scarlet Letters*, pp. 134–45 (p. 142).

12. In *The Name of the Mother: Writing Illegitimacy* (London and New York: Routledge, 1994), Marie Maclean identifies three possible motives for a husband acknowledging children not fathered by himself: 'convenience, such as acquiring an heir', 'hypocrisy, such as not losing face', and 'love' (p. 50). Balzac's novel gives no priority to the third reason and little to the second.

13. See Kathryn J. Crecelius, *Family Romances: George Sand's Early Novels* (Bloomington and Indianapolis: Indiana University Press, 1987), pp. 127–40.

14. *Le Dernier amour* is discussed in *Novel of Female Adultery*, pp. 109–116.

15. For detailed argument to this effect, see *Novel of Female Adultery*, pp. 85–91.

16. See C. J. G. Turner, 'Divorce and *Anna Karenina*', *Forum for Modern Language Studies*, 23 (1987), 97–116; and *A Karenina Companion* (Waterloo, Ont.: Wilfrid Laurier University Press, 1993), pp. 150, 158, 162.

17. See, e.g., J. P. Stern, *Re-Interpretations: Seven Studies in Nineteenth-Century German Literature* (London: Thames and Hudson, 1964; repr. Cambridge and New York: Cambridge University Press, 1981), p. 322; and F. W. J. Hemmings, 'Realism in Spain and Portugal', in *The Age of Realism*, ed. by F. W. J. Hemmings (Harmondsworth: Penguin, 1974), pp. 265–322 (p. 317).

18. For a discussion of Eça's relation to Naturalism and other movements of the time, see Alexander Coleman, *Eça de Queirós and European Realism* (New York and London: New York University Press, 1980).

19. Partly on this ground, Alison Sinclair argues that '*La Regenta* is a novel only apparently about adultery' ('The Need for Zeal and the Dangers of Jealousy: Identity and Legitimacy in *La Regenta*', in *Scarlet Letters*, pp. 174–85 [p. 175]). It is, however, undeniable that the action of the whole novel pivots on the heroine's seduction, and that the novel has much in common with previous adultery fiction.

20. See Harriet S. Turner, 'Family Ties and Tyrannies: A Reassessment of Jacinta', *Hispanic Review*, 51 (1983), 1–22; and *Benito Pérez Galdós: Fortunata and Jacinta* (Cambridge and New York: Cambridge University Press, 1992), pp. 62–70.

21. Jacobsen translated *On the Origin of Species* and *The Descent of Man* between 1871 and 1874; he also published articles summarizing Darwin's theories.

22. Quoted from a letter by Jacobsen in Hanna Astrup Larsen's

Introduction to her translation of *Marie Grubbe* (New York: American-Scandinavian Foundation; London: Oxford University Press, 1917; 2nd edn, rev. by Robert Raphael, The Library of Scandinavian Literature, 30 [Boston: G. K. Hall, 1975]), p. xi.

23. As Niels Lyhne Jensen has remarked, 'Jacobsen unquestionably held progressive views on women's rights, but his insistence in the novel that Marie's disposition for humiliation and subjection to a man is an element of what is most valuable in woman's nature reflects a decidedly masculine view of the female psyche.' See *Jens Peter Jacobsen* (Boston: G. K. Hall, 1980), p. 68.

24. Judith Armstrong mentions provisions for divorce and their absence in the historical survey with which she opens *Novel of Adultery*, e.g. on pp. 3–6 and 13–15, but she makes no direct connection between divorce and adultery fiction; the topic is given a little more importance in the Introduction and two of the essays in *Scarlet Letters* (e.g. pp. 3, 62–6, 86 and 94), but it deserves more extended treatment.

25. See Roderick Phillips, *Putting Asunder*, pp. 40, 51–2, 200–1, and 430–1.

26. *Two Novellas: The Woman Taken in Adultery and The Poggenpuhl Family*, trans. by Gabriele Annan (Chicago and London: University of Chicago Press, 1979; repr. Harmondsworth: Penguin, 1995); *Theodor Fontane: Werke und Schriften*, 54 vols, ed. by Walter Keitel and Helmuth Nürnberger, VII, *L'Adultera* (Carl Hanser: Munich, 1971; repr. in Fontane Bibliothek, Frankfurt am Main, Berlin, Vienna: Ullstein, 1991).

27. See, e.g., J. P. Stern, *Re-Interpretations*, pp. 316–39.

28. *Effi Briest*, trans. by Hugh Rorrison and Helen Chambers (London and New York: Penguin Books, 2000); *Werke und Schriften*, XVII (1974), repr. in Fontane Bibliothek (1979).

29. See *Novel of Female Adultery*, pp. viii, 10–11 and 96–119, and pp. 6–10 respectively. Judith Armstrong suggests in more general terms that 'adultery fails to seize the English imagination in the way it does the French' (*Novel of Adultery*, p. 30; see also p. 165).

30. E. Ann Kaplan, *Motherhood and Representation: The Mother in Popular Culture and Melodrama* (London and New York: Routledge, 1992), pp. 76–106; Lyn Pykett, *The 'Improper' Feminine: The Women's Sensation Novel and the New Woman Writing* (London and New York: Routledge, 1992), pp. 117–34.

31. See Pykett, *'Improper' Feminine*, pp. 128–9; and Sally Shuttleworth, 'Demonic Mothers: Ideologies of Bourgeois Motherhood in the Mid-Victorian era', in *Rewriting the Victorians: Theory, History and the Politics of Gender*, ed. by Linda M. Shires (New York and London: Routledge, 1992), pp. 31–51 (pp. 48–9).

32. Michel Foucault, *The History of Sexuality* [3 vols; vol. 1], trans. by R. Hurley (New York: Pantheon Books, 1978; London: Allen Lane, 1979).

33. See *Naturalist Fiction: The Entropic Vision* (Cambridge: Cambridge University Press, 1990).
34. 'Smiles of the Sphinx: Zola and the Riddle of Femininity', in *Breaking the Chain: Women, Theory, and French Realist Fiction* (New York: Columbia University Press, 1985), pp. 29–47 (p. 40). *A Love Affair* is discussed in Chapter 7. Schor also suggests that the novel presents the daughter in the 'preoedipal phase' of her psychic development, but this seems inconsistent with the fact that, as she acknowledges, this daughter is not an infant but at the age of puberty.
35. 'Carnal Knowledge in French Naturalist Fiction', in *Scarlet Letters*, pp. 123–33 (pp. 126, 129); *Family in Crisis*, pp. 98–109.
36. '*Une Vie* or the Name of the Mother', in *Breaking the Chain*, pp. 48–77 and p. 170, n. 17 (p. 59). Schor's discussion of this question is considered further on pp. 210, 214 below.
37. 'The Traffic in Women: Notes on the "Political Economy" of Sex', in *Toward an Anthropology of Women*, ed. by Rayna R. Reiter (New York and London: Monthly Review Press, 1975), pp. 157–210 (p. 183).

4 ADULTERY IN EARLY BRITISH FICTION

1. See *Novel of Female Adultery*, pp. 6–10. Barbara Leckie has argued that the theme of adultery was by no means absent from nineteenth-century British fiction, even before Meredith, Hardy and James, but the examples from the 1860s that she cites are not novels of adultery. See *Culture and Adultery* and the discussion above on pp. 16–17. She refers only in passing to Ellen Wood's *East Lynne*, a novel of adultery first published in 1861, and discussed above on pp. 63–5.
2. See Judith Kegan Gardiner, 'The First English Novel: Aphra Behn's *Love-Letters*, The Canon, and Women's Tastes', *Tulsa Studies in Women's Literature*, 8 (1989), 201–22.
3. *Novel of Female Adultery*, e.g. pp. vi, viii, 10–11, 96–119, 211–12.
4. *Family, Sex and Marriage*, p. 648.
5. See especially the reviews by E. P. Thompson, 'Happy families', *New Society*, 41 (1977), 499–501, and by Alan Macfarlane in *History and Theory*, 18 (1979), 103–26. Caroline Gonda summarizes the main issues at stake in *Reading Daughters' Fictions 1709–1834: Novels and Society from Manley to Edgeworth* (Cambridge and New York: Cambridge University Press, 1996), pp. 3–4.
6. *Family, Sex and Marriage*, p. 530.
7. See Warren Chernaik, *Sexual Freedom in Restoration Literature* (Cambridge: Cambridge University Press, 1995).
8. *Les Lettres Portugaises* was translated by Sir Roger L'Estrange as *Five Love-Letters from a Nun to a Cavalier* (1678); *La Princesse de Clèves* anonymously as *The Princess of Cleves* (1679).

9. The chief French precedents were the romance, the *nouvelle*, the scandal history and the epistolary novel. Ros Ballaster discusses the influence of these on English fiction in *Seductive Forms: Women's Amatory Fiction from 1684 to 1740* (Oxford: Clarendon Press, 1992), pp. 42–66, 100–13, 123–31.

10. No plays by Behn were performed from 1682, when she was imprisoned for slander, until 1686. See Chernaik, *Sexual Freedom in Restoration Literature*, p. 162.

11. *Love-Letters Between a Nobleman and his Sister*, ed. by Janet Todd (London and New York: Penguin, 1996).

12. 'Unguarded Hearts: Transgression and Epistolary Form in Aphra Behn's *Love-Letters* and the *Portuguese Letters*', *Journal of English and Germanic Philology*, 97 (1998), 13–33 (p. 14).

13. Ellen Pollak discusses the role of incest in the novel, and some of its possible implications, in 'Beyond Incest: Gender and the Politics of Transgression in Aphra Behn's *Love-Letters Between a Nobleman and his Sister*', in *Rereading Aphra Behn: History, Theory, and Criticism*, ed. by Heidi Hutner (Charlottesville and London: University of Virginia Press, 1993), pp. 151–86.

14. Janet Todd outlines the historical facts in *Love-Letters Between a Nobleman and his Sister*, pp. xi–xiv, and includes part of a transcript of Grey's trial, pp. 443–61.

15. *Love-Letters Between a Nobleman and His Sister*, ed. by Maureen Duffy (London: Virago, 1987), p. vi. The earliest example of the name cited by *OED* to signify an accomplished lover dates from 1709, and of the verb 'to philander' from 1737.

16. H. J. Habbakuk, 'Marriage Settlements in the Eighteenth Century', *Transactions of the Royal Historical Society*, 4th series, 32 (1950), 15–30; cited by Christopher Hill in 'Clarissa Harlowe and Her Times', *Essays in Criticism*, 5 (1955), 315–40, repr. in *Samuel Richardson: A Collection of Critical Essays*, ed. by John Carroll (Englewood Cliffs, NJ: Prentice-Hall, 1969), pp. 102–23.

17. *Family, Sex and Marriage*, pp. 277–9, 504–6, 529–34, 657.

18. *The Fair Jilt*, in *Oroonoko and Other Writings*, ed. by Paul Salzman (Oxford and New York: Oxford University Press, 1994), pp. 93–6. As the final volume of *Love-Letters* was published in 1687, and *The Fair Jilt* was first published in 1688, it seems fair to assume that the story was written later than the novel, especially as Behn's need for money at the time is likely to have hastened rather than delayed publication.

19. For this reason, too, John Richetti's inference that the novel conveys 'a longing for a meaningful, valid public life where ritual and communal expression correct the corrosive private hedonism the novel has relentlessly chronicled' is preferable to Bradford K. Mudge's contention that the characters in the novel 'who approach love theologically (love can be only either true or false, right or

wrong) are foolish victims'. Richetti derives his comment in part from the scene of Octavio's ordination. See *'Love Letters Between a Nobleman and His Sister*: Aphra Behn and Amatory Fiction', in *Augustan Subjects: Essays in Honor of Martin C. Battestin*, ed. by Albert J. Rivero (Newark, NJ: University of Delaware Press; London: Associated University Presses, 1997), pp. 13–28 (p. 26); *The Whore's Story: Women, Pornography, and the British Novel, 1684–1830* (Oxford and New York: Oxford University Press, 2000), p. 134. In 'Aphra Behn, Libertine', *Restoration: Studies in English Literary Culture, 1660–1700*, 24 (2000), 75–97, M. L. Stapleton argues convincingly that 'Behn excoriates the libertine as she depends utterly on him for the life of her plays, poems, and fiction' (p. 77), though his view that Silvia illustrates 'the corrosive effects of libertinism on women' (p. 88) does not take sufficient account of the extent to which Behn dramatizes her heroine's exploitation.

20. *Seductive Forms*, p. 107.
21. *Madame Bovary: Provincial Lives*, trans. by Geoffrey Wall (London and New York: Penguin, 1992); *Madame Bovary: moeurs de province*, ed. by Claudine Gothot-Mersch (Paris: Garnier, 1971).
22. '"Parents can oppose their children's marriages, but children cannot prevent the follies of parents in their second childhood," said Maître Hulot to Maître Popinot, the second son of the former Minister of Commerce, who mentioned the marriage to him' (*Cousin Bette*, trans. by Sylvia Raphael [Oxford and New York: Oxford University Press, 1992], p. 462; *Balzac: La Comédie humaine*, 12 vols, ed. by Pierre-Georges Castex and others [Paris: Gallimard, 1976–81], VII, 451). Balzac not only mocks the speaker's bourgeois sententiousness but deftly suggests how the lawyers are taking over. I owe this point to Arnold Kettle.
23. *The Women of Grub Street: Press, Politics, and Gender in the London Literary Marketplace 1678–1730* (Oxford and New York: Clarendon Press, 1998), pp. 19, 263.
24. *Women of Grub Street*, p. 245.
25. *Nobody's Story: The Vanishing Acts of Women Writers in the Marketplace, 1670–1820* (Oxford: Clarendon Press, 1994), p. 103.
26. *Broken Lives: Separation and Divorce in England 1660–1857* (Oxford and New York: Oxford University Press, 1993), p. 78.
27. See G. B. Needham, 'Mary de la Rivière Manley: Tory Defender', *Huntington Library Quarterly*, 12 (1948–9), 255–89. John J. Richetti notes that the so-called seventh edition of 1736 appeared also in weekly instalments; see *Popular Fiction Before Richardson: Narrative Patterns 1700–1739* (Oxford: Clarendon Press, 1969), p. 123.
28. *Women of Grub Street*, p. 223.
29. *Secret Memoirs and Manners of several Persons of Quality, of Both Sexes, from the New Atalantis, an Island in the Mediteranean*, 2 vols (London: J.

Morphew, 1709), repr. in *The Novels of Mary Delariviere Manley 1705–1714*, ed. by Patricia Köster, 2 vols (Gainesville, FL: Scholars' Facsimiles & Reprints, 1971), I, 265–804, and as *The New Atalantis*, ed. by Rosalind Ballaster (London: Pickering and Chatto, 1991; London and New York: Penguin, 1992). Page references are given to both editions.

30. *Seductive Forms*, p. 137.
31. *The Secret History, of Queen Zarah, and the Zarazians*, repr. in *Novels of Mary Delariviere Manley*, I, 1–119 (p. 158).
32. *Popular Fiction Before Richardson*, p. 152.
33. See John Cairncross, *After Polygamy Was Made a Sin: The Social History of Christian Polygamy* (London: Routledge and Kegan Paul, 1974); and Ballaster, 'Introduction', *New Atalantis*, pp. viii–ix.
34. This was with her cousin, John Manley. Two different versions of the story appear in Manley's work, first in the *New Atalantis* under the name of Delia, and later under the name of the eponymous heroine in *The Adventures of Rivella*.
35. Manley has the male narrator of her fictionalized autobiography remark: 'the Charter of that Sex being much more confin'd than ours, what is not a Crime in Men is scandalous and unpardonable in Woman, as she herself has very well observ'd in divers Places, throughout her own Writings' (*The Adventures of Rivella; or, the History of the Author of the Atalantis* [London: n.p., 1714], repr. in *Novels of Mary Delariviere Manley*, II, 729–856 [pp. 743–4]).
36. *Adultery in the Novel*, p. 13.
37. This point is made by Ros Ballaster in her edition of *The New Atalantis*, though she overstates it when she claims that 'they appear to be two entirely different and discrete novels that share only their author and their propagandistic zeal for the Tory party' (p. xvi).
38. *Seductive Forms*, p. 143. I do not follow Ballaster in finding equal significance in the sex of the two dedicatees.
39. *Seductive Forms*, p. 144.
40. See, e.g., Richetti, *Popular Fiction Before Richardson*, pp. 121–2.
41. *Women of Grub Street*, p. 258, referring to J. Paul Hunter, '"News, and new Things": Contemporaneity and the Early English Novel', *Critical Inquiry*, 14 (1988), 493–515 (p. 501).
42. *Memoirs of Europe, Towards the Close of the Eighth Century. Written by Eginardus, Secretary and Favourite to Charlemagne*, 2 vols (London: J. Morphew, 1710), repr. in *Novels of Mary Delariviere Manley*, II, 1–724.
43. *Seductive Forms*, p. 137. Irene is one of Manley's many satirical portraits of Sarah Churchill, Duchess of Marlborough.
44. See McDowell, *Women of Grub Street*, pp. 242–4, 276.
45. *The Spectator*, no. 81 (2 June 1711), cited in *Women of Grub Street*, p. 277. McDowell documents this campaign on pp. 273–81.
46. *Women of Grub Street*, p. 292. Manley's later publications were '*Lucius*

(1717), a tragic drama, and *The Power of Love in Seven Novels* (1720), a reworking of a number of stories found in John Painter's *The Palace of Pleasure*' (Ballaster, 'Introduction', *New Atalantis*, p. xviii).

47. *Seductive Forms*, p. 156.

48. *Seductive Forms*, p. 157.

49. 2 vols, vol. I dated 1725, vol. II 1726 (London: Booksellers of London and Westminster; vol. 1 repr. New York and London: Garland, 1972).

50. For Manley's view of male inconstancy, see pp. 81, 86 above; for her refusal to accept that sex depraves a woman permanently, p. 90.

51. 'Mrs. Penelope Aubin and the Early Eighteenth-Century English Novel', *Huntington Library Quarterly*, 20 (1956–7), 245–67 (p. 250).

52. See *Licensing Entertainment: The Elevation of Novel Reading in Britain, 1684–1750* (Berkeley and London: University of California Press, 1998), pp. 111–16 (p. 112).

53. *Living by the Pen: Women Writers in the Eighteenth Century* (London and New York: Routledge, 1992), p. 38.

54. *Love in Excess; or, The Fatal Enquiry*, ed. by David Oakleaf, 2nd edn (Peterborough, Ont., and Orchard Park, NY: Broadview Press, 2000).

55. *Licensing Entertainment*, pp. 149–75.

56. *Moll Flanders*, ed. by G. A. Starr (Oxford and New York: Oxford University Press, 1971); *Roxana: The Fortunate Mistress*, ed. by Jane Jack (Oxford and New York: Oxford University Press, 1964).

57. *Family, Sex and Marriage*, p. 40. See also *Road to Divorce*, pp. 141–3. Roxana's servant Amy makes the case for cohabitation following desertion in *Roxana*, pp. 36–7.

58. *Licensing Entertainment*, pp. 174, 151–2.

59. See John Cleland, *Memoirs of a Woman of Pleasure*, ed. by Peter Sabor (Oxford and New York: Oxford University Press, 1985), pp. xxii–xxvi.

60. Bradford K. Mudge relates *Memoirs of a Coxcomb* to this new climate, especially its changing attitudes to prostitution, in *Whore's Story*, pp. 223–30.

61. The Memoirs occupy nearly all of Chapter LXXXVIII of *Peregrine Pickle*. The estimate of their length is James L. Clifford's, in the Introduction to his edition of the novel, revised by Paul-Gabriel Boucé (Oxford and New York: Oxford University Press, 1964; rev. edn, 1983), p. xxvi.

62. 'Controversy or Collusion? The "Lady Vane" Tracts', *Notes and Queries*, n.s., 19 (1972), 375–8 (p. 376), citing Rufus Putney, 'Smollett and Lady Vane's Memoirs', *Philological Quarterly*, 25 (1946), 120–6.

63. 'Controversy or Collusion?', p. 375. Contemporary reviews and comments are collected in *Tobias Smollett: The Critical Heritage*, ed. by Lionel Kelly (London and New York: Routledge and Kegan Paul, 1987), pp. 47–89.

64. *Memoirs of Mrs. Laetitia Pilkington* (1748–9, 1754); *An Apology for the Conduct of Mrs. Teresia Constantia Phillips* (1748–9); *A Narrative of the*

Life of Mrs. Charlotte Charke (1755). These and other scandalous memoirs by women, including Lady Vane's, are discussed by Felicity A. Nussbaum in *The Autobiographical Subject: Gender and Ideology in Eighteenth-Century England* (Baltimore and London: Johns Hopkins University Press, 1989), pp. 178–200.

65. *Critical Heritage*, p. 7.

66. *Tobias Smollett: Novelist* (Athens and London: University of Georgia Press, 1998), p. 85. I do not share Beasley's view, expressed in the rest of the sentence, that the result is to validate both the actual and the imagined 'in a relation of mutuality and reciprocity'.

67. *Critical Heritage*, p. 47; from *Selected Letters of Samuel Richardson*, ed. by John Carroll (Oxford: Clarendon Press, 1964), p. 173.

68. Howard Swazey Buck provides a complete account of the revisions in *A Study in Smollett* (New Haven: Yale University Press; London: Oxford University Press, 1925), pp. 123–207; they are summarized by James L. Clifford in the notes to his edition.

69. *Critical Heritage*, p. 293. Barbauld's slip in rendering the title as *Memoirs of a Lady of Pleasure* is revealing.

5 IDEOLOGY OF FEMININITY AND CRIMINAL CONVERSATION: 1728–71

1. See *The London Stage, 1660–1800*, ed. by William Van Lennep and others, 5 Parts in 11 vols (Carbondale: University of Illinois Press, 1960–8), Part I, *1660–1700*, ed. by William Van Lennep (1965), pp. lxiv–lxv, xxix–xxx; and Donald Thomas, *A Long Time Burning: The History of Literary Censorship in England* (London: Routledge and Kegan Paul, 1968), pp. 67–8.

2. *The Rise of the Woman Novelist: From Aphra Behn to Jane Austen* (Oxford and New York: Basil Blackwell, 1986), p. 15.

3. *The Spectator*, ed. by Donald F. Bond, 5 vols (Oxford: Clarendon Press, 1965), III, 271–2 (no. 342).

4. 'The daughters of Behn and the problem of reputation', in *Women, Writing, History 1640–1740*, ed. by Isobel Grundy and Susan Wiseman (London: B. T. Batsford, 1992), pp. 33–54 (pp. 34–5).

5. 'Addison', *The Lives of the English Poets*, ed. by George Birkbeck Hill, 3 vols (Oxford: Clarendon Press, 1905; repr. New York: Octagon Books, 1967), II, 95.

6. *The Rape of Clarissa: Writing, Sexuality and Class Struggle in Samuel Richardson* (Oxford: Basil Blackwell, 1982), p. 13.

7. *The Rape of Clarissa*, p. 14.

8. *Desire and Domestic Fiction: A Political History of the Novel* (New York and Oxford: Oxford University Press, 1987), p. 133.

9. *Friendship in Death: In Twenty Letters from the Dead to the Living*, 3rd

edn (London: T. Worrall, 1733; repr. New York and London: Garland, 1972). Since this collection paginates each of its four parts separately, references to *Letters Moral and Entertaining*, printed in three parts following *Letters from the Dead to the Living*, are to part, letter number, and page.

10. *Popular Fiction Before Richardson*, pp. 239–61 (p. 253).

11. See William H. McBurney, 'Mrs. Penelope Aubin and the Early Eighteenth-Century English Novel', pp. 266–7. Sarah Prescott has recently argued that the fiction of Aubin and Rowe does not so much reject Haywood's as exploit some of its basic conventions for more traditionally moral purposes. See 'The Debt to Pleasure: Eliza Haywood's *Love in Excess* and women's fiction of the 1720s', *Women's Writing*, 7 (2000), 427–45.

12. *Licensing Entertainment: The Elevation of Novel Reading in Britain, 1684–1750*, p. 184.

13. *Rise of the Woman Novelist*, pp. 81, 88.

14. *Rise of the Woman Novelist*, p. 88.

15. *Desire and Domestic Fiction*, p. 109.

16. *Rise of the Woman Novelist*, pp. 112–13.

17. *The Fair Adultress: or, the Treacherous Brother. Being the Secret Memoirs of a certain Noble Family in the Island of Cyprus. Interspersed with Several Original Letters. Translated from the Greek* (London: A. Miller, 1743).

18. For Richardson's use of traditional emblems in *Pamela*, see Margaret Anne Doody, *A Natural Passion: A Study of the Novels of Samuel Richardson* (Oxford: Clarendon Press, 1974), pp. 58–61, 83–4.

19. *Adultery Anatomized: in a select collection of tryals, for criminal conversation*, 2 vols (London: n.p., 1761), II, 210–25 (p. 210).

20. G. E. C[okayne] and others, *The Complete Peerage of England, Scotland, Ireland, Great Britain and the United Kingdom*, rev. edn, 14 vols (London: St. Catherine Press, 1910–59). The entry includes a reference to the case from Mary Delany's diary dated March 1743/4.

21. See A. P. W. Malcolmson, *The Pursuit of the Heiress: Aristocratic Marriage in Ireland 1750–1820* (Ulster Historical Foundation, 1982), p. 37. Malcolmson points out that Lady Belvidere was not an heiress, and that the affair was 'immortalized in anecdote'. Lawrence Stone refers to the case briefly in *Road to Divorce*, pp. 167, 269, citing Malcolmson but not *Adultery Anatomized*.

22. *The Fair Adulteress. A Novel. A Story Founded on Real Facts, and Intended to Encourage Virtue, by Exposing Vice in its Proper Colours: Being the Genuine History of the Late Amours of Two Persons of the First Rank* (London: W. Bickerton, 1744).

23. For discussion of trial reports, the action for criminal conversation and Parliamentary divorce, see pp. 126–7 below.

24. *Broken Lives*, pp. 136, 137. For further details, see the entries for Beaufort and Talbot in *Complete Peerage* and those for Beaufort, Talbot

and Scudamore in *DNB*. The novel refers in flattering terms to Talbot's father, Charles, who was Lord Chancellor at his death in 1737, as 'Justinian'.

25. *Broken Lives*, p. 117.
26. *Long Time Burning*, p. 86.
27. *Eros Revived: Erotica of the Enlightenment in England and America* (London: Martin Secker & Warburg, 1988), p. 210.
28. *The Sign of Angellica: Women, Writing and Fiction, 1660–1800* (London: Virago, 1989), p. 126.
29. *The History of Miss Betsy Thoughtless* (Oxford and New York: Oxford University Press, 1997). In another modern edition of the novel, Christine Blouch cautions against the view that Haywood '"repented" of her early sensational fiction' and suggests that she had learned 'that the most essential virtue is appearing to be virtuous'. See her Introduction to *The History of Miss Betsy Thoughtless* (Peterborough, Ont., and Orchard Park, NY: Broadview Press, 1998), pp. 11, 12.
30. 'Introduction', *The Female Spectator: Selections*, ed. by Gabrielle M. Firmager (London: Bristol Classical Press, 1993), p. 8.
31. *Rise of the Female Novelist*, Chapter 5.
32. There are two such examples, both involving D'Elmont, in *Love in Excess*. While he succumbs to the first, he successfully resists the second, offered by the Italian Ciamara.
33. See Stone, *Family, Sex and Marriage*, pp. 272–90.
34. *The History of the Countess of Dellwyn*, 2 vols (London: A. Millar, 1759; repr. New York and London: Garland, 1974).
35. Spencer, *Rise of the Woman Novelist*, pp. 118–22; Linda Bree, *Sarah Fielding* (New York: Twayne Publishers; London: Prentice Hall International, 1996), pp. 122–34.
36. *Sarah Fielding*, p. 130.
37. *Sarah Fielding*, p. 127.
38. See Roderick Phillips, *Putting Asunder*, pp. 227–41; and, on divorce law in Scotland and how it worked during this period, Leah Leneman, *Alienated Affections: The Scottish Experience of Divorce and Separation, 1684–1830* (Edinburgh: Edinburgh University Press, 1998).
39. *Sarah Fielding*, p. 166, n. 9, citing *Road to Divorce*, p. 432.
40. *Sarah Fielding*, p. 8, citing *Living by the Pen: Women Writers in the Eighteenth Century* (London and New York: Routledge, 1992), p. 38.
41. The phrase is Spencer's (*Rise of the Woman Novelist*, p. 15); see also Todd, *Sign of Angellica*, p. 2 and passim. Poovey, who deals mainly with works of the late eighteenth and early nineteenth century, remarks that 'the paradigm of femininity had come to dominate the experience of most middle-class Englishwomen by the last half of the eighteenth century'. See *The Proper Lady and the Woman Writer: Ideology as Style in the Works of Mary Wollstonecraft, Mary Shelley, and Jane Austen* (Chicago and London: University of Chicago Press, 1984), p. 30.

42. *Sarah Fielding*, p. 145.
43. See Janet Todd, *Sensibility: An Introduction* (London and New York: Methuen, 1986); and G. J. Barker-Benfield, *The Culture of Sensibility: Sex and Society in Eighteenth-Century Britain* (Chicago and London: University of Chicago Press, 1992).
44. *Rise of the Woman Novelist*, pp. 122–3 (p. 122).
45. *Memoirs of Miss Sidney Bidulph*, ed. by Patricia Köster and Jean Coates Cleary (Oxford and New York: Oxford University Press, 1995). In *A Vindication of the Rights of Woman*, Mary Wollstonecraft was to criticize two of these works: Fordyce's *Sermons to Young Women* (1765) in Chapter V, Section II; Gregory's *A Father's Legacy to his Daughters* (1774) in Chapter II and Chapter V, Section III.
46. 'Frances Sheridan: Morality and Annihilated Time', in *Fetter'd or Free? British Women Novelists 1670–1815*, ed. by Mary Anne Schofield and Cecilia Macheski (Athens: Ohio University Press, 1986), pp. 324–58 (p. 342).
47. Sheridan's *Conclusion of the Memoirs of Miss Sidney Bidulph* (1767) is discussed by Doody in 'Frances Sheridan: Morality and Annihilated Time', pp. 346–50.
48. Frances Sheridan: Morality and Annihilated Time', p. 345.
49. *Family, Sex and Marriage*, p. 35; *Road to Divorce*, pp. 350, 137.
50. *Rise of the Woman Novelist*, pp. 124–5.
51. *Rise of the Woman Novelist*, p. 124.
52. *The History of Lady Barton, A Novel, in Letters*, 3 vols (London: T. Davies and T. Cadell, 1771).
53. Marla Harris finds in the novel a critical, proto-feminist message but does not acknowledge its caution over female desire. See '"How Nicely Circumspect Must Your Conduct Be": Double Standards in Elizabeth Griffith's *The History of Lady Barton*', in *Eighteenth-Century Women and the Arts*, ed. by Frederick M. Keener and Susan E. Lorsch (New York and London: Greenwood Press, 1988), pp. 277–82.
54. *Road to Divorce*, p. 233. Subsequent page references are given in parentheses.
55. 'The pornographer in the courtroom: trial reports about cases of sexual crimes and delinquencies as a genre of eighteenth-century erotica', in *Sexuality in Eighteenth-Century Britain*, ed. by Paul-Gabriel Boucé (Manchester: Manchester University Press; Totowa, NJ: Barnes and Noble, 1982), pp. 120–40 (p. 128). See also Wagner's 'Trial Reports as a Genre of Eighteenth-Century Erotica', *British Journal for Eighteenth-Century Studies*, 5 (1982), 117–21, and *Eros Revived*, pp. 113–32, which incorporates most of the two earlier articles.
56. London; repr. in facsimile in the series Marriage, Sex, and the Family in England 1660–1800, ed. by Randolph Trumbach, 44 vols (New York: Garland, 1985).
57. 'Pornographer in the courtroom', p. 127; *Eros Revived*, p. 127.

Collected in *Trials for Adultery*, the report occupies over 300 pages in Volume 5 and over 200 in Volume 6.

58. *Free Thoughts on Seduction, Adultery, and Divorce. [. . .] Occasioned by the late intrigue between his Royal Highness the Duke of Cumberland, and Henrietta, wife of the Right Honourable Richard Lord Grosvenor. [. . .] By a Civilian* (London: J. Bell, 1771).

59. Anon, 2 vols, London: J. Brough; anon, 2 vols, London: R. Baldwin.

60. Anon, 2 vols, London: R. Baldwin and J. Bew, 1779.

61. *Eros Revived*, p. 3.

62. 'Pornographer in the courtroom', p. 134; *Eros Revived*, p. 129.

63. *Culture and Adultery: The Novel, the Newspaper, and the Law, 1857–1914* (Philadelphia: University of Pennsylvania Press, 1999).

6   ADULTERY, REVOLUTION AND REACTION: 1773–1814

1. Stone, *Road to Divorce*, p. 288. There were four such bills, in 1771, 1779, 1800, and 1809. See pp. 257, 287–8, 335–9.

2. *Novellettes, Selected for the Use of Young Ladies and Gentlemen* (London: Fielding & Walker, 1780). The story was first published in *The Westminster Magazine*, 13 vols (1773–85), I, 525–35.

3. Respectively, 'The History of Louisa', 'Story of Lady Fanny Beaumont and Lord Layton', 'The Story of Sir William Sidney'; 'Story of Valmore and Julia', 'The Story of the Comte De Bernis', 'The Triumph of Constancy'; 'The Story of Miss Warner', 'Story of Rosalie'; 'The Dupe of Love and Friendship: or, The Unfortunate Irishman', 'The Dangerous Effects of a Wrong Education: or, The Fatal Contest'; 'The Story of Miss Williams'. Griffith's 13 stories in *Novellettes* appeared in the *Magazine* between 1773 and 1779. Of the other three stories in the collection, one is a virtue-in-distress story with a happy ending by a Mr. McMillan, and the other two are slight anecdotal pieces by Goldsmith.

4. *Women, Writing, and Revolution 1790–1827* (Oxford and New York: Clarendon Press, 1993), p. 1.

5. See, respectively, Susan Skedd, 'Women Teachers and the Expansion of Girls' Schooling in England, *c.* 1760–1820', in *Gender in Eighteenth-Century England: Roles, Representations, and Responsibilities*, ed. by Hannah Barker and Elaine Chalus (London and New York: Longman, 1997), pp. 101–25; Turner, *Living by the Pen*, pp. 31–9, 212–16.

6. 5 vols, London: G. G. J. and J. Robinson.

7. See note 1 above.

8. Loraine Fletcher, *Charlotte Smith: A Critical Biography* (London: Macmillan; New York: St Martin's Press, 1998), p. 1.

9. *Charlotte Smith: A Critical Biography*, pp. 1, 193.

10. *Emmeline, the Orphan of the Castle*, ed. by Anne Henry Ehrenpreis

(London and New York: Oxford University Press, 1971).

11. See *Emmeline*, pp. viii, 529, 530; and Loraine Fletcher, *Charlotte Smith*, pp. 26–7, 59, 77, 99–101.

12. *Rise of the Woman Novelist*, p. 128.

13. *Charlotte Smith: A Critical Biography*, p. 98.

14. *Charlotte Smith: A Critical Biography*, p. 94.

15. Introduction to her edition, *A Simple Story* (Oxford and New York: Oxford University Press, 1967; rev. edn, 1988), p. vii.

16. *Desire and Truth: Functions of Plot in Eighteenth-Century English Novels* (Chicago and London: University of Chicago Press, 1990), p. 198.

17. *Desire and Truth*, p. 200.

18. *Memoirs of Miss Emma Courtney*, ed. by Eleanor Ty (Oxford and New York: Oxford University Press, 1996).

19. *Unsex'd Revolutionaries: Five Women Novelists of the 1790s* (Toronto, Buffalo, NY, and London: University of Toronto Press, 1993), p. 46.

20. Hays drew freely in the novel on her correspondence with William Frend, with whom she was in love, and with Godwin, who advised her. See the Introduction and Explanatory Notes in Ty's edition, and also Kelly, *Women, Writing, and Revolution 1790–1827*, pp. 93–4, 100–2.

21. 'A Different Voice: Mary Hays's *The Memoirs of Emma Courtney*', *Women's Writing*, 8 (2001), 139–67, especially pp. 141–3, 151–2.

22. See, e.g., Sharma, 'A Different Voice', pp. 141–3. Ty points out that, although the novel 'was received favourably by contemporary reviewers', after 1797, 'With Wollstonecraft gone, Hays bore the brunt of the anti-Jacobin attacks' ('Introduction', pp. xxxiv, xxxv).

23. *Mary and The Wrongs of Woman*, ed. by Gary Kelly (Oxford and New York: Oxford University Press, 1976; repr. 1998). The quotation is from Matthew 22.30, and the emphasis is the author's.

24. 'Wild nights: pleasure/sexuality/feminism', in *Sea Changes: Culture and Feminism* (London: Verso, 1987), pp. 31–56 (p. 47), repr. in *The Ideology of Conduct: Essays in Literature and the History of Sexuality*, ed. by Nancy Armstrong and Leonard Tennenhouse (New York and London: Methuen, 1987), pp. 163–84 (p. 177). Kaplan's essay was first published in *Formations of Pleasure* (1983); see also Mary Poovey, *The Proper Lady and the Woman Writer*, pp. 69–81.

25. See their respective essays in *Women's Writing*, 4 (1997): 'Criminal Conversation: Mary Wollstonecraft's *The Wrongs of Woman*', pp. 221–34; 'Wollstonecraft's Secrets', pp. 247–60. The remark quoted is Moore's (p. 249).

26. As Jordan points out in 'Criminal Conversation', p. 222.

27. The square brackets enclose material added to Wollstonecraft's manuscript by her editor William Godwin.

28. *Rise of the Woman Novelist*, p. 132.

29. *Rise of the Woman Novelist*, p. 136. For the reaction to Godwin's *Memoirs of the Author of a Vindication of the Rights of Woman*, see R. M.

Janes, 'On the Reception of Mary Wollstonecraft's *A Vindication of the Rights of Woman*', *Journal of the History of Ideas*, 39 (1978), 293–302; repr. in *A Vindication of the Rights of Woman*, ed. by Carol H. Poston, 2nd edn (New York: W. W. Norton, 1988), pp. 297–307 (pp. 302–5).

30. *Women, Writing, and Revolution*, p. 25.
31. *Eve and the New Jerusalem: Socialism and Feminism in the Nineteenth Century* (London: Virago Press, 1983), pp. 12, 13.
32. 'Reform or Ruin: "A Revolution in Female Manners"', *Studies in Eighteenth-Century Culture*, 11 (1982), 199–216, repr. in *A Vindication of the Rights of Woman*, pp. 328–43.
33. *Revolutionary Feminism: The Mind and Career of Mary Wollstonecraft* (Basingstoke: Macmillan, 1992), p. 227.
34. Works by Sand, Tristan and Chernyshevsky are discussed in *Novel of Female Adultery*, pp. 96–117, 117–19, 129–32 respectively.
35. *Seductive Forms*, pp. 200–4 (p. 201).
36. *Seductive Forms*, p. 204.
37. *Seductive Forms*, p. 205; *Nobody's Story*, p. 1. The anecdote appears in a letter of 1826 quoted in John Gibson Lockhart, *Memoirs of the Life of Sir Walter Scott*, 10 vols (Edinburgh: Adam and Charles Black, 1853), VI, 406–7; and in Lockhart's abridged *Life of Sir Walter Scott* (repr. London: Dent; New York: Dutton, 1906), p. 412.
38. *Seductive Forms*, pp. 198–9.
39. *Lost Illusions*, trans. by Herbert J. Hunt (Harmondsworth and Baltimore: Penguin, 1971), p. 213, TM; *Balzac: La Comédie humaine*, 12 vols, ed. by Pierre-Georges Castex and others (Paris: Gallimard, 1976–81), V, 313.
40. Preface to *The Human Comedy*, trans. by Petra Morrison, in *The Nineteenth-Century Novel: Critical Essays and Documents*, ed. by Arnold Kettle, 2nd edn (London: Heinemann, 1981), pp. 134–147 (p. 142); 'Avant-propos', *Balzac: La Comédie humaine*, I, 15.
41. *Long Time Burning*, p. 189. Subsequent page references are given in parentheses.
42. The passage quoted is in *The Friend*, ed. by Barbara E. Rooke, 2 vols (London: Routledge and Kegan Paul; Princeton, NJ: Princeton University Press, 1969), II, 28–9.
43. *Women, Writing, and Revolution*, p. 181.
44. *The Novels of Jane Austen*, 5 vols, ed. by R. W. Chapman, 3rd edn, I, *Sense and Sensibility* (London and New York: Oxford University Press, 1933; repr. 1967).
45. *Novels of Jane Austen*, III, *Mansfield Park* (1934; repr. 1966). For an interesting discussion of the subject, chiefly addressing *Mansfield Park*, see Claire Lamont, '"Let other pens dwell on guilt and misery": Adultery in Jane Austen', in *Scarlet Letters*, pp. 70–81.
46. *Revolution and the Form of the British Novel 1790–1825*, pp. 94–5.

7 AFTER *MADAME BOVARY*: FEMALE ADULTERY IN ZOLA

1. See Thomas, *Long Time Burning*, pp. 267–9.
2. *Family in Crisis*, p. 3.
3. 'Preface, Written Twenty Years After the Novel', in *Against the Grain* [trans. by John Howard, pseud.] (New York: Three Sirens Press, 1931; repr. Dover, 1969), p. xxxv; *Oeuvres complètes de J.-K. Huysmans*, ed. by Charles Grolleau, 18 vols (Paris: Crès, 1928–34), VII, *A rebours*, p. x.
4. '*Madame Bovary*, by Gustave Flaubert', in *Madame Bovary*, ed. by Paul de Man, pp. 336–43; *Baudelaire: Oeuvres complètes*, II, 76–86.
5. *Toward an Aesthetic of Reception*, trans. by Timothy Bahti (Brighton, Sussex: Harvester, 1982), pp. 27–8; for discussion of the nature of Feydeau's innovation, see *Novel of Female Adultery*, pp. 91–4. Naomi Segal discusses the French Romantic confession in *Adulteress's Child*, passim, and 'Our Lady of the Flowers', in *Violetta and her Sisters*, pp. 161–7.
6. Paris: Michel Lévy Frères.
7. 'Our Lady of the Flowers', p. 163.
8. See, e.g., André Maurois, *Three Musketeers: A Study of the Dumas Family*, trans. by Gerard Hopkins (London: Jonathan Cape, 1957).
9. *Revue des deux mondes*, 5 parts, 15 April – 15 June, 1867; 'Monsieur de Camors', *Revue des deux mondes*, 15 January 1868, 63 (1868), 497–510; *Grand dictionnaire universel du dix-neuvième siècle*, 17 vols (Paris: Larousse et Boyer, 1866–86), VIII (1872), 310.
10. 'Monsieur de Camors', p. 499.
11. *Camors; or, Life under the New Empire* (New York: Blelock and Co., 1868). The chapter divisions in this translation differ in some places from those in the original.
12. *Monsieur de Camors*, 7th edn (Paris: Michel Lévy Frères, 1867).
13. *Grand dictionnaire universel*, XI (1874), 473.
14. *Grand dictionnaire universel*, XI (1874), 473. Caderousse was the Duc de Gramont-Caderousse, notorious for high living; he killed the English editor of *Le Sport* in a duel in 1862. See *Grand dictionnaire universel*, VIII (1872), 1442. Morny was indeed instrumental to Louis Napoleon's coup in 1851. See William E. Echard, *Historical Dictionary of the French Second Empire* (Westport, CT: Greenwood Press; London: Aldwych Press, 1985), pp. 418–21.
15. *Grand dictionnaire universel*, XI (1874), 575; *Historical Dictionary of the French Second Empire*, p. 418.
16. See I.i.19, 24 (Juliette); I.iii.64, I.vi.186, II.i.208–9 (Charlotte); I.iv.109, I.vi.162–3 (Elise).
17. 'his smile of a young tiger' (I.v.125–6); 'he had been cruelly fooled by his nervous system' (I.vi.171); 'if there is, as we hope, a divine hand which weighs in just balances our sufferings in comparison with our faults' (II.xi.361).

18. *Émile Zola*, 2nd edn (Oxford: Clarendon Press, 1966), p. 243.
19. *Émile Zola: Les Rougon-Macquart*, ed. by Henri Mitterand, IV (1966), 1718–19, 1722. The whole of Zola's *Ébauche* or preliminary outline for the novel has been reprinted in *Zola, 'La Bête humaine': texte et explications*, ed. by Geoff Woollen (Glasgow: University of Glasgow French and German Publications, 1990), pp. 25–62 (see pp. 28, 33).
20. *Émile Zola: Oeuvres complètes*, ed. by Henri Mitterand, 15 vols (Paris: Cercle du Livre Précieux, 1966–9), I, 95.
21. *Thérèse Raquin*, ed. by Henri Mitterand (Paris: Garnier-Flammarion, 1970), pp. 14–17.
22. *Naturalist Fiction*, p. 89, citing Alastair Fowler, *Kinds of Literature: An Introduction to the Theory of Genres and Modes* (Harvard University Press, 1982), p. 158.
23. *Thérèse Raquin*, trans. by Andrew Rothwell (Oxford and New York: Oxford University Press, 1992); *Émile Zola: Oeuvres complètes*, I.
24. *Ventriloquized Bodies: Narratives of Hysteria in Nineteenth-Century France* (Ithaca, NY, and London: Cornell University Press, 1994).
25. *Ventriloquized Bodies*, p. 41.
26. *Ventriloquized Bodies*, especially Chapter 3, 'Reading Women: The Novel in the Text of Hysteria'.
27. E.g. by David Baguley, in *Naturalist Fiction*, p. 90.
28. 'La Femme adultère', in *Les Français peints par eux-mêmes: encyclopédie morale du dix-neuvième siècle*, 8 vols (Paris: Curmer, 1840–2), III, 265–72. Lucas's article is discussed in *Novel of Female Adultery*, pp. 67–8, 77–82.
29. *Madame Bovary*, ed. by Paul de Man, p. 338; *Baudelaire: Oeuvres complètes*, II, 79–80.
30. *Ventriloquized Bodies*, p. 154.
31. For extended analysis of this paradox, and discussion of the whole subject, see Brian Nelson, *Zola and the Bourgeoisie: A Study of Themes and Techniques in Les Rougon-Macquart* (London: Macmillan, 1983).
32. For discussion of the influence of the libertine text on the novel of female adultery, see *Novel of Female Adultery*, pp. 12, 20, 36–45.
33. *Oeuvres complètes*, IX, 272.
34. *Les Rougon-Macquart*, IV, 1710–17 (p. 1710).
35. *Les Rougon-Macquart*, IV, 1727, 1741.
36. *Émile Zola*, pp. 243; 241, n. 2; 244.
37. For the first idea of murdering Roubaud, see *La Bête humaine*, trans. by Roger Pearson (Oxford and New York: Oxford University Press, 1996), VIII.239; *Les Rougon-Macquart*, IV, 1214. For the passages in which Thérèse and Séverine propose murder, see *Thérèse Raquin*, IX.50; 558, XXI.119; 606, and *La Bête humaine*, IX.260–1; 1233–4.
38. Early in his outline for the novel, Zola wrote that the woman with whom the novel's main character would fall in love would 'then drive him to kill' (*Les Rougon-Macquart*, IV, 1719; *'La Bête humaine'*:

texte et explications, p. 29).

39.   *Les Rougon-Macquart*, IV, 1722.
40.   *Les Rougon-Macquart*, IV, 1747; Zola's letter of thanks is on p. 1751.
41.   *Les Rougon-Macquart*, IV, 1766. Pearson also discusses Lombroso's influence in his Introduction, pp. xvi–xviii.
42.   See *L'Homme criminel: étude anthropologique et médico-légale*, trans. from the fourth Italian edition by G. Regnier and A. Bornet (Paris: Félix Alcan; Turin: Bocca Frères, 1887), pp. 660–8.
43.   'Jacques the Ripper', in *Emile Zola Centenary Colloquium 1893–1993*, ed. by Patrick Pollard (London: Emile Zola Society, 1995), pp. 73–82 (p. 77).
44.   *Les Rougon-Macquart*, IV, 1718; *'La Bête humaine': texte et explications*, p. 28. He uses a similar phrase a few pages later (IV, 1722; p. 33).
45.   'A question of motives: heredity and inheritance in *La Bête humaine*', in *'La Bête humaine': texte et explications*, pp. 184–95 (pp. 185–6).
46.   See Pearson, 'Introduction', *La Bête humaine*, p. xviii.
47.   'Codes en conflit dans *La Bête humaine*', in *'La Bête humaine': texte et explications*, pp. 136–48 (p. 137), referring to Cesare Lombroso and Guillaume Ferrero, *La Femme criminelle et la prostituée*, trans. of 4th edn of 1887 by Louise Meille (Paris: Félix Alcan, 1896).
48.   See p. 4 above.
49.   'The Man-Eater', in *Critical Essays on Emile Zola*, ed. by David Baguley (Boston, MA: G. K. Hall, 1986), pp. 90–3 (p. 90).
50.   *Nana*, trans. by George Holden (Harmondsworth and New York: Penguin Books, 1972); *Nana*, in *Les Rougon-Macquart*, II, 1093–1485.
51.   Zola may have considered syphilis too obvious a choice; more to the point, its impact would have been slower and so much less dramatic.
52.   *Reflecting on Nana* (London and New York: Routledge, 1991); compare Valerie Minogue, who sees Nana as representing 'the lost innocence of humanity at large', and therefore as being endowed 'with a certain tragic grandeur' ('Venus Observing – Venus Observed: Zola's *Nana*', in *Emile Zola Centenary Colloquium 1893–1993*, pp. 57–72 [p. 63]).
53.   In the introduction to his translation of the novel, pp. 11–13, George Holden gives a translation of Zola's preliminary description of Nana.
54.   'A question of motives: heredity and inheritance in *La Bête humaine*', p. 192.
55.   'Introduction', Émile Zola, *Pot-Bouille*, ed. by Robert Lethbridge (London and Rutland, VT: J. M. Dent, 2000), p. xxvi.
56.   *Les Rougon-Macquart*, III, 1619.
57.   'Introduction', *Pot-Bouille*, p. xix.
58.   *Les Rougon-Macquart*, III, 1607.
59.   *Les Rougon-Macquart*, III, 1610, 1619.
60.   'Introduction', *Pot-Bouille*, p. xxiii.
61.   *Émile Zola: Oeuvres complètes*, ed. by Henri Mitterand, XIV, 531–7 (pp. 533, 535, 535).

62. 'Introduction', *Pot-Bouille*, p. xxiii.
63. *Zola and the Bourgeoisie*, p. 51.
64. *Oeuvres complètes*, III, 531.
65. *Family in Crisis*, pp. 7–8, 25–40, 51–7, 69.
66. Introduction to Émile Zola, *Pot Luck*, trans. by Brian Nelson (Oxford and New York: Oxford University Press, 1999), p. xv.
67. *Les Rougon-Macquart*, III, 1619; Zola's emphasis.
68. *Pot Luck*, trans. by Brian Nelson; *Les Rougon-Macquart*, III.
69. See, e.g., F. W. J. Hemmings, *Émile Zola*, pp. 139–41, 146, 148–50, 179–80.
70. *Ventriloquized Bodies*, p. 192, citing Susanna Barrows, *Distorting Mirrors: Visions of the Crowd in Late Nineteenth-Century France* (New Haven: Yale University Press, 1981).
71. *Ventriloquized Bodies*, pp. 196, 194–5.
72. 'Introduction', *Pot Luck*, p. x. However, what Nelson says about 'the nineteenth-century novel of adultery' applies more to the tradition in France than elsewhere, especially in countries where divorce was not available.
73. 'Introduction', *Pot-Bouille*, p. xxv; 'Carnal Knowledge in French Naturalist Fiction', in *Scarlet Letters*, p. 128. White is much nearer the mark when he says elsewhere: 'the ambivalence of Zola's position is revealed in the way that he indulges in the adulterous motif as much as he parodies its cultural predominance' (*Family in Crisis*, p. 56).
74. *Émile Zola: Les Rougon-Macquart*, II, 1610.
75. *A Woman of Thirty* first acquired its definitive title in 1842; see the discussion in *Novel of Female Adultery*, pp. 56–60.
76. 'She was Lady Rowena, she was in love, with the deep peaceful passion of a noble soul' (*A Love Affair*, trans. by Jean Stewart [London: Paul Elek, 1958; repr. Arrow Books, 1967], I.v.67); *Une Page d'amour*, in *Émile Zola: Les Rougon-Macquart*, II, 797–1092 (p. 855). See also the example from *Thérèse Raquin* referred to on p. 161 above.
77. See *Ventriloquized Bodies*, e.g. pp. 40–8, 78–82, 154–61. As Brian Nelson has observed, 'Images of liquidity [. . .] are used to evoke Hélène's passion and also imply inner dissolution' (*Zola and the Bourgeoisie*, p. 119).
78. *Les Rougon-Macquart*, II, 1610.
79. *Les Rougon-Macquart*, II, 1610; Zola's emphasis.
80. See Chapter 3 above.
81. *Émile Zola*, p. 129.
82. *Zola and the Bourgeoisie*, p. 127; quoting *Novel of Adultery*, p. 86.
83. In a letter to Zola of April 1878, repr. in *Les Rougon-Macquart*, II, 1624–5 (p. 1624); Flaubert's emphasis.
84. *Zola and the Bourgeoisie*, p. 99.
85. *Les Rougon-Macquart*, II, 1624–5 (p. 1624); Flaubert's emphasis.
86. *Zola and the Bourgeoisie*, p. 128.

87. *Zola and the Bourgeoisie*, pp. 104–111, 119–20, 124–5.
88. *Breaking the Chain*, p. 47.

8 PARODY, ENTROPY, ECLIPSE: HUYSMANS, CÉARD, MAUPASSANT

1.   *Family in Crisis*, p. 1.
2.   *Family in Crisis*, p. 159.
3.   *Naturalist Fiction*, p. 136; *Family in Crisis*, p. 30.
4.   'The Golden Age of Male Adultery: The Third Republic', *Journal of Social History*, 28 (1995), 469–90 (p. 483).
5.   'Golden Age of Male Adultery', p. 485, n. 9.
6.   'Le Divorce et la littérature', in *Émile Zola: Oeuvres complètes*, ed. by Henri Mitterand, 15 vols (Paris: Cercle du Livre Précieux, 1966–70), XIV, 543–7 (p. 545). The article appeared in *Le Figaro* on 14 February 1881, two weeks before Zola's 'Adultery among the Bourgeoisie'.
7.   'Le Divorce et le théâtre', *Le Figaro*, 12 June 1884, repr. in *Chroniques*, 3 vols (Paris: Union générale d'éditions, 1980), II, 408–15. Edward D. Sullivan discusses and quotes from the article in *Maupassant the Novelist* (Princeton: Princeton University Press, 1954; repr. Westport, CT: Greenwood Press, 1978), pp. 80–1.
8.   See *Maupassant: Romans*, ed. by Louis Forestier (Paris: Gallimard, 1987), p. 1427. Forestier notes that, although the Naquet law was not passed until 27 July 1884, it was preceded by considerable public discussion, including several articles by Maupassant.
9.   *Naturalist Fiction*, p. 207.
10. See Baguley, *Naturalist Fiction*, passim.
11. 'Note', in *En Ménage, Oeuvres complètes de J.-K. Huysmans*, IV, 387–95 (p. 394); for discussion of Zola's article see above, pp. 175–6.
12. *Naturalist Fiction*, p. 132.
13. *Living Together*, trans. by J. W. G. Sandiford-Pellé (London: Fortune Press, 1969); *En Ménage, Oeuvres complètes de J.-K. Huysmans*, IV.
14. *J.-K. Huysmans: Novelist, Poet, and Art Critic* (Ann Arbor, MI: UMI Research Press, 1987), p. 33.
15. 'Huysmans's *En Ménage* and the Unwritable Naturalist Text', *Forum for Modern Language Studies*, 29 (1993), 18–30 (p. 28).
16. 'Huysmans's *En Ménage* and the Unwritable Naturalist Text', p. 29.
17. 'Huysmans's *En Ménage* and the Unwritable Naturalist Text', p. 19.
18. This is a further parallel with Zola's heroine in *A Love Affair*.
19. *A Lovely Day*, trans. by Ernest Boyd (New York: Alfred A. Knopf, 1924); *Une Belle Journée* (Paris: Charpentier, 1881; repr. Geneva: Slatkine, 1970).
20. *The Physiology of Marriage* is discussed in *Novel of Female Adultery*, pp. 15–23.

21. A famous pictorial representation of the symbol is *Girl with a Broken Pitcher* by Jean-Baptiste Greuze (1725–1805), to which Zola refers in *Pot Luck* (III.54; 55). Janet Beizer illustrates the painting and analyses its significance in *Ventriloquized Bodies*, pp. 197–200.
22. *Madame Bovary*, ed. by Paul de Man, p. 211; *Madame Bovary*, ed. by Claudine Gothot-Mersch, p. 296.
23. *Naturalist Fiction*, p. 136.
24. For a discussion of Schopenhauer's long-recognized influence on Naturalism, see *Naturalist Fiction*, pp. 134–5, 251 n. 34, and passim.
25. *Naturalist Fiction*, p. 136.
26. 'A Harmless Liaison: On Céard's *Une belle journée*', *Nineteenth-Century French Studies*, 18 (1990), 482–91 (pp. 482–3).
27. O. R. Morgan, 'Léon Hennique (1851–1935). His Life and Works. A contribution to the history of the Naturalist School in French Literature' (unpublished MA thesis, University of Nottingham, 1961), pp. 71–2; *Émile Zola: Correspondance*, ed. by B. H. Bakker and others, 10 vols (Montreal: Presses de l'Université de Montréal; Paris: Éditions du Centre National de la Recherche Scientifique, 1978–95), III (1982), 212. The letter is dated 20 August 1878.
28. 'Léon Hennique', pp. 95–6.
29. *Family in Crisis*, p. 154.
30. White analyses this scene in detail in *Family in Crisis*, pp. 159–67.
31. *Family in Crisis*, p. 157.
32. Maupassant, *Contes et nouvelles*, 2 vols, ed. by Louis Forestier (Paris: Gallimard, 1974), I, 1334.
33. 'The Love of Long Ago', in *Short Stories of the Tragedy and Comedy of Life, The Life Work of Henri René Guy de Maupassant*, 17 vols, trans. anon. (London and New York: M. Walter Dunne, 1903), V, 9–14; *Maupassant: Contes et nouvelles*, I, 181–5.
34. *Maupassant the Novelist*, pp. 17–18.
35. *Maupassant: Contes et nouvelles*, I, 1338.
36. 'L'Adultère', *Le Gaulois*, 23 January 1882, 1–2 (p. 1), repr. in *Chroniques*, I, 397–402 (p. 398).
37. *Maupassant: Romans*, p. 1239.
38. *Naturalist Fiction*, p. 129; *The Historical Novel*, trans. by Hannah and Stanley Mitchell (London: Merlin Press, 1962), p. 199.
39. 'Introduction', *Bel-Ami*, trans. by Margaret Mauldon (Oxford and New York: Oxford University Press, 2001), pp. ix, xiv–xvi, xxviii, xxx–xxxi; the novel by Marivaux is *Le Paysan parvenu* (1734–5).
40. *Bel-Ami*, trans. by Margaret Mauldon; *Romans*, ed. by Louis Forestier.
41. Forestier notes the echo of Flaubert (*Romans*, p. 1428).
42. *Monsieur de Camors* is discussed on pp. 156–9 above; as Edward D. Sullivan has said, Feuillet was Maupassant's 'favorite whipping-boy'. See *Maupassant the Novelist*, p. 15.
43. *Maupassant: Pierre et Jean* (London: Grant & Cutler, 1984), p. 71.

44. '*Une Vie* or the Name of the Mother', in *Breaking the Chain*, pp. 48–77. I am indebted to this essay for my knowledge of the story 'Jadis' discussed on pp. 199–200 above.

45. *A Woman's Revenge: The Chronology of Dispossession in Maupassant's Fiction* (Lexington, KY: French Forum Publishers, 1986), p. 48.

46. *Mont-Oriol, or A Romance of Auvergne: A Novel*, in *Life Work*, VIII; *Romans*, ed. Forestier.

47. These novels are discussed in *Novel of Female Adultery*, pp. 99–109.

48. *Maupassant the Novelist*, p. 97.

49. *Pierre and Jean*, trans. by Leonard Tancock (Harmondsworth: Penguin, 1979); *Romans*, ed. Forestier.

50. As Robert Lethbridge remarks, 'the text provides ample evidence to justify the widespread critical agreement that Pierre's obsessive love can be properly described as Oedipal' (*Maupassant: Pierre et Jean*, p. 46). Less often recognized is Mary Donaldson-Evans's point that the novel also provides a successful resolution of the Oedipal crisis in Jean's marriage to Mme Rosémilly (*A Woman's Revenge*, p. 37).

51. See p. 211 above.

52. *Fort Comme la Mort, or The Ruling Passion*, in *Life Work*, XI; *Romans*, ed. Forestier. As Forestier points out, the title evokes the Song of Songs (*Romans*, pp. 1569–70; Song of Solomon, 8:6).

53. See p. 210 above.

54. *A Woman's Revenge*, pp. 13–17 and passim.

55. *Maupassant: Bel-Ami* (London: Grant & Cutler, 1988), p. 40; *Family in Crisis*, pp. 86–7.

56. *French Feminism in the Nineteenth Century* (Albany: State University of New York Press, 1984), p. 209. For an account of the passing of the 1884 divorce law, see Antony Copley, *Sexual Moralities in France, 1780–1980: New Ideas on the Family, Divorce and Homosexuality* (London: Routledge, 1989), pp. 114–33.

57. See *Maupassant: Contes et nouvelles*, I, 1338, notes 3 and 4.

58. *Notre Coeur, or A Woman's Pastime: A Novel*, in *Life Work*, IX; *Romans*, ed. Forestier.

59. Forestier notes that Mme de Burne's lesbianism is more explicit in Maupassant's manuscript (*Romans*, pp. 1617, 1661). Bram Dijkstra discusses representations of female narcissism and homosexuality in *Idols of Perversity: Fantasies of Feminine Evil in Fin-de-Siècle Culture* (New York and Oxford: Oxford University Press, 1986), pp. 135–59.

60. *Romans*, pp. 1272, 1640.

61. Forestier suggests that this novel recalls Paul Bourget's *Un Coeur de femme*, published like Maupassant's in 1890 (*Romans*, p. 1632).

62. See *Ventriloquized Bodies*, passim, and pp. 161–3, 181 above.

63. See *Romans*, e.g. pp. 1514, 1579, 1580, 1640, 1658, 1660, 1663; *A Woman's Revenge*, p. 139.

64. For discussion of the two unfinished novels, see Sullivan, *Maupassant*

the Novelist, pp. 157–64; for the texts and commentary, see Forestier, *Romans*, pp. 1185–1224, 1670–87.

65. *Naturalist Fiction*, p. 104.
66. See, for example, Jennifer Birkett, *The Sins of the Fathers: Decadence in France, 1870–1914* (London and New York: Quartet Books, 1986), and Dijkstra, *Idols of Perversity*.
67. Nancy Miller calls attention to 'what appears to be a gap between Sand and Colette' in the literary history of French women novelists, though she mentions Louise Colet, Daniel Stern, Gyp, Rachilde, and Juliette Adam. See *Subject to Change: Reading Feminist Writing* (New York: Columbia University Press, 1988), pp. 19–20, n. 9. Lucienne Frappier-Mazur points to a 'void' between erotic fiction by Frenchwomen in the first years of the nineteenth century and the Decadent period of the 1880s; see 'Marginal Canons: Rewriting the Erotic', *Yale French Studies*, 75, *The Politics of Tradition: Placing Women in French Literature* (1988), 112–28 (p. 119).
68. *Feminist Novelists of the Belle Epoque: Love as a Lifestyle* (Bloomington and Indianapolis: Indiana University Press, 1990), especially Chapter 1, 'Away from the Bourgeois Ideal'.
69. French novels that question the wife's role in bourgeois marriage are discussed by Waelti-Walters in *Feminist Novelists of the Belle Epoque*. Two North American examples are Kate Chopin, *The Awakening* (1899), and Willa Cather, *A Lost Lady* (1923). Novels that present the husband critically and ironically, though in rather different ways, are Marcellus Emants, *A Posthumous Confession* (1894), and Machado de Assis, *Dom Casmurro* (1899).

Bibliography

PRIMARY SOURCES ORIGINALLY WRITTEN IN ENGLISH

Anon, *Adultery Anatomized: in a select collection of tryals, for criminal conversation*, 2 vols (London: n.p., 1761)

——, *The Fair Adulteress. A Novel. A Story Founded on Real Facts, and Intended to Encourage Virtue, by Exposing Vice in its Proper Colours: Being the Genuine History of the Late Amours of Two Persons of the First Rank* (London: W. Bickerton, 1744)

——, *The Fair Adultress: or, the Treacherous Brother. Being the Secret Memoirs of a certain Noble Family in the Island of Cyprus. Interspersed with Several Original Letters. Translated from the Greek* (London: A. Miller, 1743)

——, *Free Thoughts on Seduction, Adultery, and Divorce. [. . .] Occasioned by the late intrigue between his Royal Highness the Duke of Cumberland, and Henrietta, wife of the Right Honourable Richard Lord Grosvenor. [. . .] By a Civilian* (London: J. Bell, 1771)

——, *A Full and Complete History of His R—l H— the D— of C—d and Lady G—r, the Fair Adultress*, 3rd edn, 2 vols (London: J. Brough, 1770)

——, *Harriet: or, The Innocent Adultress*, 2 vols (London: R. Baldwin, 1770; repr. R. Baldwin and J. Bew, 1779)

Astell, Mary, *The First English Feminist: 'Reflections upon Marriage' and Other Writings by Mary Astell*, ed. by Bridget Hill (Aldershot, Hants: Gower Publishing, 1986)

——, *Political Writings*, ed. by Patricia Springborg (Cambridge and New York: Cambridge University Press, 1996)

Austen, Jane, *Mansfield Park*, ed. by R. W. Chapman (London and New York: Oxford University Press, 1934; repr. 1966)

——, *Sense and Sensibility*, ed. by R. W. Chapman, 3rd edn (London and New York: Oxford University Press, 1933; repr. 1967)

Behn, Aphra, *Love-Letters Between a Nobleman and His Sister*, ed. by Maureen Duffy (London: Virago, 1987)

——, *Love-Letters Between a Nobleman and his Sister*, ed. by Janet Todd (London and New York: Penguin, 1996)

——, *Oroonoko and Other Writings*, ed. by Paul Salzman (Oxford and New York: Oxford University Press, 1994)

Burney, Frances, *Evelina, or, The History of a Young Lady's Entrance into the World*, ed. by Edward A. and Lillian D. Bloom (Oxford and New York: Oxford University Press, 1968)

Cleland, John, *Memoirs of a Woman of Pleasure*, ed. by Peter Sabor (Oxford and New York: Oxford University Press, 1985)

Defoe, Daniel, *Moll Flanders*, ed. by G. A. Starr (Oxford and New York: Oxford University Press, 1971)

——, *Roxana: The Fortunate Mistress*, ed. by Jane Jack (Oxford and New York: Oxford University Press, 1964)

De Forest, John William, *Miss Ravenel's Conversion From Secession to Loyalty*, ed. by Gary Scharnhorst (New York: Penguin Putnam; London: Penguin Books, 2000)

Fielding, Henry, *Amelia*, ed. by David Blewett (Harmondsworth and New York: Penguin, 1987)

——, *The History of Tom Jones*, ed. by R. P. C. Mutter (Harmondsworth and Baltimore: Penguin, 1966)

Fielding, Sarah, *The History of the Countess of Dellwyn*, 2 vols (London: A. Millar, 1759; repr. New York and London: Garland, 1974)

Goldsmith, Oliver, *The Vicar of Wakefield*, ed. by Arthur Friedman (Oxford and New York: Oxford University Press, 1974; rev. edn, 1981)

Griffith, Elizabeth, *The History of Lady Barton, A Novel, in Letters*, 3 vols (London: T. Davies and T. Cadell, 1771)

——, and others, *Novellettes, Selected for the Use of Young Ladies and Gentlemen* (London: Fielding & Walker, 1780)

Hays, Mary, *Memoirs of Miss Emma Courtney*, ed. by Eleanor Ty (Oxford and New York: Oxford University Press, 1996)

Haywood, Eliza, *The Female Spectator: Selections*, ed. by Gabrielle M. Firmager (London: Bristol Classical Press, 1993)

——, *The History of Miss Betsy Thoughtless*, ed. by Beth Fowkes Tobin (Oxford and New York: Oxford University Press, 1997)

——, *The History of Miss Betsy Thoughtless*, ed. by Christine Blouch (Peterborough, Ont., and Orchard Park, NY: Broadview Press, 1998)

——, *Love in Excess; or, The Fatal Enquiry*, ed. by David Oakleaf, 2nd edn (Peterborough, Ont., and Orchard Park, NY: Broadview Press, 2000)

——, *Memoirs of a Certain Island Adjacent to the Kingdom of Utopia*, 2 vols (London: Booksellers of London and Westminster, 1724, 1725 [dated 1725, 1726]; vol. 1 repr. New York and London: Garland, 1972)

Inchbald, Elizabeth, *A Simple Story*, ed. by J. M. S. Tompkins (Oxford and New York: Oxford University Press, 1967; rev. edn, 1988)

Johnson, Samuel, *The Lives of the English Poets*, ed. by George Birkbeck Hill, 3 vols (Oxford: Clarendon Press, 1905; repr. New York: Octagon Books, 1967)

Lee, Harriet, *The Errors of Innocence*, 5 vols (London: G. G. J. and J. Robinson, 1786)

Locke, John, *Two Treatises of Government*, ed. by Peter Laslett, 2nd edn (Cambridge and New York: Cambridge University Press, 1988)

Mackenzie, Henry, *The Man of Feeling* (New York: W. W. Norton, 1958)

Manley, Delarivier, *The Adventures of Rivella; or, the History of the Author of the Atalantis* [London: n.p., 1714]

——, *Memoirs of Europe, Towards the Close of the Eighth Century*, 2 vols (London: J. Morphew, 1710)

——, *The New Atalantis*, ed. by Rosalind Ballaster (London: Pickering and Chatto, 1991; London and New York: Penguin, 1992)

——, *The Novels of Mary Delariviere Manley 1705–1714*, ed. by Patricia Köster, 2 vols (Gainesville, FL: Scholars' Facsimiles & Reprints, 1971)

——, *Secret Memoirs and Manners of several Persons of Quality, of Both Sexes, from the New Atalantis, an Island in the Mediteranean*, 2 vols (London: J. Morphew, 1709)

Richardson, Samuel, *Clarissa; or, The History of a Young Lady*, ed. by Angus

Ross (Harmondsworth: Penguin; New York: Viking Penguin, 1985)
——, *Pamela; or, Virtue Rewarded*, ed. by Peter Sabor (Harmondsworth and Baltimore: Penguin, 1980)
——, *Selected Letters of Samuel Richardson*, ed. by John Carroll (Oxford: Clarendon Press, 1964)
Rowe, Elizabeth, *Friendship in Death: In Twenty Letters from the Dead to the Living*, 3rd edn (London: T. Worrall, 1733; repr. New York and London: Garland, 1972)
Sheridan, Frances, *Memoirs of Miss Sidney Bidulph*, ed. by Patricia Köster and Jean Coates Cleary (Oxford and New York: Oxford University Press, 1995)
Smith, Charlotte, *Emmeline, the Orphan of the Castle*, ed. by Anne Henry Ehrenpreis (London and New York: Oxford University Press, 1971)
Smollett, Tobias, *Peregrine Pickle*, ed. by James L. Clifford and Paul-Gabriel Boucé (Oxford and New York: Oxford University Press, 1983)
Spectator, The, ed. by Donald F. Bond, 5 vols (Oxford: Clarendon Press, 1965)
Trials for Adultery: or, the History of Divorces, 7 vols, in Marriage, Sex, and the Family in England 1660–1800, ed. by Randolph Trumbach, 44 vols (New York: Garland, 1985)
Westminster Magazine, or the Pantheon of Taste, The, 13 vols (London, 1773–85)
Wood, Ellen [Mrs Henry Wood], *East Lynne*, ed. by Norman Page and Kamal Al-Solaylee (London: J. M. Dent; Rutland, VT: Charles E. Tuttle, 1984; new edn, 1994)
Wollstonecraft, Mary, *Mary and The Wrongs of Woman*, ed. by Gary Kelly (Oxford and New York: Oxford University Press, 1976; repr. 1998)
——, *A Vindication of the Rights of Woman*, ed. by Carol H. Poston, 2nd edn (New York: W. W. Norton, 1988)

PRIMARY SOURCES ORIGINALLY WRITTEN IN OTHER LANGUAGES

Alas, Leopoldo ('Clarín'), *La Regenta*, trans. by John Rutherford (Harmondsworth: Penguin; New York: Viking Penguin, 1984)
Balzac, Honoré de, *Cousin Bette*, trans. by Sylvia Raphael (Oxford and New York: Oxford University Press, 1992)
——, *The Lily of the Valley*, trans. by James Waring, in *La Comédie Humaine*, 40 vols, ed. by George Saintsbury, XXI (London: Dent; New York: Macmillan, 1897)
——, *Lost Illusions*, trans. by Herbert J. Hunt (Harmondsworth and Baltimore: Penguin, 1971)
——, *The Muse of the Department*, trans. by James Waring, in *La Comédie Humaine*, 40 vols, ed. by George Saintsbury, XXVIII, *Parisians in the Country* (1898)
——, *Le Père Goriot*, trans. by A. J. Krailsheimer (Oxford and New York: Oxford University Press, 1991)
——, *The Physiology of Marriage*, trans. by Francis Macnamara (London: Casanova Society, 1925)
——, Preface to *The Human Comedy*, trans. by Petra Morrison, in *The*

Nineteenth-Century Novel: Critical Essays and Documents, ed. by Arnold Kettle, 2nd edn (London: Heinemann, 1981)

Balzac, Honoré de, *A Woman of Thirty*, trans. by Ellen Marriage, in *La Comédie Humaine*, 40 vols, ed. by George Saintsbury, XL (1897)

———, *Balzac: La Comédie humaine*, 12 vols, ed. by Pierre-Georges Castex and others (Paris: Gallimard, 1976–81)

Baudelaire, Charles, 'Madame Bovary, by Gustave Flaubert', in *Madame Bovary*, Norton Critical Edition, ed. by Paul de Man (New York: Norton, 1965)

———, 'Madame Bovary, par Gustave Flaubert', in *Baudelaire: Oeuvres complètes*, ed. by Claude Pichois, 2 vols (Paris: Gallimard, 1975–6), II, 76–86

Céard, Henri, *A Lovely Day*, trans. by Ernest Boyd (New York: Alfred A. Knopf, 1924)

———, *Une Belle Journée* (Paris: Charpentier, 1881; repr. Geneva: Slatkine, 1970)

Champfleury (pseudonym of Jules-Husson Fleury), *Les Bourgeois de Molinchart*, 2nd edn (Paris: Librairie nouvelle, 1855)

Chateaubriand, François-René, Vicomte de, *Atala and René*, trans. by Rayner Heppenstall (London and New York: Oxford University Press, 1963)

Constant, Benjamin, *Adolphe*, trans. by Margaret Mauldon (Oxford and New York: Oxford University Press, 2001)

Dumas, Alexander, the younger, *Affaire Clémenceau: mémoire de l'accusé* (Paris: Michel Lévy Frères, 1866)

Eça de Queirós, José Maria de, *Cousin Bazilio*, trans. by Roy Campbell (London: Max Reinhardt, 1953; repr. Manchester: Carcanet Press, 1992)

Feuillet, Octave, *Camors; or, Life under the New Empire*, trans. anon. (New York: Blelock and Co., 1868)

———, *Monsieur de Camors*, 7th edn (Paris: Michel Lévy Frères, 1867)

Feydeau, Ernest, *Fanny: or the Revelations of a Woman's Heart*, trans. anon (London: George Vickers, 1860)

———, *Fanny: Étude*, 4th edn (Paris: Amyot, 1858)

Flaubert, Gustave, *Madame Bovary: Provincial Lives*, trans. by Geoffrey Wall (London and New York: Penguin, 1992)

———, *Madame Bovary: moeurs de province*, ed. by Claudine Gothot-Mersch (Paris: Garnier, 1971)

———, *Sentimental Education*, trans. by Robert Baldick (Harmondsworth and New York: Penguin Books, 1964)

Fontane, Theodor, *Beyond Recall*, trans. by Douglas Parmée (London and New York: Oxford University Press, 1964)

———, *Effi Briest*, trans. by Hugh Rorrison and Helen Chambers (London and New York: Penguin Books, 2000)

———, *Two Novellas: The Woman Taken in Adultery and The Poggenpuhl Family*, trans. by Gabriele Annan (Chicago and London: University of Chicago Press, 1979; repr. Harmondsworth: Penguin, 1995)

———, *L'Adultera*, in *Werke und Schriften*, 54 vols, ed. by Walter Keitel and Helmuth Nürnberger, VII (Carl Hanser: Munich, 1971; repr. in Fontane Bibliothek, Frankfurt am Main, Berlin, Vienna: Ullstein, 1991)

Fontane, Theodor, *Effi Briest*, in *Werke und Schriften*, XVII (1974; 1979)

Fromentin, Eugène, *Dominique*, trans. by Sir Edward Marsh (London: Cresset Press, 1948; repr. Soho Book Company, 1986)

Goethe, Johann Wolfgang von, *Elective Affinities*, trans. by R. J. Hollingdale (Harmondsworth and New York: Penguin Books, 1971)

——, *Elective Affinities: A Novel*, trans. by David Constantine (Oxford and New York: Oxford University Press, 1994)

——, *Goethe: Die Wahlverwandtschaften*, ed. by H. B. Nisbet and Hans Reiss (Oxford: Basil Blackwell, 1971)

——, *Die Wahlverwandtschaften*, in *Goethes Werke*, ed. by Erich Trunz and others, 14 vols (Hamburg: Christian Wegner Verlag, 1948–60), VI

Grand dictionnaire universel du dix-neuvième siècle, 17 vols (Paris: Larousse et Boyer, 1866–86)

Hennique, Léon, *Les Héros modernes. L'Accident de Monsieur Hébert* (Paris: Charpentier, 1884)

Huysmans, Joris-Karl, *Living Together*, trans. by J. W. G. Sandiford-Pellé (London: Fortune Press, 1969)

——, 'Preface, Written Twenty Years After the Novel', in *Against the Grain*, trans. by John Howard, pseud. (New York: Three Sirens Press, 1931; repr. Dover, 1969)

——, *A rebours*, in *Oeuvres complètes de J.-K. Huysmans*, ed. by Charles Grolleau, 18 vols (Paris: Crès, 1928–34), VII

——, *En Ménage*, in *Oeuvres complètes de J.-K. Huysmans*, IV

Jacobsen, Jens Peter, *Marie Grubbe: A Lady of the Seventeenth Century*, trans. by Hanna Astrup Larsen (New York: American-Scandinavian Foundation; London: Oxford University Press, 1917); 2nd edn, rev. by Robert Raphael, The Library of Scandinavian Literature, 30 (Boston: G. K. Hall, 1975)

Laclos, Choderlos de, *Les Liaisons dangereuses*, trans. by Douglas Parmée (Oxford and New York: Oxford University Press, 1995)

Lafayette, Marie-Madeleine Pioche de la Vergne, Comtesse de, *The Princesse de Clèves, The Princesse de Montpensier, The Comtesse de Tende*, trans. by Terence Cave (Oxford and New York: Oxford University Press, 1992)

Lombroso, Cesare, *L'Homme criminel: étude anthropologique et médico-légale*, trans. from the fourth Italian edition by G. Regnier and A. Bornet (Paris: Félix Alcan; Turin: Bocca Frères, 1887)

Lucas, Hippolyte, 'La Femme adultère', in *Les Français peints par eux-mêmes: encyclopédie morale du dix-neuvième siècle*, 8 vols (Paris: Curmer, 1840–2), III, 265–72

Maupassant, Guy de, *Bel-Ami*, trans. by Margaret Mauldon (Oxford and New York: Oxford University Press, 2001)

——, *Fort Comme la Mort, or The Ruling Passion*, in *The Life Work of Henri René Guy de Maupassant*, 17 vols, trans. anon. (London and New York: M. Walter Dunne, 1903), XI

——, *A Life: The Humble Truth*, trans. by Roger Pearson (Oxford and New York: Oxford University Press, 1999)

——, 'The Love of Long Ago' ['Jadis'], in *Short Stories of the Tragedy and Comedy of Life*, in *Life Work*, V, 9–14

——, *Mont-Oriol, or A Romance of Auvergne: A Novel*, in *Life Work*, VIII

Maupassant, Guy de, *Notre Coeur, or A Woman's Pastime: A Novel*, in *Life Work*, IX

——, *Pierre and Jean*, trans. by Leonard Tancock (Harmondsworth: Penguin, 1979)

——, 'L'Adultère', *Le Gaulois*, 23 January 1882, 1–2

——, *Chroniques*, 3 vols (Paris: Union générale d'éditions, 1980)

——, *Contes et nouvelles*, 2 vols, ed. by Louis Forestier (Paris: Gallimard, 1974)

——, *Maupassant: Romans*, ed. by Louis Forestier (Paris: Gallimard, 1987)

Musset, Alfred de, *A Modern Man's Confession*, trans. by G. F. Monkshood, pseudonym of W. J. Clarke (London: Greening, 1907)

Pérez Galdós, Benito, *Fortunata and Jacinta: Two Stories of Married Women*, trans. by Agnes Moncy Gullón (Athens: University of Georgia Press, 1986; repr. Harmondsworth: Penguin, 1988)

——, *That Bringas Woman* [*La de Bringas*], trans. by Catherine Jagoe (London: J. M. Dent; Rutland, VT: Charles E. Tuttle, 1996)

Rousseau, Jean-Jacques, *Eloisa: or a series of original letters*, trans. by William Kenrick, 4 vols (London, 1761), repr. in 2 vols (Oxford: Woodstock Books, 1989)

——, *Julie, or the New Heloise: Letters of Two Lovers Who Live in a Small Town at the Foot of the Alps*, trans. by Philip Stewart and Jean Vaché (Hanover, NH, and London: University Press of New England, 1997)

——, *La Nouvelle Héloïse: Julie, or The New Eloise*, trans. by Judith H. McDowell (University Park and London: Pennsylvania State University Press, 1968)

——, *Julie, ou La Nouvelle Héloïse*, ed. by Michel Launay (Paris: Garnier-Flammarion, 1967)

——, *Rousseau: Oeuvres complètes*, ed. by Bernard Gagnebin and Marcel Raymond, 5 vols (Paris: Gallimard, 1959–95), II, *La Nouvelle Héloïse; Théâtre; Poésies; Essais littéraires*, ed. by Henri Coulet and Bernard Guyon (1964)

Sand, George (pseudonym of Aurore Dudevant), *Le Dernier amour* (Paris: Michel Lévy, 1867; repr. Éditions des femmes, 1991)

——, *Jacques*, trans. by Anna Blackwell, 2 vols (New York: J. S. Redfield, 1847)

Stendhal (pseudonym of Marie-Henri Beyle), *The Charterhouse of Parma*, trans. by Richard Howard (New York: Modern Library, 1999)

——, *The Red and the Black*, trans. by Catherine Slater (Oxford and New York: Oxford University Press, 1991)

Tolstoy, Lev Nikolayevich, *Anna Karenin*, trans. by Rosemary Edmonds, rev. edn (Harmondsworth: Penguin, 1978)

——, *The Kreutzer Sonata and Other Stories*, trans. by David McDuff (London and New York: Penguin Books, 1983)

Zola, Émile, *La Bête humaine*, trans. by Roger Pearson (Oxford and New York: Oxford University Press, 1996)

——, *Emile Zola: Thérèse Raquin*, ed. by Brian Nelson (London: Bristol Classical Press, 1993)

——, *The Ladies' Paradise*, trans. by Brian Nelson (Oxford and New York: Oxford University Press, 1995)

Zola, Émile, *A Love Affair*, trans. by Jean Stewart (London: Paul Elek, 1958; repr. Arrow Books, 1967)

——, *Nana*, trans. by George Holden (Harmondsworth and New York: Penguin Books, 1972)

——, *Pot-Bouille*, trans. by Percy Pinkerton, rev. and ed. by Robert Lethbridge (London and Rutland, VT: J. M. Dent, 2000)

——, *Pot Luck*, trans. by Brian Nelson (Oxford and New York: Oxford University Press, 1999)

——, *Thérèse Raquin*, trans. by Andrew Rothwell (Oxford and New York: Oxford University Press, 1992)

——, *Émile Zola: Correspondance*, ed. by B. H. Bakker and others, 10 vols (Montreal: Presses de l'Université de Montréal; Paris: Éditions du Centre National de la Recherche Scientifique, 1978–95)

——, *Émile Zola: Oeuvres complètes*, ed. by Henri Mitterand, 15 vols (Paris: Cercle du Livre Précieux, 1966–9)

——, *Émile Zola: Les Rougon-Macquart*, ed. by Henri Mitterand, 4 vols (Paris: Garnier-Flammarion, 1960–7)

——, *Thérèse Raquin*, ed. by Henri Mitterand (Paris: Garnier-Flammarion, 1970)

SECONDARY SOURCES

Anderson, Stuart, 'Legislative Divorce – Law for the Aristocracy?', in *Law, Economy, and Society, 1750–1914: Essays in the History of English Law*, ed. by G. R. Rubin and David Sugarman (Abingdon, Oxon.: Professional Books, 1984), pp. 412–44

Armstrong, Judith, *The Novel of Adultery* (London: Macmillan, 1976)

Armstrong, Nancy, *Desire and Domestic Fiction: A Political History of the Novel* (New York and Oxford: Oxford University Press, 1987)

Baguley, David (ed.), *Critical Essays on Emile Zola* (Boston, MA: G. K. Hall, 1986)

——, 'A Harmless Liaison: On Céard's *Une belle journée*', *Nineteenth-Century French Studies*, 18 (1990), 482–91

——, *Naturalist Fiction: The Entropic Vision* (Cambridge and New York: Cambridge University Press, 1990)

Ballaster, Ros, *Seductive Forms: Women's Amatory Fiction from 1684 to 1740* (Oxford: Clarendon Press, 1992)

Barker-Benfield, G. J., *The Culture of Sensibility: Sex and Society in Eighteenth-Century Britain* (Chicago and London: University of Chicago Press, 1992)

Barnes, H. G., *Goethe's Die Wahlverwandtschaften: A Literary Interpretation* (Oxford: Clarendon Press, 1967)

Barthes, Roland, 'The Man-Eater', in *Critical Essays on Emile Zola*, ed. by David Baguley, pp. 90–3

——, *Writing Degree Zero*, trans. by Annette Lavers and Colin Smith (London: Jonathan Cape, 1967)

Beasley, Jerry C., *Tobias Smollett: Novelist* (Athens and London: University of Georgia Press, 1998)

Beizer, Janet, *Ventriloquized Bodies: Narratives of Hysteria in Nineteenth-Century France* (Ithaca, NY, and London: Cornell University Press, 1994)

Belsey, Catherine, *Desire: Love Stories in Western Culture* (Oxford, Eng., and Cambridge, MA: Blackwell Publishers, 1994)

Benjamin, Walter, 'Goethe's Elective Affinities', trans. by Stanley Corngold, in *Walter Benjamin: Selected Writings: Volume 1, 1913–1926*, ed. by Marcus Bullock and Michael W. Jennings (Cambridge, MA, and London: Harvard University Press, 1996), pp. 297–360

Bérenguier, Nadine, 'Unfortunate Couples: Adultery in Four Eighteenth-Century French Novels', *Eighteenth-Century Fiction*, 4 (1992), 331–50

Birkett, Jennifer, *The Sins of the Fathers: Decadence in France, 1870–1914* (London and New York: Quartet Books, 1986)

Boucé, Paul-Gabriel, 'Imagination, pregnant women, and monsters, in eighteenth-century England and France', in *Sexual Underworlds of the Enlightenment*, ed. by G. S. Rousseau and Roy Porter (Manchester: Manchester University Press, 1987), pp. 86–100

—— (ed.), *Sexuality in Eighteenth-Century Britain* (Manchester: Manchester University Press; Totowa, NJ: Barnes and Noble, 1982)

Bree, Linda, *Sarah Fielding* (New York: Twayne Publishers; London: Prentice Hall, 1996)

Buck, Howard Swazey, *A Study in Smollett* (New Haven: Yale University Press; London: Oxford University Press, 1925)

Cairncross, John, *After Polygamy Was Made a Sin: The Social History of Christian Polygamy* (London: Routledge and Kegan Paul, 1974)

Carroll, John (ed.), *Selected Letters of Samuel Richardson* (Oxford: Clarendon Press, 1964)

Chernaik, Warren, *Sexual Freedom in Restoration Literature* (Cambridge: Cambridge University Press, 1995)

——, 'Unguarded Hearts: Transgression and Epistolary Form in Aphra Behn's *Love-Letters* and the *Portuguese Letters*', *Journal of English and Germanic Philology*, 97 (1998), 13–33

Chitnis, Beatrice, *Reflecting on Nana* (London and New York: Routledge, 1991)

Clack, Beverley (ed.), *Misogyny in the Western Philosophical Tradition: A Reader* (Basingstoke: Macmillan, 1999)

Cohen, Margaret, *The Sentimental Education of the Novel* (Princeton, NJ: Princeton University Press, 1999)

C[okayne], G. E., and others, *The Complete Peerage of England, Scotland, Ireland, Great Britain and the United Kingdom*, rev. edn, 14 vols (London: St. Catherine Press, 1910–59)

Coleman, Alexander, *Eça de Queirós and European Realism* (New York and London: New York University Press, 1980)

Coleridge, Samuel Taylor, *The Friend*, ed. by Barbara E. Rooke, 2 vols (London: Routledge and Kegan Paul; Princeton, NJ: Princeton University Press, 1969)

Constantine, David, 'Rights and Wrongs in Goethe's *Die Wahlverwandtschaften*', in *German Life and Letters: A Quarterly Review*, n.s., 47 (1994), 387–99

Copley, Antony, *Sexual Moralities in France, 1780–1980: New Ideas on the Family, Divorce and Homosexuality* (London: Routledge, 1989)

Corbin, Alain, *Women for Hire: Prostitution and Sexuality in France after 1850*, trans. by Alan Sheridan (Cambridge, MA, and London: Harvard University Press, 1990)

Cousins, Russell, *Zola: Thérèse Raquin* (London: Grant & Cutler, 1992)

Crecelius, Kathryn J., *Family Romances: George Sand's Early Novels* (Bloomington and Indianapolis: Indiana University Press, 1987)

Darnton, Robert, *The Corpus of Clandestine Literature in France, 1769–89* (New York and London: W. W. Norton, 1995)

——, *The Forbidden Best-Sellers of Pre-Revolutionary France* (London: Harper Collins, 1996)

DeJean, Joan, 'Notorious Women: Marriage and the Novel in Crisis in France 1690–1710', in *Scarlet Letters*, ed. by Nicholas White and Naomi Segal, pp. 56–69

——, *Tender Geographies: Women and the Origins of the Novel in France* (New York: Columbia University Press, 1991)

Dijkstra, Bram, *Idols of Perversity: Fantasies of Feminine Evil in Fin-de-Siècle Culture* (New York and Oxford: Oxford University Press, 1986)

Donaldson-Evans, Mary, *A Woman's Revenge: The Chronology of Dispossession in Maupassant's Fiction* (Lexington, KY: French Forum Publishers, 1986)

Doody, Margaret M., 'Frances Sheridan: Morality and Annihilated Time', in *Fetter'd or Free? British Women Novelists 1670–1815*, ed. by Mary Anne Schofield and Cecilia Macheski (Athens: Ohio University Press, 1986)

——, *A Natural Passion: A Study of the Novels of Samuel Richardson* (Oxford: Clarendon Press, 1974)

Eagleton, Terry, *The Rape of Clarissa: Writing, Sexuality and Class Struggle in Samuel Richardson* (Oxford: Basil Blackwell, 1982)

Echard, William E., *Historical Dictionary of the French Second Empire* (Westport, CT: Greenwood Press; London: Aldwych Press, 1985)

Eikhenbaum, Boris, *Tolstoi in the Seventies*, trans. by Albert Kaspin (Ann Arbor, MI: Ardis, 1982)

Fletcher, Loraine, *Charlotte Smith: A Critical Biography* (London: Macmillan; New York: St Martin's Press, 1998)

Fraisse, Geneviève, *Reason's Muse: Sexual Difference and the Birth of Democracy*, trans. by Jane Marie Todd (Chicago and London: University of Chicago Press, 1994)

Frappier-Mazur, Lucienne, 'Marginal Canons: Rewriting the Erotic', *Yale French Studies*, 75, *The Politics of Tradition: Placing Women in French Literature* (1988), 112–28

Fuchs, Rachel G., *Poor and Pregnant in Paris: Strategies for Survival in the Nineteenth Century* (New Brunswick, NJ: Rutgers University Press, 1992)

Gallagher, Catherine, *Nobody's Story: The Vanishing Acts of Women Writers in the Marketplace, 1670–1820* (Oxford: Clarendon Press, 1994)

Gardiner, Judith Kegan, 'The First English Novel: Aphra Behn's *Love-Letters*, The Canon, and Women's Tastes', *Tulsa Studies in Women's*

Literature, 8 (1989), 201–22

Gonda, Caroline, *Reading Daughters' Fictions 1709–1834: Novels and Society from Manley to Edgeworth* (Cambridge and New York: Cambridge University Press, 1996)

Habbakuk, H. J., 'Marriage Settlements in the Eighteenth Century', *Transactions of the Royal Historical Society*, 4th series, 32 (1950), 15–30

Harris, Marla, '"How Nicely Circumspect Must Your Conduct Be": Double Standards in Elizabeth Griffith's *The History of Lady Barton*', in *Eighteenth-Century Women and the Arts*, ed. by Frederick M. Keener and Susan E. Lorsch (New York and London: Greenwood Press, 1988), 277–82

Harsin, Jill, *Policing Prostitution in Nineteenth-Century Paris* (Princeton, NJ, and Guildford: Princeton University Press, 1985)

Harvey, A. D., *Sex in Georgian England: Attitudes and Prejudices from the 1720s to the 1820s* (London: Gerald Duckworth, 1994)

Hemmings, F. W. J., *Culture and Society in France, 1789–1848* (Leicester: Leicester University Press, 1987)

——, *Culture and Society in France, 1848–1898: Dissidents and Philistines* (London: B. T. Batsford, 1971)

——, *Émile Zola*, 2nd edn (Oxford: Clarendon Press, 1966)

——, 'Realism in Spain and Portugal', in *The Age of Realism*, ed. by F. W. J. Hemmings (Harmondsworth: Penguin, 1974), pp. 265–322

Hill, Christopher, 'Clarissa Harlowe and Her Times', *Essays in Criticism*, 5 (1955), 315–40, repr. in John Carroll (ed.), *Samuel Richardson: A Collection of Critical Essays* (Englewood Cliffs, NJ: Prentice-Hall, 1969), pp. 102–23

Hunter, J. Paul, '"News, and new Things": Contemporaneity and the Early English Novel', *Critical Inquiry*, 14 (1988), 493–515

Hutner, Heidi (ed.), *Rereading Aphra Behn: History, Theory, and Criticism* (Charlottesville and London: University of Virginia Press, 1993)

Janes, R. M., 'On the Reception of Mary Wollstonecraft's *A Vindication of the Rights of Woman*', *Journal of the History of Ideas*, 39 (1978), 293–302; repr. in *A Vindication of the Rights of Woman*, ed. by Carol H. Poston, 2nd edn (New York: W. W. Norton, 1988), pp. 297–307

Jauss, Hans Robert, *Toward an Aesthetic of Reception*, trans. by Timothy Bahti (Brighton, Sussex: Harvester, 1982)

Jensen, Niels Lyhne, *Jens Peter Jacobsen* (Boston: G. K. Hall, 1980)

Jordan, Elaine, 'Criminal Conversation: Mary Wollstonecraft's *The Wrongs of Woman*', *Women's Writing*, 4 (1997), 221–34

Kahn, Annette, *J.-K. Huysmans: Novelist, Poet, and Art Critic* (Ann Arbor, MI: UMI Research Press, 1987)

Kamuf, Peggy, *Fictions of Feminine Desire: Disclosures of Heloise* (Lincoln and London: University of Nebraska Press, 1982; repr. 1987)

Kaplan, Cora, 'Wild nights: pleasure/sexuality/feminism', in *Sea Changes: Culture and Feminism* (London: Verso, 1987), pp. 31–56; repr. in *The Ideology of Conduct: Essays in Literature and the History of Sexuality*, ed. by Nancy Armstrong and Leonard Tennenhouse (New York and London: Methuen, 1987), pp. 163–84

Kaplan, E. Ann, *Motherhood and Representation: The Mother in Popular*

Culture and Melodrama (London and New York: Routledge, 1992)

Kelly, Gary, '(Female) Philosophy in the Bedroom: Mary Wollstonecraft and female sexuality' in *Women's Writing*, 4 (1997), 143–54

——, *Revolutionary Feminism: The Mind and Career of Mary Wollstonecraft* (Basingstoke: Macmillan, 1992)

——, *Women, Writing, and Revolution 1790–1827* (Oxford and New York: Clarendon Press, 1993)

Kelly, Lionel (ed.), *Tobias Smollett: The Critical Heritage* (London and New York: Routledge and Kegan Paul, 1987)

Krieger, Leonard, *The German Idea of Freedom: History of a Political Tradition* (Chicago and London: University of Chicago Press, 1957; repr. 1972)

LaCapra, Dominick, *'Madame Bovary' on Trial* (Ithaca, NY, and London: Cornell University Press, 1982)

Lamont, Claire, '"Let other pens dwell on guilt and misery": Adultery in Jane Austen', in *Scarlet Letters*, ed. by Nicholas White and Naomi Segal, pp. 70–81

Leckie, Barbara, *Culture and Adultery: The Novel, the Newspaper, and the Law, 1857–1914* (Philadelphia: University of Pennsylvania Press, 1999)

Leneman, Leah, *Alienated Affections: The Scottish Experience of Divorce and Separation, 1684–1830* (Edinburgh: Edinburgh University Press, 1998)

Lethbridge, Robert, *Maupassant: Pierre et Jean* (London: Grant & Cutler, 1984)

Lewes, G. H., *The Life and Works of Goethe*, 2 vols (London: David Nutt, 1855)

Lisboa, Maria Manuel, 'Machado de Assis and the Beloved Reader: Squatters in the Text', in *Scarlet Letters*, ed. by Nicholas White and Naomi Segal, pp. 160–73

Lloyd, Christopher, *Maupassant: Bel-Ami* (London: Grant & Cutler, 1988)

Lockhart, John Gibson, *Memoirs of the Life of Sir Walter Scott*, 10 vols (Edinburgh: Adam and Charles Black, 1853)

——, *The Life of Sir Walter Scott* (abr. edn, repr. London: Dent; New York: Dutton, 1906)

Lukács, Georg, *The Historical Novel*, trans. by Hannah and Stanley Mitchell (London: Merlin Press, 1962)

Maccubbin, Robert Purks (ed.), *'Tis Nature's Fault: Unauthorized Sexuality during the Enlightenment* (Cambridge and New York: Cambridge University Press, 1987)

Macfarlane, Alan, review of Stone, *The Family, Sex and Marriage*, in *History and Theory*, 18 (1979), 103–26

MacLean, Marie, *The Name of the Mother: Writing Illegitimacy* (London and New York: Routledge, 1994)

——, 'The Heirs of Amphitryon: Social Fathers and Natural Fathers', in *Scarlet Letters*, ed. by Nicholas White and Naomi Segal, pp. 13–33

MacPike, Loralee, 'The Fallen Woman's Sexuality: Childbirth and Censure', in *Sexuality and Victorian Literature*, ed. by Don Richard Cox, Tennessee Studies in Literature, 27 (Knoxville: University of Tennessee Press, 1984), pp. 54–71

McBurney, William H., 'Mrs. Penelope Aubin and the Early Eighteenth-Century English Novel', *Huntington Library Quarterly*, 20 (1956–57), 245–67

McDowell, Paula, *The Women of Grub Street: Press, Politics, and Gender in the London Literary Marketplace 1678–1730* (Oxford and New York: Clarendon Press, 1998)

McKnight, Natalie J., *Suffering Mothers in Mid-Victorian Novels* (Basingstoke: Macmillan, 1997)

McMillan, James F., *Housewife or Harlot: The Place of Women in French Society, 1870-1940* (Brighton, Sussex: Harvester, 1981)

Malcolmson, A. P. W., *The Pursuit of the Heiress: Aristocratic Marriage in Ireland 1750–1820* (Ulster Historical Foundation, 1982)

Mann, Thomas, 'Goethe's Career as a Man of Letters', in *Essays of Three Decades*, trans. by H. T. Lowe-Porter (London: Secker and Warburg, n.d. [1947]), pp. 43–65

——, 'Goethes Laufbahn als Schriftsteller' in *Gesammelte Werke*, 12 vols (Oldenburg: S. Fischer Verlag, 1960), IX, 333–62

——, 'Fantasy on Goethe', in *Last Essays*, trans. by Richard and Clara Winston and Tania and James Stern (London: Secker and Warburg, 1959), pp. 96–140

——, 'Phantasie über Goethe' [1948], in *Gesammelte Werke*, IX, 713–54

Maurois, André, *Three Musketeers: A Study of the Dumas Family*, trans. by Gerard Hopkins (London: Jonathan Cape, 1957)

Medoff, Jeslyn, 'The daughters of Behn and the problem of reputation', in *Women, Writing, History 1640–1740*, ed. by Isobel Grundy and Susan Wiseman (London: B. T. Batsford, 1992), pp. 33–54

Miller, Nancy K., *The Heroine's Text: Readings in the French and English Novel, 1722–1782* (New York: Columbia University Press, 1980)

——, 'Men's Reading, Women's Writing: Gender and the Rise of the Novel', *Yale French Studies*, 75, *The Politics of Tradition: Placing Women in French Literature* (1988), 40–55

——, *Subject to Change: Reading Feminist Writing* (New York: Columbia University Press, 1988)

Milne, C. Audrey, 'The Elective Affinities in Exile: *Der Ehering*', *German Life and Letters: A Quarterly Review*, n.s., 47 (1994), 456–68

Minogue, Valerie, 'Venus Observing – Venus Observed: Zola's *Nana*', in *Emile Zola Centenary Colloquium 1893–1993*, ed. by Patrick Pollard, pp. 57–72

Montégut, Émile, 'Monsieur de Camors', *Revue des deux mondes*, 15 January 1868, 63 (1868), 497–510

Moore, Jane, 'Wollstonecraft's Secrets', *Women's Writing*, 4 (1997), 247–60

Moretti, Franco, *Atlas of the European Novel 1800–1900* (London and New York: Verso, 1978)

Morgan, O. R., 'Léon Hennique (1851–1935). His Life and Works. A contribution to the history of the Naturalist School in French Literature' (unpublished MA thesis, University of Nottingham, 1961)

Moses, Claire Goldberg, *French Feminism in the Nineteenth Century* (Albany: State University of New York Press, 1984)

Mudge, Bradford K., *The Whore's Story: Women, Pornography, and the British Novel, 1684–1830* (Oxford and New York: Oxford University Press, 2000)

Myers, Mitzi, 'Reform or Ruin: "A Revolution in Female Manners"', *Studies in Eighteenth-Century Culture*, 11 (1982), 199–216, repr. in *A Vindication of the Rights of Woman*, ed. by Carol H. Poston, pp. 328–43

Needham, G. B., 'Mary de la Rivière Manley: Tory Defender', *Huntington Library Quarterly*, 12 (1948–9), 255–89

Nelson, Brian, *Zola and the Bourgeoisie: A Study of Themes and Techniques in Les Rougon-Macquart* (London: Macmillan, 1983)

Nussbaum, Felicity A., *The Autobiographical Subject: Gender and Ideology in Eighteenth-Century England* (Baltimore and London: Johns Hopkins University Press, 1989)

Okin, Susan Moller, *Women in Western Political Thought* (Princeton, NJ: Princeton University Press, 1979)

Overton, Bill, *The Novel of Female Adultery* (Basingstoke: Macmillan; New York: St Martin's Press, 1996)

Pflanze, Otto, *Bismarck and the Development of Germany: The Period of Unification, 1815–1871* (Princeton, NJ: Princeton University Press, 1963)

Phillips, Roderick, *Putting Asunder: A History of Divorce in Western Society* (Cambridge and New York: Cambridge University Press, 1988)

Plenderleith, H. Jane, 'Sex, Lies, and *Die Wahlverwandtschaften*', *German Life and Letters: A Quarterly Review*, n.s., 47 (1994), 407–17

Pollak, Ellen, 'Beyond Incest: Gender and the Politics of Transgression in Aphra Behn's *Love-Letters Between a Nobleman and his Sister*', in Heidi Hutner (ed.), *Rereading Aphra Behn: History, Theory, and Criticism* (Charlottesville and London: University of Virginia Press, 1993), pp. 151–86

Pollard, Patrick (ed.), *Emile Zola Centenary Colloquium 1893–1993* (London: Emile Zola Society, 1995)

Poovey, Mary, *The Proper Lady and the Woman Writer: Ideology as Style in the Works of Mary Wollstonecraft, Mary Shelley, and Jane Austen* (Chicago and London: University of Chicago Press, 1984)

Porter, Roy, and G. S. Rousseau (eds), *Sexual Underworlds of the Enlightenment* (Manchester: Manchester University Press, 1987)

Prendergast, Christopher, *Balzac: Fiction and Melodrama* (London: Edward Arnold; New York: Holmes and Meier, 1978)

Prescott, Sarah, 'The Debt to Pleasure: Eliza Haywood's *Love in Excess* and women's fiction of the 1720s', *Women's Writing*, 7 (2000), 427–45

Putney, Rufus, 'Smollett and Lady Vane's Memoirs', *Philological Quarterly*, 25 (1946), 120–6

Pykett, Lyn, *The 'Improper' Feminine: The Women's Sensation Novel and the New Woman Writing* (London and New York: Routledge, 1992)

Ray, William, *Story and History: Narrative Authority and Social Identity in the Eighteenth-Century French and English Novel* (Cambridge, MA, and Oxford: Basil Blackwell, 1990)

Richetti, John J., '*Love Letters Between a Nobleman and His Sister*: Aphra Behn and Amatory Fiction', in *Augustan Subjects: Essays in Honor of Martin C. Battestin*, ed. by Albert J. Rivero (Newark, NJ: University of Delaware Press; London: Associated University Presses, 1997), pp. 13–28

——, *Popular Fiction Before Richardson: Narrative Patterns 1700–1739* (Oxford: Clarendon Press, 1969)

Roulston, Christine, *Virtue, Gender, and the Authentic Self in Eighteenth-*

Century Fiction: Richardson, Rousseau, and Laclos (Gainesville: University Press of Florida, 1998)

Rousseau, G. S., 'Controversy or Collusion? The "Lady Vane" Tracts', *Notes and Queries*, n.s., 19 (1972), 375–8

Rubin, Gayle, 'The Traffic in Women: Notes on the "Political Economy" of Sex', in *Toward an Anthropology of Women*, ed. by Rayna R. Reiter (New York and London: Monthly Review Press, 1975), pp. 157–210

Schofield, Mary Anne, and Macheski, Cecilia (eds), *Fetter'd or Free? British Women Novelists 1670–1815* (Athens: Ohio University Press, 1986)

Schor, Naomi, *Breaking the Chain: Women, Theory, and French Realist Fiction* (New York: Columbia University Press, 1985)

——, 'Mother's Day: Zola's Women', in *Critical Essays on Emile Zola*, ed. by David Baguley, pp. 130–42

Schumacher, Claude, *Zola: Thérèse Raquin* (Glasgow: University of Glasgow French and German Publications, 1990)

Segal, Naomi, *The Adulteress's Child: Authorship and Desire in the Nineteenth-Century Novel* (Cambridge, Eng., and Cambridge, MA: Polity Press, 1992)

——, 'The Adulteress's Children', in *Scarlet Letters*, ed. by Nicholas White and Naomi Segal, pp. 109–22

——, 'Our Lady of the Flowers', in *Violetta and her Sisters: The Lady of the Camellias, Responses to the Myth*, ed. by Nicholas John (London and Boston: Faber and Faber, 1994), pp. 161–5

Sharma, Anjana, 'A Different Voice: Mary Hays's *The Memoirs of Emma Courtney*', *Women's Writing*, 8 (2001), 139–67

Shuttleworth, Sally, 'Demonic Mothers: Ideologies of Bourgeois Motherhood in the Mid-Victorian era', in *Rewriting the Victorians: Theory, History and the Politics of Gender*, ed. by Linda M. Shires (New York and London: Routledge, 1992), pp. 31–51

Sinclair, Alison, 'The Need for Zeal and the Dangers of Jealousy: Identity and Legitimacy in *La Regenta*', in *Scarlet Letters*, ed. by Nicholas White and Naomi Segal, pp. 174–85

Sirc, Susan, 'Monkeys, Monuments and Miracles: Aspects of Imitation of Word and Image in *Die Wahlverwandtschaften*', *German Life and Letters*, n.s., 47 (1994), 432–48

Skedd, Susan, 'Women Teachers and the Expansion of Girls' Schooling in England, *c.* 1760–1820', in *Gender in Eighteenth-Century England: Roles, Representations, and Responsibilities*, ed. by Hannah Barker and Elaine Chalus (London and New York: Longman, 1997), pp. 101–25

Sohn, Anne-Marie, 'The Golden Age of Male Adultery: The Third Republic', *Journal of Social History*, 28 (1995), 469–90

Spacks, Patricia Meyer, *Desire and Truth: Functions of Plot in Eighteenth-Century English Novels* (Chicago and London: University of Chicago Press, 1990)

Spencer, Jane, *The Rise of the Woman Novelist: From Aphra Behn to Jane Austen* (Oxford and New York: Basil Blackwell, 1986)

Sponsler, Lucy A., 'The Status of Married Women under the Legal System of Spain', *Journal of Legal History*, 3 (1982), 125–52

Stapleton, M. L., 'Aphra Behn, Libertine', *Restoration: Studies in English*

Literary Culture, 1660–1700, 24 (2000), 75–97
Stephens, Anthony, 'The Essential Vulgarity of Benjamin's Essay on Goethe's *Elective Affinities*', in *'With the Sharpened Axe of Reason': Approaches to Walter Benjamin*, ed. by Gerhard Fischer (Oxford and Herndon, VA: Berg, 1996), pp. 149–60
Stern, J. P., *Re-Interpretations: Seven Studies in Nineteenth-Century German Literature* (London: Thames and Hudson, 1964; repr. Cambridge and New York: Cambridge University Press, 1981)
Stone, Lawrence, *Broken Lives: Separation and Divorce in England 1660–1857* (Oxford and New York: Oxford University Press, 1993)
——, *The Family, Sex and Marriage In England 1500–1800* (London: Weidenfeld and Nicolson, 1977)
——, *Road to Divorce: England 1530–1987* (Oxford and New York: Oxford University Press, 1990)
Sullivan, Edward D., *Maupassant the Novelist* (Princeton, NJ: Princeton University Press, 1954; repr. Westport, CT: Greenwood Press, 1978)
Tanner, Tony, *Adultery in the Novel: Contract and Transgression* (Baltimore and London: Johns Hopkins University Press, 1979)
Taylor, Barbara, *Eve and the New Jerusalem: Socialism and Feminism in the Nineteenth Century* (London: Virago Press, 1983)
Thomas, Donald, *A Long Time Burning: The History of Literary Censorship in England* (London: Routledge and Kegan Paul, 1968)
Thomas, Keith, 'The Double Standard', *Journal of the History of Ideas*, 20 (1959), 195–216
Thompson, E. P., 'Happy familes', review of Stone, *The Family, Sex and Marriage*, in *New Society*, 41 (1977), 499–501
Til Rusthoven, Thea van, 'Codes en conflit dans *La Bête humaine*', in *Zola, 'La Bête humaine': texte et explications*, ed. by Geoff Woollen, pp. 136–48
Todd, Janet, *Sensibility: An Introduction* (London and New York: Methuen, 1986)
——, *The Sign of Angellica: Women, Writing and Fiction, 1660–1800* (London: Virago, 1989)
Traer, James F., *Marriage and the Family in Eighteenth-Century France* (Ithaca, NY, and London: Cornell University Press, 1980)
Turner, C. J. G., 'Divorce and *Anna Karenina*', *Forum for Modern Language Studies*, 23 (1987), 97–116
——, *A Karenina Companion* (Waterloo, Ont.: Wilfrid Laurier University Press, 1993)
Turner, Cheryl, *Living by the Pen: Women Writers in the Eighteenth Century* (London and New York: Routledge, 1992)
Turner, Harriet S., *Benito Pérez Galdós: Fortunata and Jacinta* (Cambridge and New York: Cambridge University Press, 1992)
——, 'Family Ties and Tyrannies: A Reassessment of Jacinta', *Hispanic Review*, 51 (1983), 1–22
Ty, Eleanor, *Unsex'd Revolutionaries: Five Women Novelists of the 1790s* (Toronto, Buffalo and London: University of Toronto Press, 1993)
Van Lennep, William, *The London Stage, 1660–1800*, Part I, *1660–1700* Carbondale: University of Illinois Press, 1965)
Waelti-Walters, Jennifer, *Feminist Novelists of the Belle Epoque: Love as a*

Lifestyle (Bloomington and Indianapolis: Indiana University Press, 1990)

Wagner, Peter, *Eros Revived: Erotica of the Enlightenment in England and America* (London: Secker and Warburg, 1988)

——, 'The pornographer in the courtroom: trial reports about cases of sexual crimes and delinquencies as a genre of eighteenth-century erotica', in *Sexuality in Eighteenth-Century Britain*, ed. by Paul-Gabriel Boucé, pp. 120–40

——, 'Trial Reports as a Genre of Eighteenth-Century Erotica', *British Journal for Eighteenth-Century Studies*, V (1982), 117–21

Warner, James H., 'Eighteenth-Century English Reactions to the *Nouvelle Héloïse*', *PMLA*, 52 (1937), 803–19

Warner, William B., *Licensing Entertainment: The Elevation of Novel Reading in Britain, 1684–1750* (Berkeley and London: University of California Press, 1998)

Watson, Nicola J., *Revolution and the Form of the British Novel 1790–1825: Intercepted Letters, Interrupted Seductions* (Oxford and New York: Clarendon Press, 1994)

Weisser, Susan Ostrov, *Women and Sexual Love in the British Novel, 1740–1880: A 'Craving Vacancy'* (London: Macmillan, 1997)

White, Nicholas, 'Carnal Knowledge in French Naturalist Fiction', in *Scarlet Letters*, ed. by Nicholas White and Naomi Segal, pp. 123–33

——, *The Family in Crisis in Late Nineteenth-Century French Fiction* (Cambridge: Cambridge University Press, 1999)

——, 'Introduction: The Present State of Affairs', in *Scarlet Letters*, ed. by Nicholas White and Naomi Segal, pp. 1–10

——, and Naomi Segal (eds), *Scarlet Letters: Fictions of Adultery from Antiquity to the 1990s* (Basingstoke: Macmillan; New York: St Martin's Press, 1997)

Williams, Tony, 'Champfleury, Flaubert and the Novel of Adultery', *Nineteenth-Century French Studies*, 20 (1991–2), 145–57

——, 'Introduction: Flaubert Studies 1983–96', in *New Approaches in Flaubert Studies*, ed. by Tony Williams and Mary Orr (Lewiston, NY, Queenston, Ont., and Lampeter, Wales: The Edwin Mellen Press, 1999), pp. 1–31

——, 'Patriarchal Ideology and French Fictions of Adultery 1830–57', in *Scarlet Letters*, ed. by Nicholas White and Naomi Segal, pp. 134–45

Wilson, Nelly, 'A question of motives: heredity and inheritance in *La Bête humaine*', in *Zola, 'La Bête humaine': texte et explications*, ed. by Geoff Woollen, pp. 184–95

Winkelmann, John, *Goethe's Elective Affinities: An Interpretation* (New York, Bern, Frankfurt am Main, Paris: Peter Lang, 1987)

Wolfram, Sybil, 'Divorce in England 1700–1857', *Oxford Journal of Legal Studies*, 5 (1985), 155–86

Woollen, Geoff (ed.), *Zola, 'La Bête humaine': texte et explications* (Glasgow: University of Glasgow French and German Publications, 1990)

——, 'Jacques the Ripper', in *Emile Zola Centenary Colloquium 1893–1993*, ed. by Patrick Pollard, pp. 73–82

Ziegler, Robert E., 'Huysmans's *En Ménage* and the Unwritable Naturalist Text', *Forum for Modern Language Studies*, 29 (1993), 18–30

Index